WISDOM OF

MAN, WOMAN & GOD
IN JEWISH CANONICAL LITERATURE

JUDAISM AND JEWISH LIFE

ACADEMIC
STUDIES
PRESS

Wisdom of Love

MAN, WOMAN & GOD
IN JEWISH CANONICAL LITERATURE

Naftali Rothenberg

Boston
2009

Translated by Shmuel Sermoneta-Gertel

On the cover: Riki Rothenberg, *Love of the Cherubim*

ISBN 978-1-934843-55-0

Book design by Yuri Alexandrov
Published by Academic Studies Press in 2009
28 Montfern Avenue
Brighton, MA 02135, USA
press@academicstudiespress.com
www.academicstudiespress.com

CONTENTS

Section III
THE SAGE OF UNCONSUMMATED LOVE:
JUDAH ABRAVANEL'S *DIALOGHI D'AMORE*

Section IV
WRITTEN FOR MEN BY MEN: FEMINIST REVOLUTION
AND INNOVATION IN THE CANONICAL SOURCES

Section V
CONTRAST AND HARMONY IN MARRIED LIFE:
ON SPIRITUALITY AND ABSTINENCE

Dedicated
to the beloved memory
of Karen A. Shapira

PREFACE

> Let thy fountain be blessed: and rejoice with
> the wife of thy youth. Let her be as the beloved
> doe and graceful hind; let her breasts satisfy
> thee at all times; and be thou ravished always
> with her love. And why wilt thou, my son, be
> ravished with a strange woman, and embrace
> the bosom of a stranger?
>
> *Proverbs* 5:18-20

Love is wisdom. Beyond being one of the faculties of the spirit, expressed in emotion, desire and self-awareness, i.e. in recognising one's lover as such, love — like all forms of wisdom — requires study and deeper understanding. The wisdom of love can be acquired in two ways: The first is theoretical study and contemplation, in the sense of "study that leads to action". The second is study by experience, learning through the reality of a love relationship. Either way, each and every man and woman should devote time to the study of this subject, which is as neglected as it is important. Many take love for granted, and fail to devote any time at all to it. This is absurd, since love is the least understood of all disciplines. No one can say: I will leave the study of love to those who are interested in the subject — it does not concern me. The wisdom of love is unique in that it concerns everyone.

Most people are familiar with two apparently contradictory approaches to love: the puritanical and the permissive. In studying Jewish sources on the subject, I have come to adopt a harmonious approach, rejecting both conservatism and promiscuity, perceiving love as a harmonious convergence of mind, soul and body.

Research on the wisdom of love requires a special inspiration. First and for most I would like to thank my wife Riki, wife of my youth, beloved doe and source of my inspiration. The Hebrew version of this book (Ayelet Ahavim — Iyunim Bekhokhmat HaAhava) published in Israel in 2004 was dedicated to her.

I would like to thank my teacher, Prof. W. Zeev Harvey from the Hebrew University of Jerusalem, the first to introduce me to the wisdom of love. My colligues, friends and teachers have read all or part of the manuscript, and have offered helpful and instructive comments. I would like to thank Prof. Rachel Elior, Dr. David Satran, Prof. Eliezer Schweid, and Prof. Jacques Schlanger.

Shlomo Tikochinski read the entire (Hebrew) manuscript, making necessary corrections and helpful suggestions regarding both content and form, and prepared the bibliography and indices.

Thank you Shlomo for your scholarly support and participation.

Susan Elster-Zecher read the entire manuscript, making necessary corrections and helpful suggestions. Her help is very much appreciated.

The Van Leer Jerusalem Institute is my scholarly and creative home, so I would like to thank my colleagues and friends in the Institute for providing me with a permanent intellectual and friendly environment.

The English edition is an outcome of an initiative by a very special person and friend: *Karen A. Shapira*. She became interested in my various spheres of research, especially that of love. I found Karen to be a thinking person. She was curious and hungry for knowledge and willing to investigate every matter thoroughly and to deal with complexities in her own special fashion. She comprehended reality in various ways. In the ethical realm, for instance, she was always clear, acute, and uncompromising. In the intellectual sphere, her approach was one of experimentation and searching. She understood the cognitive structures of the rational method but also studied, with respect, curiosity, and a modest detachment, the worlds of mysticism and psychology. Above all, though, she will be remembered for her good heart and loving nature.

She very much wanted to read this book and initiated its translation into English. By the time the translation was completed Karen was unable to read it, and passed away three weeks later. Her desire and initiative have made these ideas accessible to an English readership. I would like to dedicate the English edition of the book to the beloved memory of Karen A. Shapira.

Thank you very much to Shmuel Sermoneta-Gertel for the translation from the Hebrew.

Working with Academic Studies Press was a pleasant experience. I like to thank Prof. Simcha Fishbane, Dr. Igor Nemirovsky and all who made this book published.

Wisdom of Love: Man, Woman & God in Jewish Canonical Literature introducing readers to the extensive, profound and significant treatment of love in the Jewish canon. Thus, although certain elements within Jewish society over the generations may have adopted approaches far from the rabbinical ideal of love, there has always been the possibility that they might return to the wisdom of love as expressed in the canonical sources. The prevailing view throughout these sources is that love, marriage, spiritual and physical harmony are in fact, the height of human perfection.

Naftali Rothenberg
The Van Leer Jerusalem Institute

Wisdom of Love

MAN, WOMAN & GOD
IN JEWISH CANONICAL LITERATURE

LOVE IN THE CANONICAL LITERATURE: DEALING WITH COGNITIVE DISSONANCE

I

Love between the sexes is a central and recurring theme in all of the Jewish canonical sources. The Bible, the Talmuds, the halakhic and midrashic literature, as well as mystical works such as the *Zohar*, devote considerable attention to the concept of love in all its manifestations, treating both the spiritual and physical aspects of love without inhibition or complexes of any kind. Surprisingly, the centrality and pervasiveness of love in the canonical writings, and particularly love between the sexes, has been largely ignored, even by those familiar with this corpus — as if their minds had filtered, censored or reinterpreted what their eyes had read. There is thus a considerable discrepancy between what people believe or expect the Bible and other canonical works to say on the subject of love, and the ideas that they actually express.

Wisdom of Love: Man, Woman & God in Jewish Canonical Literature strives to challenge this discrepancy between the way in which source texts relate to love and the way in which they are perceived to do so, introducing readers to the extensive, profound and significant treatment of love in the Jewish canon. It addresses some of the questions and dilemmas raised by this discrepancy, while disregarding others. There is no exhaustive discussion, for example, of the reasons behind the phenomenon. My intention was to challenge the discrepancy rather than analyse it. In other words, this is a book about love, not its repression; an opportunity to study the wisdom of love, not those who lack such wisdom and are unlikely to ever acquire it.

In dealing with the dissonance between the canonical sources and the way in which they are generally perceived, I have employed the following strategies:

1) Presenting one of the main reasons for the phenomenon and demonstrating its incongruousness with the content of the canon.

2) Offering an extensive and systematic review of canonical sources that run counter to prevailing views of biblical and other texts on the subject of love.

In terms of methodology, I have borrowed from a number of disciplines, including hermeneutics and, infrequently — where I felt it would contribute significantly to understanding or heightening an idea — comparative philology. *Wisdom of Love: : Man, Woman & God in Jewish Canonical Literature* comprises five studies, each focusing on a different facet of love in the canonical sources, although touching upon many of the same questions and issues throughout. All five studies employ the above strategies in addressing the discrepancy between the canon and perceptions of it.

II

The discussion of the dichotomous approach employs the first strategy. One of the reasons that readers are unaware of Scripture's extensive treatment of the subject of love between the sexes is that they simply do not expect it. They expect Scripture to address the sublime and the spiritual, not the base and the physical, and to their minds, love between the sexes belongs squarely in the latter category.

According to the dichotomous approach, spiritual development is contingent upon detachment from materialism and corporeality. Couple relationships are seen as an impediment to spiritual and intellectual growth — widely believed to require a commensurate renunciation of physical pursuits. At higher levels of spirituality one is expected to limit such activities to the minimum necessary to sustain the body and the soul it harbours within. One physical need that can be denied without jeopardising physical existence is the need for sex. This view is deeply entrenched in human consciousness in general and western culture, shaped by Christianity, in particular. The positions that derive from the dichotomous approach are addressed at length in a variety of Jewish sources. In this book you will find Jewish views supporting the dichotomous approach, as well as the prevailing belief in Judaism, that love between the sexes, spiritual development, holiness and prophecy are entirely compatible. This prevailing view in fact aspires to harmony between physical love and spirituality, as we shall see below.

III

The harmonious approach thus appears as a counterweight to the dichotomous view. The general lack of awareness regarding the centrality of love in the canonical writings is easily addressed by introducing readers to things they would not expect to find in Scripture, certainly not to such an extent, while freely discussing and analysing them, without inhibitions or complexes that might interfere with a clear and direct understanding of the texts. My intention however, was not to provide an anthology of traditional sources on the subject of love, for readers to judge for themselves. The selection here is far from exhaustive, and many sources were intentionally left out. The goal of the present work is to study the systematic association between these sources, to explore prevailing views on love in the canonical sources and the important questions the Rabbis sought to answer.

The harmonious approach to love between man and woman, which pervades the entire book, is a clear example of this systematic association. Most people are familiar with two possible approaches to love: the puritanical, which they ascribe to religion, Scripture and "spirituality"; and the permissive — generally considered materialistic and anti-spiritual, even in the eyes of its own exponents. In other words, whether one adopts a puritanical or permissive approach of lifestyle, one subscribes to a worldview based on the dichotomy between "spirit" and "matter", merely aligning oneself with one or the other side of the equation. The harmonious approach on the other hand — shown here to be the prevailing view on love in the canonical sources — rejects both puritanism and permissiveness. Love exists within the harmony of spirit and matter, mind and body. The sources seek to promote just such a relationship between man and woman — on the cognitive-intellectual, spiritual-emotional and physical planes. Accordingly, the repudiation of any of these three elements is seen to undermine and even abolish the love bond. Love's survival depends upon the constant effort to maintain harmony between mind, spirit and body.

The present study posits the existence of a systematic harmonious approach to love in the canonical sources. I would point out however, that to speak of "the thought of the Sages of the Talmud" is somewhat imprecise, due to the difficulty in establishing a comprehensive rabbinic position on most of the central philosophical issues.[1] Among the reasons for this difficulty is the fact that the sages of that era were concerned primarily with matters of Halakhah, to which they devoted the greater part of their work, from which we may, in turn, extrapolate their views on philosophical matters. Ideological, ethical, philosophical and other, non-halakhic ideas are expressed, for the most part, in the form of legends and homilies — later compilations of which, constitute the bulk of extant sources on such matters. Furthermore, we cannot reconstruct a comprehensive, philosophical system to which the Sages themselves never pretended. We lack sufficient knowledge of the historical context of many of the Rabbis' statements, and generally speaking, we have no idea of the specific circumstances in which they were made: to whom they were addressed, why, and

---

[1] See Urbach 1969.

what they actually meant at the time. The statements included in what is known as "Aggadah", that is the non-halakhic literature of the Talmud and Midrash, are thus extremely malleable and in a perpetual process of interpretation and reinterpretation. The sources themselves are generally fragmented, comprising only a few words or sentences rather than ordered and coherent paragraphs, not to mention chapters or longer works, which simply do not exist. There is thus no real substance that can be termed a "philosophical system". I have dwelt on the difficulty in ascribing a comprehensive philosophical system to the Sages of the Talmud in most areas of thought; in order highlight the very different situation with regard to the subject of love, as I hope to show in the chapters that follow. The fact is that sources from the mishnaic and Talmudic periods afford a surprisingly broad and stable foundation for a comprehensive system one might call the "position of the Sages" on the subject of love between the sexes. The harmonious approach, as noted above, lies at the heart of this philosophical method.[2]

IV

The second strategy in dealing with the dissonance between canonical sources on love and the way in which they are perceived pertains to the establishment of love as an independent discipline, a branch of wisdom to which all — or at least those who seek wisdom — must aspire. *Wisdom of Love* offers readers an introduction to the wisdom of love, including discussions of the following topics:

1) The difficulties, dilemmas and even absurdities that lovers may encounter.
2) Different expressions and manifestations of love, such as love of God, love of one's fellow, love of wisdom — and the relationship between these and love between man and woman.
3) The various components of love between the sexes and the relationship between its intellectual, emotional and physical aspects.
4) The philosophy and character of the sage of love, as found in the figures of Rabbi Akiva (from the Jewish canon) and Socrates (from the world of Greek philosophy).

This approach strives to bring about not only a change in perception — recognising the existence of the wisdom of love *per se* — but also the realisation, based on the following premises, that this wisdom is the very foundation of religious wisdom as a whole, rather than a peripheral branch of it:

[2]　See Rothenberg 2000, pp. 51-52.

1) All love derives from a single source: love between man and woman. It is from this source that all other manifestations of love, such as love of God, love of wisdom, love of one's fellow, draw their meaning.
2) The love and harmony between partners in a love relationship are the foundation upon which all morality, divine service and efforts to "repair" the world are built.
3) In the Kabbalah, human love relationships, desire and matchmaking are the concepts from which descriptions of the relationship between the divine world and the world of action are drawn, and as such are the very basis of mystical theology.

The above premises offer some explanation of how love became such a broad, comprehensive and central theme in the canonical sources.

V

The book comprises five sections — five separate studies that can, in theory, be read independently of one another. Together however, they create an overall picture of the wisdom of love and its many different facets. The main feature of this overall picture — stressed repeatedly throughout the book — is the harmonious approach to love relations between the sexes. In emphasising a single, central approach, I have neither ignored the existence of alternative views nor implied that this approach is without difficulties or lacunae. The scholarship in each of the sections attempts to address the difficulties, dilemmas and lacunae posed by the harmonious method, or to present positions based upon the rival, dichotomous approach.

The harmonious approach is constructed like a philosophical, moral or ideological system, based on a number of key elements. The most important of these is the androgyne myth, which in its Greek source actually represents an anti-harmonious approach. In Plato's *Symposium*, the androgynous attachment between male and female is a negative one that leads to rebellion against the gods, who represent perfection and harmony. Rabbinic sources adopted the androgyne myth as a founding myth, representing the ideal of the whole that derives from the unity of its two parts, man and woman. In the process, the Jewish canon reversed the story's anti-harmonious meaning.

The first section looks into the appearance of the androgyne myth in the Jewish canon, along with the messages, ideals and problems it presents. I have chosen this topic for the book's opening discussion, because it is the foremost element in the development of the harmonious approach. The title of this section, "The Androgyne — Unity; Separation; Desire and Unity", reflects the philosophical paradigm embodied in the myth, as it appears in the canon. The androgynous unity of male and female preceded the state of separation and is an expression of the harmonious whole. The source of this unity is the Godhead, the souls created from it, and the first "man" — made male and female in a single body. Epistemic awareness of the precedence of the androgynous whole is the source of the desire experienced by both male and female following their separation, which leads them to reunite. This positive approach to desire and reunion is unique to the rabbinic interpretation of the androgyne myth, and in fact sets Judaism apart from Christianity. Paul and the Church Fathers accept and stress the anti-harmonious aspect of the myth, which influenced the development of the concept of *original sin*. The myth is cited by the Rabbis in many different sources, dating from various periods. In these sources, the myth appears in entirely new contexts, conveying a variety of new messages; from the creation of the first human being as an androgyne to descriptions of God and divine harmony in terms of the union between male and female. The importance of the androgyne myth thus lies not in its explanation of the attraction between men and women — the reason they fall in love and seek unity and harmony in love — but in its view of love as the basis for a harmonious approach to all existence: between man and woman, heaven and earth, man and wisdom, man and God, and within the Godhead itself.

Nothing undermines the harmonious approach to love more than reality itself. Crises and failures, expected and unexpected difficulties, stand in the way of anyone who seeks to approach love from a harmonious perspective. The harmonious approach cannot remain an abstract concept, an idea that exists beyond the realm of reality. The entire force of the claim upon which it is based lies in the fact that it can be implemented in the real world that it flows from a harmonious reality that can be restored. Even a man and woman united in love must face the task of realising the love they share throughout their lives. The practical realisation of love is the greatest challenge to the harmonious approach, since reality often leaves love unrealised. The desire for the kind of union that expresses wholeness is frustrated by the desire for immediate gratification; the desire for conciliation and acceptance, by illness, misfortune and finally death.

The following sections, the second and the third, offer a thorough examination of the reasons behind the difficulty in realising love. Before the harmonious approach to love can be presented, we must first understand the obstacles that stand in the way of its realisation. The question of realisation is best explained by means of individual figures, whose reality we can envisage. (Such figures need not be historically accurate, or even real. For the purposes of this philosophical inquiry, fictional or fictionalised characters will do just as well.) The realisation of harmonious love is best explored through the words and behaviour of exemplary figures, rather than men and women selected at random. I sought paragons of wisdom, with coherent and consistent views on love as the wisdom of love. To this end, I chose two sages of love: Rabbi Akiva ben Joseph, and Philo, protagonist of Judah Abravanel's *Dialoghi d'Amore*.

The word "philosopher" is generally understood to mean one who loves wisdom and consequently pursues a life of study and contemplation in the hope of attaining knowledge for its own sake. Plato however, at the end of the fifth and beginning of the sixth book of his *Politics*, describes the philosopher not as one who seeks wisdom, but as one who has already attained it, one who knows the good. Some have therefore suggested that the platonic philosopher is not in fact one who loves wisdom, but one who is wise in love. Socrates, who famously asserted that he knows that which he does not know — indicating awareness of the infinity of knowledge and wisdom — also said of himself that he "understand[s] nothing but matters of love". The two figures whose work and lives I have chosen to present here, are worthy of the name philosopher both in the general sense and in the sense that they are versed in the wisdom of love.

The second section, entitled "**A Profile of the Sage of Love**", discusses Rabbi Akiva's philosophy of love, in light of his personal experience: the trials he encountered, his relationship with his wife Rachel, and ultimately, his torture and death. This mixture of philosophy and adversity makes Rabbi Akiva the ideal subject for a through study of the feasibility of the harmonious approach to love in truly difficult circumstances. The practical realisation of love is affected by factors such as the lapse of desire into lust, coping with adversity and death, and so forth. This section introduces readers to the wisdom of love, not only in a theoretical or abstract sense, but in the context of the contradictions and difficulties that arise in the course of its practical application. Rabbi Akiva was a theoretician of love, whose theoretical knowledge derived from, and was constantly measured against, his experiences throughout life, and even at the time of his death. He believed that all expressions of love — love of one's fellow, love of wisdom, love of man and love of God — ultimately flow from a single source: love between man and woman. Rabbi Akiva sought to complement his theory of love with a practical guide to its application — a behavioural code within the framework of Halakhah. The sage of love thus became the lawmaker of love, in the belief that the wisdom of love can serve as the basis for all human ethics.

The fact that Rabbi Akiva is presented in the Talmud as the sage of love par excellence is indicative of the centrality of the wisdom of love in the Jewish canon as a whole. Rabbi Akiva is not just another sage. He is the ultimate sage; the cornerstone upon which the entire body of tannaitic literature depends.

As noted above, it is reality that poses the greatest challenge to the harmonious approach to love. Unrealised love is far more common than realised love; or rather the period in which love is actually realised in a relationship is generally short-lived. The sources concerning Rabbi Akiva, cited and analysed in this section, afford only limited opportunity for discussion of the question of non-realisation. Rabbi Akiva's own remarkable achievements are the product of realised love, of Rachel's love for him, which enabled him to overcome all obstacles in love's path.

The third section, **"The Sage of Unconsummated Love: Judah Abravanel's** *Dialoghi d'amore*", takes a close look at Abravanel's work and the questions it raises. The book's most remarkable assertion is that the greatest impediments to the realisation of love between a man and a woman stem from the very love they feel for one another. The *Dialoghi d'amore* explore the tension between love and desire, including the age-old question whether love itself fades once it has been consummated. Is there a contradiction between the fulfilment of desire and the realisation of love? While Philo and Sophia debate this issue, readers discover one of the greatest obstacles to love's realisation: the paradox of abstract perception.

Abstract perception occurs when the image of a certain person is imprinted upon the soul or mind of another. Those who experience it need not physically see or touch the object of their perception in order to experience its presence. This type of perception is usually the result of a strong emotional bond, most commonly associated with love. The image imprinted upon the lover's soul is so compelling that the actual physical presence of the beloved may go unnoticed. Although it is love that creates the capacity for abstract perception, such perception may stand in the way of love's realisation. This is perhaps the greatest obstacle of all, since abstract perception leaves lovers convinced of their devotion, when the object of their attention is in fact an abstract image within their own souls. In this state of delusion, they are unaware of the obstacle they face and are thus unable to extricate themselves from it. The paradox lies in the fact that abstract perception is both the result of love and an impediment to its realisation.

The sage of unrealised love is extremely knowledgeable on the subject of love, yet is unable to realise his own love. He is the product of European Christian culture — like the readers for whom the book was intended. The obstacles faced by the sage of unrealised love are complex, as he swings, like a pendulum, in and out of the Christian world and its concepts. Even the definition of love's "realisation" differs from world to world. Abravanel's study offers significant insight into the relationship between Christian and post-Christian thought, as well as the relationship between Christianity and Judaism in this matter. He does not however, portray Judaism and Christianity as separate and antithetical cultures. In the *Dialoghi d'amore*, Abravanel carefully explores European culture as a whole, without pitting religion against religion or culture against culture. His criticism of Christian Puritanism is cleverly disguised as criticism of non-Christian thinkers or circles, such as those of ancient Greece, similar to those espoused by Christianity. Nowhere in the entire book is Christianity criticised directly. The author thus avoided accusations of anti-Christian polemic. The dialectic structure of the work lends itself to the simultaneous presentation of opposing views, leaving it up to the reader to decide between them. The book takes the discussion of love from the abstract and the conceptual to the practical experiences of real men and women; addressing issues such as sexual attraction, the relationship between love and beauty, and the different manifestations of love in the world.

While the third section explores extra-Christian views on love in relation to prevailing views within ecclesiastical culture, the fourth section examines the possible rediscovery of a modern idea in the Jewish canon. I refer to the feminist idea — to this day considered the most threatening of all modern ideas to the traditional norms that lie at the heart of religious attitudes.

The fourth section is entitled **"Written by Men for Men: Feminist Revolution and Innovation in the Canonical Sources".**[3] My intention was neither to project extraneous ideas upon the sources, nor to offer a "feminist reading" of the Bible, Talmud or Zohar. The question I asked was: Can we ascribe feminist innovation and even feminist revolution to these texts, as they stand? I do not want readers to imagine for one second that this literature was not created within a particular cultural and class context. It is a body of literature written by men for men, from which women are wholly excluded — whether as thinkers, authors or readers. That is not to say that the men who wrote these works took the gender reality of their time for granted. They tried to change it, daring to innovate, serving as messengers to their own cultural milieus.

A primary example of this is the opposition we find in the canon, to polygamy — a social norm that persisted for many centuries after the canonical texts first questioned its validity, right up to the Modern Era. The men, who wrote this literature, carried the message of monogamy to a polygamous society. The union of one woman and one man also reflects the view that perfection is achieved through the unification of male and female. The novelty in this approach lay in its assertion that man too is incomplete without woman — thereby creating space for the female experience in a hitherto male world. This extraordinary idea was given a solid theological foundation in the inclusion of the gender phenomenon — male and female equally — in the concept of *"imago dei"*, and later in the Godhead itself and the bi-sexual souls that emanate from it. Reciprocity and harmony between the sexes are thus afforded the greatest possible legitimacy, and a strong ideological and theological basis established for change and improvement in the status of women. This reduction of male territory results in the portrayal of the human male as a divided, imperfect creature, whose intellectual, moral, spiritual and certainly physical perfection is contingent upon a female partner and

---

[3] An earlier version of this section appeared in: R. Elior ed., *Men and Women: Gender, Judaism and Democracy*, the Van Leer Jerusalem Institute and Urim Publications, Jerusalem and New York, 2004.

a harmonious, reciprocal relationship. Such harmony is reflected in the ideal relationship delineated in the canon: a reciprocal bond that is physical as well as emotional and intellectual. To this end, the Torah gave husbands the special obligation of sex for the sake of pleasure — theirs and their wives'.

Surprisingly, this study of ostensibly feminist positions in the canon complements the idea of a harmonious approach to love and adds to our understanding of the wisdom of love.

A study on the wisdom of love cannot end on a simplistic note, with harmonious love and equality between the sexes. Reality is far more complex and *Wisdom of Love: Man, Woman & God in Jewish Canonical Literature* is not a romance novel, but a study of philosophical approaches and ideas. Moreover, harmonious love is not a permanent state but a constant challenge, far from universally accepted. The dichotomous approach to love has not vanished into thin air simply because we have introduced readers to the harmonious approach — in itself unstable, undermined by every setback in a relationship.

The fifth and final section of the book is entitled "**Contrast and Harmony in the Love Relationship — On Spirituality and Abstinence**". I have included this study primarily to give voice to alternatives to the harmonious approach, and to explore central themes in the canonical literature and mediaeval Jewish philosophy that do not coincide with the position I have adopted throughout the book. Three of the section's eight chapters relate to issues treated in the canonical literature: the dilemma of marriage versus individual intellectual development, sexual abstinence in general, and the specific case of Moses. Two further chapters address the issue of abstinence in mediaeval thought: abstinence as a precondition for love in the thought of Rabbi Bahya Ibn Pakuda, and the rejection of abstinence in the thought of Rabbi Judah Halevi.

This section sheds light on one of the causes of the cognitive dissonance noted at the beginning of this introduction: the large epistemic gap between what the Bible and the canonical literature actually say about love, and what people believe or expect them to say. The dichotomous approach is deeply ingrained in the minds of most people, and Jews are no exception, although — as I have tried to show in the first four sections of the book — this approach runs counter to the prevailing view in the Jewish canon. Once readers have been introduced to the harmonious approach, the book gives voice (retrospectively, from the reader's point of view) to the dichotomous approach, directly addressing those canonical sources in which it has become firmly established.

The dichotomous school does not go as far as presenting total abstinence as a worthy goal, even for Torah sages. Such a goal runs counter to halakhic principles, which is why we do not find the concept of celibacy in Jewish tradition, since the Torah obligates each and every Jew to marry and have sex not only for the sake of procreation, but also for the sake of the sexual pleasure of both partners. Any real-life attempt to apply the principles deriving from the dichotomous approach would clearly face halakhic constraints. The dichotomous school thus advocated abstinence to the limit of the permissible — based on the principle of minimum physical need — rather than complete abstinence.

The idea of inbuilt, total abstinence within the boundaries of Halakhah appears in Bahya Ibn Pakuda's *Duties of the Heart* (*Hovot Halevavot*). The fact that he is perhaps the only one of the great philosophers unequivocally associated with the dichotomous school speaks for itself. We must not however, underestimate his influence or that of earlier members of the school. Interestingly, many of those who embraced Ibn Pakuda's philosophical views were also influenced by those of the opposing school, without noticing the fundamental incompatibility of the two positions. There are three possible explanations for this: 1) Most people are receptive to Ibn Pakuda's ideas, because the dichotomy they represent confirms their own a priori perceptions. 2) Ibn Pakuda presents a clear spiritual and intellectual goal, as well as gradual path to its achievement. 3) His adherence to the principles of Halakhah and the limits it imposes on abstinence result in a moderate philosophy with broad public appeal.

The dichotomous school focuses primarily on the contradiction between material life in general and married life in particular, and the attainment of spiritual and intellectual goals. Since complete abstinence from marriage is not an option, it argues that one must engage in Torah study and intellectual development before taking on the yoke of marriage and family. This position stands at the heart of a Talmudic debate regarding the issue of sexual abstinence during marriage. A number of the exponents of the dichotomous approach suggest that a husband may temporarily abstain from sexual relations with his wife, for the sake of Torah study and the attainment of lofty intellectual goals. This approach is vehemently rejected by the exponents of the harmonious approach, who caution that abstinence after marriage places the abstainer, as pure as his intentions may be, in no less than a life-threatening situation. Abstinence, according to this view, undermines human existence and is a complete distortion of man's duty to God.

The dichotomous approach draws its strongest support from the greatest figure in the Jewish canon — Moses — who abstained from relations with his wife, thereby demonstrating that spiritual stature such as his is incompatible with conjugal life. Maimonides, in the *Guide for the Perplexed*, writes: "The object of this Law is that all men should be like that man [Moses]". In other words, Moses is the human figure all must strive to emulate, although none will ever reach his spiritual-prophetic level. Is Moses also a role model in the matter sexual abstinence? This is highly doubtful, judging by the sources that address the issue of Moses' abstinence — some of which even imply cautious criticism of the great man's behaviour.

VI

A study of love in the canonical sources cannot be confined to the philosophical or the theological, but must explore practical aspects as well. The wisdom of love in the canon draws its strength from the way in which legend, myth and philosophy converge with halakhic practice in the daily lives of men and women. This connection between the realm of thought and imagination on the one hand, and practical behaviour on the other, produces a winning formula; one that is virtually impossible to reject or ignore. Legends, myths and theories are constantly contradicted, rejected and even forgotten over time, while principles applied to everyday existence — in love as in other matters — give substance to the abstract and make ideas solid facts of life.

The wisdom of love is universal, and although it is addressed here from a Jewish perspective, it is by no means limited to any one culture. Specific cultural context offers far greater insight into a given phenomenon than its universalisation. I have therefore chosen to discuss the wisdom of love with people of all backgrounds through the medium of Jewish culture and its sources. The androgyne myth, which came to Judaism from ancient Greece, can be found in other mythologies as well — some quite removed from one another. At first glance, the figure of the sage of love, represented here by Rabbi Akiva, appears to be a specifically Jewish phenomenon, until a comparison with Socrates places it in a different cultural context. Philo — the literary creation of the Jewish sage Leone Ebreo or Judah Abravanel — is emblematic of the universality of the wisdom and the sage of love. It is my sincere hope that readers of all backgrounds will come to see this book as a guide to the wisdom of love. Whether or not they accept the conclusions I have reached in the studies presented here, may they continue to grapple with the questions that should trouble all who do not take love for granted.

THE ANDROGYNE UNITY; SEPARATION; DESIRE AND UNITY

Chapter One

THE ANDROGYNE MYTH ACCORDING TO PLATO

A group of men gathered at the home of Agathon, writes Plato in the "*Symposium*", including Socrates, Eryximachus son of Acumenus, Phaedrus, Pausanius, Aristophanes, their host, and others. Eryximachus suggests that they devote their banquet to speeches in honour of *Eros*, who in his opinion does not receive the recognition he deserves: ". . . to this day no one has ever dared worthily to hymn Love's praises! So entirely has this great deity been neglected" (Plato's *Symposium*, 177c). Eryximachus' suggestion is welcomed with great enthusiasm, especially after Socrates' adds his support: "No one will vote against you, Eryximachus, said Socrates. How can I oppose your motion, who professes to understand nothing but matters of love?" (*ibid.* 177d-e).

The various speakers praise Eros and extol his might, not only as the deity charged with arousing love between human beings, but as the source of universal love "to be found in the bodies of all animals and productions of the earth". They accept Eryximachus' suggestion that they devote their speeches to praise of Eros, but ignore the problem that had given rise to the suggestion: the fact that human beings do not give Eros his due. Aristophanes is the only one to devote the greater part of his speech to the question of why men fail to recognize the power and blessings of Eros. According to Aristophanes the problem is neither one of neglect nor of ingratitude toward the god who is "of all the gods . . . the best friend of men, the helper and the healer of the ills which are the great impediment to the happiness of the race" (*ibid.* 189d), but that mankind has never understood the power of Eros or the good that he has bestowed upon them. The reason for this lies in man's ancient androgynous nature. Here Plato affords his readers a first account of the myth — a long and detailed account to which the myth owes its great fame:

"For the original human nature was not like the present, but different. The sexes were not two as they are now, but originally three in number; there was man, woman, and the union of the two, having a name corresponding to this double nature, which had once a real existence, but is now lost, and the word "Androgynous" is only preserved as a term of reproach. In the second place, the primeval man was round, his back and sides forming a circle; and he had four hands and four feet, one head with two faces, looking opposite ways, set on a round neck and precisely alike; also four ears, two privy members, and the remainder to correspond."

Ibid. 189d-190a

This legend goes far beyond other accounts of mythological beings: dragons as big as mountains, birds as big as fortresses, sea-monsters as big as islands, flying horses and other winged creatures — all breathing fire wreaking havoc and sowing destruction and death. These beings arouse anxiety and wonder due to their strangeness, and touch upon reality only as its antithesis, threatening to undermine it. Reality is defined independently of the spectacular phenomena of legend, and it is this independent existence that evokes wonder at the sudden appearance of such outlandish creatures.

The androgyne myth however, does not belong to this genre of spectacular legend. It neither challenges known reality with its strangeness nor attempts to introduce that strangeness into reality. It is more far-reaching and revolutionary than other myths in that it changes reality itself: "for the original human nature was not like the present, but different". It is no longer the same reality, the world as we know it; but a previous world, different from ours in two ways. First, there were three genders: male, female and androgynous. Mankind was not as we know it — divided into two sexes, with the attendant gender relations — but formed a three-gendered triangle. Second, the appearance of human beings of all three sexes differed from that of the human form we know. From our perspective (which is of course Plato's perspective as well), these beings were round rather than elongated, possessed two sets of organs rather than one, and "terrible was their might and strength".

These mighty human creatures lived without fear or threat to their survival. They were able to rely on their own terrible strength, and this filled them with such pride that they rebelled against the gods: "and the thoughts of their hearts were great, and they made an attack upon the gods". Plato cites the ancient tale of the giants Otus and Ephialtes who rebelled against the gods and drove them from Olympus. Not satisfied with this, they tried to set Mount Ossa atop Mount Olympus, and Mount Pelion atop of Ossa, that they might attack the gods in heaven itself.

The rebellion of course angered the gods, and Zeus foremost: "Doubt reigned in the celestial councils. Should they kill them . . . there would be an end of the sacrifices and worship which men offered to them; but, on the other hand, the gods could not suffer their insolence to be unrestrained." Finally, after much deliberation, Zeus decided to punish them by splitting them in half, thereby diminishing their strength and causing them to behave more humbly and cease the insolence that had brought them to rise up against the gods.

There were two stages to the operation performed on the humans punished by Zeus. First came the punishment itself—splitting in half—implemented by Zeus, with the assistance of Apollo. Each half longed for its other half, seeking it out, and once found, the two would sit embracing one another, dying of hunger and neglect since they did not wish to do anything apart. Then came the second stage, mitigation of their punishment: Zeus in his mercy moved their genitalia to the front of their bodies "and they sowed the seed no longer as hitherto like grasshoppers in the ground, but in one another; and after the transposition the male generated in the female," that they might have sex and "go their ways to the business of life".

The ancient androgyne myth answers a number of important questions: What is the secret of the attraction between men and women? Why do men and women desire one another, fall in love and seek to become one in their love? In the words of Plato, spoken by Aristophanes:

> "So ancient is the desire of one another which is implanted in us, reuniting our original nature, making one of two, and healing the state of man. Each of us when separated, having one side only . . . and the desire and pursuit of the whole is called love . . . But my words have a wider application — they include men and women everywhere; and I believe that if our loves were perfectly accomplished, and each one returning to his primeval nature had his original true love, then our race would be happy. And if this would be best of all, the best in the next degree and under present circumstances must be the nearest approach to such a union; and that will be the attainment of a congenial love. Wherefore, if we would praise him who has given to us the benefit, we must praise the god Love, who is our greatest benefactor, both leading us in this life back to our own nature, and giving us high hopes for the future, for he promises that if we are pious, he will restore us to our original state, and heal us and make us happy and blessed."
>
> *Ibid.* 191c-193d

Plato approaches this legend with the skill of a master storyteller who is loathe to detract from the unique character of the story, yet wishes to bring the ancient myth to the philosophical discussion table, and to use it to support universal assertions pertaining to human beings of his day and age. Such is the power of a legend that has become myth—there is no need to awaken from its charm to grim reality. The attraction we have for the opposite sex was implanted in us in ancient times, inherited from the previous human condition, when two of us were one. Eros' gift to mankind after the separation of the androgyne into man and woman, was the desire for perfection. It is not merely a primal desire to reunite, an ancient characteristic cast in our nature since the division of androgynous man, a meaningless animal instinct, but rather a quality of the spirit, soul and mind, linked first and foremost to the wisdom of desire for perfection. There is a transcendent idea involved, associated therefore with Eros, who blessed us by implanting in us the desire for perfection, guiding us and indicating the path to its achievement. The passage from myth to philosophical discussion is thus made possible through the use of a terminological structure reflected in the present case by two concepts: perfection and wisdom.

If the lovers' desire for unity derives only from their ancient androgynous condition, why does that necessarily imply a desire for perfection? It is true that the androgyne constitutes a whole relative to its component halves, but one need not claim that it is perfect and that a return to one's natural state is perfection. The distinction is fine, but the concept of perfection is unnecessary here. It is an addition, a divine gift that affords the attraction that stems from the condition described in the ancient tale, its transcendence: a desire for perfection. Transferring the desire for unity between the sexes from the plane of primordial nature to the transcendent plane further requires the concept of wisdom. The transcendent ideal cannot be attained without wisdom, and the consummation of the desire for perfection thus lies in wisdom: "the human race will be happy if we bring wisdom to perfection".

We must further understand the concept of rebellion against the gods. An attack on the gods is an attack on transcendent ideals, on the good and the sublime, on wisdom and perfection. All immoral behaviour on the part of an individual is in fact an attack on transcendent ideals, but when the phenomenon involves all of humanity, like the rebellion described here; it is far more than that. The struggle against the rule of the gods was in truth a struggle against the desire for perfection, against the aspiration to lofty ideals and to making such ideals ever-present in man's actions.

Plato sheds little light on the motivation behind man's rebellion. The rebellion against the gods is not the main subject of Aristophanes' discourse, but an important element through which he wishes the unfolding story to be understood — the act that brought androgynous man the punishment of separation into male and female. Let us examine the little information Plato offers us in this matter:

> "Terrible was their might and strength, and the thoughts of their hearts were great, and they made an attack upon the gods; of them is told the tale of Otus and Ephialtes who, as Homer says, dared to scale heaven, and would have laid hands upon the gods."
>
> *Ibid.* 190c

Mankind's tremendous power led to the sin of hubris, which in turn led to rebellion against the gods, with the apparent intention of replacing them.

Did all mankind rebel against the gods, or only the androgynes?

There is no clear answer to this question. Judging by the punishment — human beings of all three genders were cut in two by Zeus — we might infer that all had sinned. It is possible however that only the androgynes had rebelled against the gods, and that the reason all were cut in two was primarily aesthetic, so that all human beings might have the same appearance, "they shall walk upright on two legs" (*ibid.* 190d).

At the end of the description of man's ancient nature, which comprised three genders, we read:

> "Now the sexes were three, and such as I have described them; because the sun, moon, and earth are three; and the man was originally the child of the sun, the woman of the earth, and the man-woman of the moon, which is made up of sun and earth, and they were all round and moved round and round: like their parents. Terrible was their might and strength, and the thoughts of their hearts were great, and they made an attack upon the gods; of them is told the tale of Otus and Ephialtes who, as Homer says, dared to scale heaven, and would have laid hands upon the gods."
>
> *Ibid.* 190b-c

The androgyne — the gender comprising both male and female — derived from the moon, which in turn comprised both sun and earth. The story implies that only the androgynes rebelled, although it is not stated explicitly in the text. Earlier, Aristophanes says of this gender: ". . . and the union of the two, having a name corresponding to this double nature, which had once a real existence, but is now lost, and the word "Androgynous" is only preserved as a term of reproach." The "reproach" would appear to refer to the unaesthetic union of male and female in a single body, but is perhaps also a reminder of the androgynes of antiquity, who rebelled against the gods.

Furthermore, the explicit reference to Homer as the source of the rebellion story does not imply a general rebellion by man, but rather a rebellion conducted by a number of specific individuals: ". . . of them is told the tale of Otus and Ephialtes who, as Homer says, dared to scale heaven, and would have laid hands upon the gods."[1]

---

[1] Homer, *Odyssey*, 11, 305-320. Otus and Ephialtes were the illegitimate sons of Iphimedeia, daughter of Triops, and her father-in-law Poseidon. Ephialtes and Otus, called Aloadae after their mother's husband Aloeus, became great giants who were completely fearless as a result of a prophecy that neither man nor god could kill them. They piled the mountains Ossa and Pelion on Olympus in order to ascend to heaven and fight the gods. Artemis lured them to the island of Naxos and leapt between them in the form of a beautiful doe. They cast their spears at her, but hit each other instead, thus dying at the hand of neither man nor god. The Homeric text gives no indication that Otus and Ephialtes were androgynous. Plato however, appears to have identified Homer's account with the androgyne myth or the myth of primordial human nature in general.

This reference supports the premise that only the androgynes rebelled against the gods.[2]

The fact that the androgynes and their descendants are perceived in a negative light appears later on in Aristophanes words, in reference to the attraction the separated creatures' descendants have for one another. "The women who are a section of the woman do not care for men, but have female attachments; the female companions are of this sort." "They who are a section of the male . . . hang about men and embrace them, **and they are themselves the best of boys and youths.**" Male homosexuality enjoys a certain amount of approval; female homosexuality is reported in a neutral fashion. The descendants of the androgynes however — women who are attracted to men and men who are attracted to women — are described in a critical fashion:

> "Men who are a section of that double nature which was once called Androgynous are lovers of women; adulterers are generally of this breed, and also adulterous women who lust after men."
>
> *Ibid.* 191d-e

Despite the natural attraction men are destined to feel toward women and vice versa, Aristophanes perceives an inherent negativity in the necessary relationship between man and woman. This negativity also existed when both sexes were united in the body of the ancient androgyne, and that is what drove them to rise up against transcendent ideals, virtue and the sublime, and to rebel against the gods. Since the punishment of separation, the force of this inherent negativity in these men and women has been directed toward undermining the social order and the family unit: i.e. adultery. Only revering the gods will preserve us from further punishment, lest we be divided in two once more.

Chapter Two
MALE AND FEMALE UNITY, PRIMORDIAL SIN AND REBELLION AGAINST THE GODS

This mythological tradition and particularly its platonic interpretation — whereby the androgyne is perceived as inherently negative in its opposition to virtue, spirituality and the sublime — may have influenced the doctrine of "original sin" that later developed in Pauline Christianity.[3] Paul asserted that Adam's

---

[2]   Most exponents of Plato have understood that only the androgynes rebelled against the gods. See also Abravanel (Hebrew edition, M. Dorman ed.) p. 406, and the beginning of this section.

[3]   See *Romans* 1:22-27. Paul's words have aroused considerable theological debate among Christians. Modern commentators have explained this passage in various ways.

sin affected all of his descendants, since in his sin he bequeathed to them flesh tainted with lust and passions, thereby condemning them to sin.[4] Sin is inevitable, and complete liberation from sin is impossible as long as one lives within a human body. It is ingrained in the body (perhaps is the body itself), and is reflected in the body's desires, such as the physical relationship between man and woman. Not only is this desire wholly devoid of spirituality, it is the essence of sin inherited from Adam.

Later, it was Augustine of Hippo,[5] one of the Church Fathers, who made the important distinction between lust, and sex for the sake of procreation. He asserts that Adam and Eve would have procreated in the Garden of Eden had they not sinned and been banished from the Garden. Their sin added the negative dimension — that of lust — to their relationship. Lust is therefore the result of original sin, and not of sex for the sake of procreation.[6] Augustine's disapprobation of lust should not be seen as recommending that one follow in the footsteps of the stoics, who called for the suppression of desire and the emotions that arouse it. Augustine sees emotions as positive elements of human nature, since they are God-given. One must control one's emotions, according to Augustine, by channelling them in a positive direction, rather than by repressing them. Love, for example, exists within every person, but one must know how to channel it in an appropriate fashion. The correct manner in which to direct love, in Augustine's opinion, is toward love of one's fellow man and love of God.[7] Original sin is not the only way in which to neutralise

---

[4] See Urbach 1969, p. 373 and nn. 7, 8. See also *Dictionary of the History of Ideas*, vol. 4, pp. 228-230; Bultmann [1949] 1950, pp. 46-92; Gutrie 1950; and D. Flusser, *Judaism and the Origins of Christianity*, Magnes Press, Jerusalem 1988, pp. 60–71. Flusser compares the Dead Sea Scrolls and the New Testament. In both of these religious movements, he perceives the influence of those Greek schools of thought (eg Plato) that juxtaposed the physical and the spiritual, emphasising man's corporeal nature. Flusser also claims a certain Gnostic influence upon both movements.

[5] Aurelius Augustinus (354-430), bishop of the port of Hippo — now Annaba, Algeria. His rather extensive writings have greatly influenced Christian theology and western culture in general.

[6] *City of God*, XIV, pp. 22-24, 26. The androgyne myth clearly influenced Augustine, who admired Plato but criticised the Neo-Platonism of his day. This influence can be seen in Augustine's perception of an inherent negativity in the purely libidinous union of man and woman, on the one hand, and the legitimacy of sex for the sake of procreation on the other. This approach corresponds to that of Plato. In the Platonic story, Aristophanes emphasises the negative aspect of the attraction between men and women, but also recounts how Zeus in pity turned the parts of generation round to the front, that male might generate in female, and the race might continue.

[7] H. Chadwick, *Augustine*, Oxford University Press, New York, 1986, p. 98. Earlier (p. 2), Chadwick writes: "The aspirations of all western mystics have never escaped his [Augustine's] influence, above all because of the centrality of the love of God in his thinking. He first saw the paradox that love, which is in quest of personal happiness, necessarily implies some self-renunciation and the pain of being made what one is not."

the centrality and significance of the relationship between male and female. Messianic Christian belief, according to Paul, creates a dichotomy between earthly reality and lofty spirituality, raising up humanity as a whole, beyond its individual corporeal parts:

> "For ye are all the children of God by faith in Christ Jesus. For as many of you as have been baptized into Christ have put on Christ. There is neither Jew nor Greek, there is neither bond nor free, **there is neither male nor female**: for ye are all one in Christ Jesus."
>
> *Galatians 3:26-8*

Paul is not referring of course to the relationship between man and woman, but to the Christian gospel preached to all of mankind, and to the equality conferred by baptism. Nevertheless, he points out an important theological principle beyond the gospel itself — the significance of the level attainable by all through baptism, in its ability to take people to a spiritual plane on which the differences between them are eliminated, and consequently also the relationships deriving from these differences. The elimination of differences includes, as noted in the above passage, "neither male nor female". Paul was undoubtedly aware of the biblical precepts governing relations between different types of people, including those pertaining to husband and wife: not only the commandment to be fruitful and multiply, but also the commandment of *onah*, i.e. sex for the sake of pleasure. It is in reference to such precepts, *inter alia*, that he offers his explanation regarding the completion of the role of the Torah, or more precisely the precepts of the Torah, following Jesus' revelation: "Wherefore then serveth the law? It was added because of transgressions, till the seed should come to whom the promise was made;" (*Galations* 3:19) and "But the scripture hath concluded all under sin, that the promise by faith of Jesus Christ might be given to them that believe. But before faith came, we were kept under the law . . ." (*ibid.* 22). Now, once faith in Jesus Christ has become possible, says Paul, the precepts in general, and those pertaining to conjugal relations in particular, no longer release man from sin. On the contrary, the precepts were added because of transgressions, and deliver man to sin, so that he will always be a sinner, safeguarding himself through the precepts. Only belief in Jesus Christ will release one from sin as well as from the need for the precepts of the Torah — based upon a profound dichotomy and aspiration to complete liberation from the sin ingrained within the flesh: "But put ye on the Lord Jesus Christ, and make not provision for the flesh, to fulfil the lusts thereof" (*Romans* 13:14).

Views on marriage became a prominent feature in the debate between Jews and Christians.[8] One extreme position taken against Christian abstinence is

---

[8] See Jeremy Cohen, "*Mitzvat Periah Ureviah Umekomah Bapulmus Hadati*", in I. Bartal and I. Gafni (eds.), *Eros, Erusin Ve'Isurim*, 5758 (1998), and Joseph Dan, *On sanctity : religion, ethics and mysticism in Judaism and other religions* (Heb), 1998, pp. 338-339.

based upon a "reverse argument": Contrary to the belief that abstinence from physical contact between man and woman are the way to spiritual ascent and purification, it is claimed that Christians who have not married and born children should be considered impure specifically because of their abstinence. This position, appearing at the very outset of Jewish-Christian debate, is expressed as follows in a Jewish polemical text of the Middle Ages:

> "Let them be asked: If the (celibate) priest supersedes the Temple priest, why does he not take a wife and beget sons, as did the high priest Aaron son of Amram? Moreover, the first commandment given to Adam was that he be fruitful and multiply, yet you refrain from procreation, and engage in harlotry and wine-drinking that captures your hearts."
>
> *Sefer Nitzahon Yashan*, p. 178

Abstinence is denounced on the grounds that not only does it not increase purity, but in fact causes celibates to fall into a state of impurity, since their sexual desires are not satisfied within the framework of marriage and the harmony of a relationship between a man and a woman.[9] The very argument employed by Christians in defence of celibacy is turned against them.

Chapter Three

IN THE MIDRASH: ANDROGYNOUS ADAM

Midrashic references to ancient, primordial man are limited mostly to the figure of Adam and the verses in *Genesis* pertaining to the creation of man.

The story of man's creation appears three times in the Torah's book of *Genesis*. In the first chapter account of the six days of creation, three verses describe the creation of man on the sixth day. The essence of the account: Man was created in God's image — male and female. This version is repeated in two verses at the end of chapter five. Between these two accounts however, a third, more complex account of man's creation appears. The story recounted in five

---

[9]   See I. Gafni 1988, pp. 14-28. The Mesopotamian Church father Aphrahat wrote, against the Jewish approach: "I have written to you, my beloved, concerning virginity and sanctity, because I have heard about a Jewish man who shamed one of our brethren, the children of our Church, saying to him, 'You are unclean, for you do not take wives. But we are holy and excellent, who procreate and increase seed in the world'" (in J. Neusner, *Aphrahat and Judaism: The Christian-Jewish Argument in Fourth-century Iran*, Brill, Leiden 1971, p. 82). In a similar vein, John Chrysostom wrote, in the fourth century: "The Jews disdained the beauty of virginity, which is not surprising since they heaped ignominy upon Christ himself, who was born of a virgin. The Greeks admired and revered the virgin, but only the Church of God adored her with zeal" (John Chrysostom, *On Virginity*, 1, 1). See Jeremy Cohen, *ibid.* pp. 90-91.

verses in chapter two can be taken to mean that man was first created solely male, and that woman was subsequently fashioned from man's rib. In this version of the story, no reference is made to man's creation in God's image, or to the equal creation of male and female.

Genesis 1:26-28	Genesis 5:1-2	Genesis 2:7; 18; 21-24
And God said: 'Let us make man in our image, after our likeness; and let them have dominion . . . So God created man in His own image, in the image of God created He him; male and female created He them. And God blessed them; and God said unto them: 'Be fruitful, and multiply, and replenish the earth, and subdue it . . .	This is the book of the generations of Adam. In the day that God created man, in the likeness of God made He him; Male and female created He them, and blessed them, and called their name Adam, in the day when they were created.	And the Lord God formed man of the dust of the ground, and breathed into his nostrils the breath of life; and man became a living soul. And the Lord God said: 'It is not good that the man should be alone; I will make him a help meet for him.' And the Lord God caused a deep sleep to fall upon the man, and he slept; and He took one of his ribs, and closed up the place with flesh instead thereof. And the rib, which the Lord God had taken from the man, made he a woman, and brought her unto the man. And the man said: 'This is now bone of my bones, and flesh of my flesh; she shall be called Woman, because she was taken out of Man.' Therefore shall a man leave his father and his mother, and shall cleave unto his wife, and they shall be one flesh.

According to most of the midrashic literature on the subject of man's creation, the definitive version is the one appearing in chapters one and five. Man was created in the image of God, male and female. The complex story told in chapter two is interpreted by the authors of the Midrash in a fashion that preserves the uniformity and coherence of the biblical account of man's creation in chapters one and five.

The ancient Jewish sages addressed all of the elements of the mythological tradition:[10] androgyne, rebellion and punishment. They adopted the legend, but changed its messages in keeping with the principles of their beliefs. In rabbinic

---

[10]   Scholars differ as to whether *amoraim* would have had access to mythological tradition. See Urbach, *Hazal: Pirkei Emunot Vede'ot*, p. 201 n. 38.

literature, we find a reworking of all of the basic elements appearing in Plato's *Symposium*, laying the foundation in Jewish tradition **for a unifying approach to love of transcendent ideals, and physical desire.**

According to Aristophanes, our ancient nature comprised three genders: male, female and a composite of the two. The rabbis went even further in their version of the myth, asserting that all mankind, represented by the figure of Adam, once comprised both male and female in a single body:

> "Rabbi Yirmiyah ben Elazar said: When God created Adam, He created him androgynous, as it is written: 'male and female created He them'. Rabbi Shmuel bar Nahman said: When God created Adam, He created him double-faced, and sawed him [in two], giving him two backs, one back facing one direction and one back facing the other."

Midrash, Bereshit Rabbah 8, 1[11]

Adam, who was created alone and thus embodies all of mankind, was androgynous, i.e. a bi-sexual being, male and female bound together in a single male-female body: "He created him androgynous . . . He created him double-faced".

The androgyne myth is thus alive and well in ancient Jewish midrash,[12] some 1, 500 years after Homer, and a thousand years after its detailed retelling by Plato — in the fifth century CE *Bereshit Rabbah*, and as we shall see below, in a significant number of other midrashic works.[13] The essence of the story, the existence of the androgyne, appears in these rabbinic sources, as well as its division into two separate beings — one male and the other female: "and sawed him [in two], giving him two backs, one back facing one direction and one back facing the other." Plato, through Aristophanes, asserts the existence of three genders — male, female and androgynous — while the Midrash

---

[11]   Cf. *Vayikra Rabbah* 14, pass. Begin. "*o ishah*": "Rabbi Shmuel bar Nahman said: When God created Adam, he created him androgynous. Resh Lakish said: When he [Adam] was created, he was created double-faced, and [God] sawed him [in half] and he became two-backed a back for the male and a back for the female." And *Tanhuma, Tazria* 1: "Rabbi Shimon ben Gamliel says: What is the meaning of 'Thou hast beset me behind and before'? These are two faces, as it is written 'male and female created He them'." See also Babylonian Talmud, *Eruvin* 18a and *Berakhot* 61a; *Midrash Tehilim*, psalm 139, pass. begin. "*ahor vekadam*". Some of these sources will be discussed below. On the philological aspects of the discussion, see the Albek edition reading cited below.

[12]   It is not our intention here, to discuss halakhic references to androgynous individuals — those who possess both male and female reproductive organs — because such references are not relevant to the discussion at hand. Nevertheless, the halakhic approach to androgynes is not negative. For most purposes, Halakhah considers androgynes to be male, because they are perceived as being predominantly male, but as we have said, this subject is not pertinent to our discussion. For further study, see *Mishnah, Yevamot* 8, 6; *Shabbat* 136b; *Hagigah* 4a; *Yevamot* 72b; *ibid*. 81a, and Rashi *loc. cit.*, pass. beg. "*aval lo nisa*"; *ibid*. 83b; Rashi *Bava Batra* 126b, pass. beg. "*amar rabbi ami*".

[13]   The androgyne myth as it appears in the *Zohar* will be discussed separately below.

presents a version of the myth in which all of mankind, personified by Adam, was androgynous, making all of humanity descendants of the androgyne. The difference between the Greek and Jewish sources is reflected in details that do not affect the essence of the mythological narrative: the androgyne and its division into male and female. The legend became a myth that addresses love's great questions and desires: What is the secret of the attraction between men and women? Why do they long for one another, fall in love and seek to unite in their love? Above the answer to these important questions hovers, in all its exhilarating glory, the idea of complete unity of the two who were once one, who seek to be one again through the passion of their love.

The fact that the Jewish authors of the Midrash adopted the androgyne myth from Greek culture is evidenced not only by the similarity of the narratives, but also by philological examination of the story as it appears in the Midrash. Even upon first reading, use of the Greek word *androgunos* (ανδρογυνο) clearly indicates the cultural roots of this ancient legend. No less indicative of the legend's Greek origins however are the versions of the midrash that do not explicitly use the word *androgunos,* choosing in its place the expression *dio partzufin* or *dio partzuf panim,* meaning "double-faced". The word *dio,* which means "two" in Greek, is transcribed here in its Greek form δυο, rather than in its more common Aramaic form *du,* which also comes from the Greek. So too the word *partzufin,* which came to Aramaic and Hebrew from Greek (προσωπον).[14] In *Bereshit Rabbah* 5, in the Albek edition, the Greek form *diprosopos* (δι προσωπο) appears directly in the text:

> "Rabbi Shmuel bar Nahman said: When God created Adam, He created him *diprosopon* (double-faced) . . . ".

Philological study leaves no doubt that the androgyne myth in its original Greek form was well known to the Jewish sages, and they chose to include it in their homiletic interpretations of biblical passages.

The author of the midrash in *Bereshit Rabbah,* citing Rabbi Yirmiyah ben Elazar, chose to associate his assertion with *Genesis* 5:1-2: "This is the book of the generations of Adam. In the day that God created man, in the likeness of

---

[14]   *Cf. Eruvin* 18a: "Rabbi Yirmiyah ben Elazar said: Adam had two faces (*dio partzuf panim*) . . . ". The words *partzuf* and *panim* are synonomous: *partzuf* (προσωπον) in Greek, and *panim* in Hebrew. See also S. Lieberman, *Yevanim Veyavnut Be'eretz Yisrael* (Greeks and Hellenism in Jewish Palestine), Jerusalem, 5723 (1963), pp. 12-21, in the chapter "*Hayevanit shel Hehakhamim*" ("*The Greek of the Rabbis*"). Lieberman discusses the Aramaic-Greek vernacular that had developed among the Jews of Palestine. See also *Arukh Hashalem,* under *Dio-partzufin*; YZ Feintuch, *Mesorot Unus'ha'ot Batalmud,* Jerusalem 5745 (1985), pp. 193-198, on the MS variants of the word *androginos,* and their significance for the study of MS transmission.

God made He him; **Male and female created He them,** and blessed them, and called their name Adam, in the day when they were created." He prefers these verses to the verse in Gen 1 that describes man's creation in the context of the six days of creation — "So God created man in His own image, in the image of God created He him; **male and female created He them**" — although there is no significant difference between the two accounts, and it would have been more appropriate to support his statement with a verse from the creation story itself rather than a source appearing four chapters later and only as a summary leading into the genealogy of Adam's descendants.

The author of this midrash would appear to have chosen the verses from chapter 5 for two reasons. The first reason is the fine distinction that can be made between the Hebrew words *bara otam* and *bera'am* (both translated as "created He them"). The presence of two separate entities is slightly stronger in the former expression, than in the latter, which lends itself more readily to the interpretation "created He them — in a single body". The second, more convincing reason concerns the final part of the passage in chapter 5: "and called their name Adam, in the day when they were created". The simple meaning of this passage is that "Adam" is the shared name of both male and female. Male and female were thus given a single **common** name, easily paving the way for "when God created Adam, He created him androgynous". The two shared not only a single name, but a single body as well.

Other Midrashim associate the androgyne legend with *Psalms* 139:5 and the unusual spelling of the word *vayitzer* (formed) in *Genesis* 2:7:

> "Why is 'And the Lord God formed (*vayitzer*) man' written with two *yodin* (the Hebrew letter *yod*) . . . As Rabbi Yirmiyah ben Elazar said: God created two faces in Adam, as it is written: 'Thou hast beset me behind and before.'"
>
> Babylonian Talmud, *Berakhot* 61a

The above talmudic discussion begins with a homily by Rabbi Nahman bar Hisda on the good and evil inclinations (*yetzarim*), citing the doubling of the letter *yod* in the word *vayitzer* (*Genesis* 2:7), in the second account of man's creation. It is clear from the way in which the discussion unfolds that the editor preferred to associate the double *yod* in *vayitzer* with another, more ancient midrash, attributed to Rabbi Yirmiyah ben Elazar: the androgyne midrash. According to the midrash, the double *yod* implies double gender, i.e. male and female created together in the same body, as it is written in the book of *Psalms* (139:5): "Thou hast beset me behind and before".

No less interesting however, is the creation account with which the midrash is associated: not the first account of man's creation in *Genesis* 1, nor the repetition of the same account in *Genesis* 5, but the second account of man's creation in *Genesis* 2. This second account is a complex one, whereby man was created from the earth, alone and male, with woman being created later from him. The legend of androgynous man is in keeping with the creation story as it appears in *Genesis* 1 and 5, but not as it appears in *Genesis* 2. The midrash however, is not restricted to one account or the other, and the Rabbis do not take the complex story recounted in *Genesis* 2 at face value. As far as they are concerned, there is no second creation story or alternate version of man's creation. *Genesis* 2 refers to the same man, created male and female, double-faced, as intimated by the double *yod* in the word *vayitzer* — "And the Lord God formed (*vayitzer*) man of the dust of the ground, and breathed into his nostrils the breath of life; and man became a living soul". Man was not created solely male from the earth at first, but androgynous — male and female as one. The midrash thereby serves to unify the two creation stories, creating a single account with a single meaning — in chapter 2 as in chapter one and in chapter 5.

The Rabbis thus adopt the myth of androgynous man and his division in two, since which time each part longs to reunite with his/her missing half: "Therefore shall a man leave his father and his mother, and shall cleave unto his wife, and they shall be one flesh". Adopting the Greek myth however, does not mean adopting all of the legend's messages as attributed to Aristophanes in Plato's *Symposium*. There are a number of fundamental differences between the meaning and message of the androgyne legend in Greek mythology and in the Midrash. The legend as it appears in the Midrash is concise and able to convey messages different from those conveyed by the myth in its Greek source. In the Greek legend, the androgyne was a strong being that rebelled against the gods and was therefore divided in two as a punishment. In the Midrash, on the other hand, the androgyne appears to be a rather weak creature. After its creation, its division comes not as a punishment, but in order to enable the separate parts to reunite in marriage, cleave unto one another and be one flesh. The story of Adam's fall/sin and punishment, i.e. banishment from the Garden of Eden, is an entirely separate matter, in no way connected to man's creation as an androgyne and division in two — male and female.

The Rabbis do not view the physical union between male and female, whether as an androgyne or after having been separated, as an inherently negative union. On the contrary, God divided Adam, who was an androgyne, into male and female, in order to enable them to reunite of their own accord in marriage.

The androgyne myth can thus be seen as a crossroads between Judaism and Christianity. While Christianity was influenced by the idea that the union between man and woman is inherently negative, and subsequently developed the principle of original sin; the Rabbis used the androgyne legend to emphasise the idea of unity, asserting the importance and centrality of conjugal relations as the reason for which God divided Adam into man and woman. The two cultures, Jewish and Christian, began to diverge from one another,[15] and the concept of original sin in Christianity may have strengthened Jewish perceptions of conjugality and its physical expression. While Christianity presented a clear dichotomy between spiritual and physical love, the central approaches that developed within Judaism viewed physical and spiritual love as a holistic unit. Rabbinic interpretation of the androgyne myth in the Midrash provided a solid foundation for these streams in Jewish thought.

The creation of Adam as an androgyne is mentioned many times and in many different contexts in the Midrash and the Talmud, citing both *tanaim* and *amoraim*, including: Rabbi Shimon ben Gamliel, Rabbi Yirmiyah ben Elazar, Rabbi Shmuel bar Nahman, Rabbi Abahu, Rav and Shmuel. The significance of Adam's having been created male and female in a single body however — in a sense affording equal status to the two sexes — was not received with equanimity by all of the sages, nor in fact by many of the mediaeval commentators. As we shall see below, various interpretations stress the primacy of man (male) in human creation, and woman as a secondary addition. This viewpoint is not given prominence in the sources we have cited above. On the contrary, there are midrashic texts that emphasise the equal status of the two sexes:

> "Rabbi Shmuel bar Nahman said: When God created Adam he created him androgynous. Resh Lakish said: When he was created, he was created double-faced, and [God] sawed him [in half] and he became two- backed, a back for the male and a back for the female."
>
> Midrash, *Vayikra Rabbah* 14, 1

According to this midrash, God created male and female attached at the back, and when he divided them he made two backs, one for the male and one for the female. The text thus describes the equal creation of male and female in a single body called Adam, and their equal division into male and female. Most of the sources that interpret the creation story on the basis of the androgyne myth can be understood in this vein. As noted however, some of the Rabbis found the equality arising from the manner in which the myth was adopted and interpreted in the early sources unacceptable. No anachronistic criticism should be levelled at these rabbis, since it is in fact the sources expressing equality that reflect new, alternative and even utopian theories, rather than the culture in which they were created. As we shall see below, the style employed by these rabbis constitutes a more authentic expression of cultural reality and prevailing beliefs.

---

[15]   That is also how I understand Peter Brown, a scholar of early Christianity and the Church Fathers. See Brown, 1988, pp. 68-286. The Christians considered the Jews to be licentious, and oblivious to the effect of the body, the flesh, upon the spirit — as stated explicitly by Augustine (see n. 9 above).

Midrash Tehilim (Midrash on the book of *Psalms*)[16] associates the androgyne myth with the verse in Psalm 139 discussed above:

> "'Thou hast beset me behind and before' — What is the meaning of 'behind and before'? They were created double-faced. Thus behind Adam was the form of Eve. And so it is written: 'And the rib, which the Lord God had taken from the man, made He [a woman]'. That is why it is written 'thou hast beset me behind and before'."
>
> *Midrash Tehilim* 139

In a single Midrash, the author resolves two issues he perceives as problematic. The first problem is the equality between male and female that might arise from the rabbinic interpretation of the androgyne myth. This difficulty is resolved by determining that there was a primary creation, Adam, who was male and the principal part of the double-faced body created; and a secondary creation, Eve, whose form was attached to Adam **from behind**.

The second problem is how to understand the verses in *Genesis* 2 about Eve being formed from Adam's rib. This story is not consistent with the version appearing in chapter 1, which implies that God created male and female at the same time. This is easily resolved by the midrash, which explains that the rib was in fact the form of Eve, appended to the primary creation Adam. In other words, Eve already existed behind Adam, and needed only to be removed, "closed up . . . with flesh instead thereof", and brought to Adam as woman taken out of man.

Midrash Tehilim later cites the following dispute between *amoraim*:

> "And the rib, which the Lord God had taken from the man, made He [a woman]" — Rav and Shmuel: One said a face, and the other said a tail."
>
> BT, *Berakhot* 61a

In Genesis 2 we read: "And the Lord God caused a deep sleep to fall upon the man, and he slept; and he took one of his ribs, and closed up the place with flesh instead thereof. And the rib (*tzela*), which the Lord God had taken from the man, made He a woman, and brought her unto the man". What did God take from Adam and return to him as a woman?

We referred above to the talmudic midrash, according to which the "rib" was in fact a face or the form of woman attached to Adam from behind. This would appear to be precisely the subject of the dispute between Rav and Shmuel: One interprets the word "*tzela*" to mean face, as explained by the anonymous midrashist above, i.e. the woman's form attached to Adam's side

---

[16] Compiled in the early Middle Ages — tenth or eleventh century — and also known as *Midrash Shoher Tov.*

or back. The other explains that the "rib" in *Genesis* 2 was a tail, that Adam, the created male, had a certain appendage attached to his body, a kind of tail, from which woman was created. Although it is reasonable to assume that the reference here is not to a tail in the usual sense of the word, i.e. an appendage at the base of the spine, this is nonetheless a midrash that seeks to put woman "in her place" from a socio-cultural point of view: as a tail, an appendage to man, who is paramount.

Clearly, the androgyne myth, as adopted and reworked in the Midrash, together with the emphasis in *Genesis* 1 and 5, lays the foundation for an egalitarian interpretation of the story of the creation of Adam — the first couple. This is exciting for contemporary gender discourse, but almost incomprehensible in terms of the culture of the Midrash authors. Criticism of such an egalitarian interpretation that could have had no practical expression at the time these midrashim were written, due to prevailing socio-cultural conditions, thus comes as no surprise.

It is also noteworthy however, that the rabbis who criticised the egalitarian conclusions one might draw from accepted midrashic interpretation, offsetting them with midrashim more in keeping with their views on the status of women, did not question the adoption of the androgyne myth *per se*, as a basis for midrashic interpretation of the creation of Adam.

Cultural interaction takes place not only between different cultures, but also within the same culture. The fact that the androgyne myth can be found in many Jewish sources attests not only to Jewish openness to Greco-Hellenistic culture, but no less to cultural interaction among Jews: between communities, streams of thought and eras. Obviously, not every rabbinic source referring to the androgyne myth is an expression of direct Greek influence. It is reasonable to assume that in most cases such references reflect internal Jewish cultural dialogue. The cultural impact of the assimilation of an idea such as this into Jewish culture goes beyond the specific focus on interpretations of the creation story. The myth of male and female in a single body or union may re-appear in many different contexts.[17] One of the most far-reaching and surprising of these contexts is that of the cherubim in the Tabernacle and later in the Temple, as revealed to the prophet Ezekiel in his Vision.[18]

In the book of Exodus, the Children of Israel are commanded to build the Tabernacle and all its vessels. Instructions are given for the fashioning of many items, including the Ark of the Covenant, the ark-cover and the cherubim:

---

[17] See below on the divine androgyne in the Kabbalah.

[18] I thank Rachel Elior for pointing out the connection to Ezekiel and its commentary. Her new book includes a chapter on the cherubim and their significance in ancient mysticism. See Elior, *Temple and chariot, priests and angels, sanctuary and heavenly sanctuaries in early Jewish mysticism*, 2002, pp. 67-87.

"And thou shalt make two cherubim of gold, of beaten work shalt thou make them, at the two ends of the ark-cover. And make one cherub at the one end, and the other cherub at the other end: even of the ark-cover shall ye make the cherubim on the two ends thereof. And the cherubim shall stretch forth their wings on high, covering the ark-cover with their wings, and their faces shall look one to another; toward the ark-cover shall the faces of the cherubim be."

Exodus 25:18-20

The cherubim are the most problematic element in the entire Tabernacle, and later in the Temple, because they are figures, statues or reliefs[19] that can be construed as objects of idol-worship. In fact, the Midrash recounts how the heathens who destroyed the Temple carried the cherubim through the streets in order to demonstrate that the Jews, known for their opposition to idol-worship, engaged in it themselves in the inner recesses of their temple. According to rabbinic tradition, the cherubim bore the likeness of winged infants, youths, or children.[20] According to some rabbinic sources however, one of the cherubim was male and the other female. Let us look once again at the verse that stresses: ". . . two cherubim of gold, of beaten work shalt thou make them, at the two ends of the ark-cover"; and at Rashi's commentary, which reads: "You must not make them separately and affix them to the ends of the ark-cover after they are made . . . rather, cast a great deal of gold when you begin to fashion the ark-cover and beat it with a hammer at its midsection, so that it protrudes at the top, and depict the cherubim in its protruding ends". In other words, the cherubim and the ark-cover should be made from the same piece of gold, a single unit from the outset. The description of the two cherubim made from the same body (of gold), provided the Rabbis with an opportunity to call to mind once again the idea of the androgyne. There are of course those who explain that the cherubim were male and female in a single body — in the sense of a single piece, as commanded by the Torah. There is more to the application of the androgyne myth to the cherubim however, than mere repetition of the midrashim concerning the androgynous creation of Adam. As we shall see in the story below, the two applications of the myth differ from one another in a number of fundamental ways:

"Rabbi Katina said: When Israel would make the pilgrimage [to Jerusalem], the curtain [concealing the Holy of Holies] would be pulled aside and they would be

---

[19] In the Second Temple, they were apparently wall paintings, engravings or reliefs. See *Yoma* 54a-b, and Rashi *loc. cit.*, pass. beg. "*keruvim detzurta*" and "*hotzium lashuk*". Tosafot, *ibid.*, permit making drawings, and explain why this is not forbidden by the commandment "Thou shalt not make the any graven image, or any likeness . . . ".

[20] In *Sukah* 5b, Rabbi Abahu asserts that the faces of the cherubim were like that of an infant, while Abaye posits that their faces were human. *Cf.* Rashi on *Exodus* 25: "Cherubim — they bore the likeness of an infant's face".

shown the cherubim which were intertwined (*me'urim*), and they would be told: behold God's love for you, as the love of male and female.

BT, *Yoma* 54a

The Talmud in *Yoma* addresses the verses pertaining to the construction of the Tabernacle and the cherubim through a discussion of the duties of the High Priest on Yom Kippur — which included entering the Holy of Holies. It is in this context that the words of Rabbi Katina are cited. Rabbi Katina tells of a custom practised during the time of the pilgrimage to Jerusalem. The pilgrims would congregate in the permitted area before the gates leading to the Holy of Holies, and the priests would pull aside the curtain and show them the cherubim. From the words of Rabbi Katina we discover that the cherubim depicted male and female figures, and that they embraced one another. The priests explained to the pilgrims that the image they were beholding was meant to illustrate ("behold God's love for you") the love between Israel and God, which is as the love revealed in the joining of the cherubim — like the love of male and female.

In the case of Adam, who was created androgynous, male and female were attached at the back or the side, and God separated them, thus enabling the woman to "face" man.[21] The cherubim were made in a single body, but "each faced its fellow". They were made facing one another and, according to the midrash cited in the Talmud, were "intertwined".[22] To the pilgrims, before whom the cherubim were displayed when the curtain was pulled aside, they appeared to be male and female joined together, symbolising God's love for the People of Israel.

According to this interpretation, the presence of the cherubim in the Tabernacle, and later in the Temple, was problematic beyond the issue of statues and figures. The talmudic legend expresses this difficulty from the perspective of the heathens who destroyed the Temple:

"Resh Lakish said: When the heathens entered the Temple and saw the cherubim intertwined, they carried them out to the streets and said: These Israelites, whose

---

[21] The Hebrew word *kenegdo* in *Genesis* 2:18 can be understood either "meet for him", as it is usually translated, or "facing him".

[22] Rashi on *Yoma* 54a: "The cherubim — adhered, held and embraced one another, like a male embracing a female. *Me'urim* (intertwined) — means adhering." Rabbi Menahem Hame'iri rejects this interpretation, which would mean that the cherubim figures in the Holy of Holies were in a state of perpetual coupling. He therefore explains that their wings were touching, and in this symbolised God's love for Israel and evoked the image of love between male and female as portrayed in the Prophets and in Song of Songs. Hame'iri's interpretation however, is inconsistent with BT, Yoma 54b, which states explicitly in its description of the cherubim that they embraced one another "like a man intertwined with his companion", and Rashi explains: "adhering to and embracing his wife in his arms".

blessing is a blessing and whose curse is a curse, occupy themselves with these things? They immediately despised them, as it is written (*Lamentations* 1:8): 'All that honoured her despise her, because they have seen her nakedness.'"

Ibid., ibid. b

The words of Resh Lakish cited here support the assertion in the tractate of *Yoma* that the cherubim were male and female, perhaps a boy and girl, locked in an embrace. Unlike the androgyne in the Garden of Eden, in which the male and female parts faced away from one another — "Thou hast beset me behind and before" — in the androgyne of the Tabernacle and the Holy of Holies "each faced its fellow". Unlike Adam, who had to be separated in order to allow its parts to unite face to face, the cherubim were already "intertwined", joined in perpetuity, like God's love for the People of Israel.

For the Rabbis, Rabbi Katina, Resh Lakish and others, this was not merely a possible interpretation, an intellectual idea, a way in which to understand the biblical verses, but a historical fact, what the cherubim were truly like. One can assume that Rabbi Katina ascribed moral significance to the presence of a statue or relief depicting the cherubim as male and female joined together: "Behold God's love for you, as the love of male and female". Resh Lakish on the other hand alludes to the complexities arising from the legend of the intertwined cherubim, heightening the difficulties that lie in the cherubim statue's very presence in God's Temple. What appears to the People of Israel as an expression of God's love for them, according to Rabbi Katina, appears to the heathens as the uncovered nakedness that increases their contempt for Israel. The heathens' perspective is recounted uncritically, and one might understand that the cherubim were indeed the nakedness of Israel, as in the verse from Lamentations cited in this context: "All that honoured her despise her, because they have seen her nakedness". It is also possible to explain however, that the nakedness of Israel is not the form of the cherubim, but Israel's own sins. The Midrash, in another context,[23] asserts that the direction in which the cherubim faced changed in response to Israel's behaviour — positive or negative — and it may be to this that Resh Lakish was referring.

Applying the androgyne idea to the cherubim in the Holy of Holies reflects the power of the myth. Adam's androgynous existence in the Garden of Eden ended when male and female were separated, and following their banishment, the androgynous essence remained there, embodied by the cherubim:

---

[23] See BT, *Bava Batra* 99a: "And according to he who said that their faces look one to another — but it is written 'and their faces were inward'? This poses no difficulty; one is when Israel does the will of God, and the other when Israel does not do the will of God." See also Rashbam *loc. cit.*.

"So he drove out the man; and he placed at the east (*mikedem*) of the garden of Eden the cherubim, and the flaming sword which turned every way, to keep the way of the tree of life."

Genesis 3:24

The androgynous past of man and woman explains their mutual attraction, while the myth's application to the cherubim provides a paradigm for their ambition to re-unite. The androgyne did not disappear from the world when Adam was divided into male and female. It continues to exist in the cherubim, which symbolise the unification of many different essences, as described in *Bereshit Rabbah*:

"'Before' (*mikedem* can be translated "at the east" or "before" — tr) — The angels were created before the Garden of Eden, as it is written (*Ezekiel* 10): 'This is the living creature that I saw under the God of Israel by the river of Chebar; and I knew that they were the cherubim'. 'And the flaming [sword]' — After (*Psalms* 104) 'his ministers a flaming fire'. 'Which turned every way' — For they are **sometimes men, sometimes women**, sometimes spirits, sometimes angels.

Midrash, *Bereshit Rabbah* 21, 10

Thus the return to the androgyne legend in the teachings of Rabbi Katina and Resh Lakish in *Yoma* is not a coincidence, but is directly linked to the legend's source: the androgynous creation of Adam — an expression of the unification of the male and female essences, which preceded creation and emanates from the unity of God. In the creation process, androgynous unity was brought into being even before the world was created; in the unification of essences that marked the creation of the angels.[24] After Adam's banishment from the Garden of Eden, these angels remained there, these cherubim that the prophet Ezekiel saw in his vision in various forms — embodying various essences in their androgynous existence: "sometimes men, sometimes women, sometimes spirits, sometimes angels".

The principle whereby the unification of the male and female essences preceded the creation of mankind, is fundamental in the Kabbalah.[25] The above midrashim were therefore embraced by the *Zohar* as well:

"Come and see. It is written (*Exodus* 23): 'Behold, I send an angel before thee . . .' This is the angel who is the redemption of the world and the guardian of mankind. And it is he who brings blessings upon the entire world, for it is he who receives them first, and then brings them upon the world. It is therefore written: 'Behold, I

---

[24]   That is why these midrashim were embraced by the *Zohar* as well. See *Zohar* on *Leviticus* 19; p. 282; *Parshat Va'era* p. 27; and below on the androgyne myth in the *Zohar*.

[25]   See discussion below on the androgyne in the Kabbalah.

send an angel before thee'; and it is written: 'And I will send an angel before thee'. And this is the angel who is sometimes male and sometimes female . . . and it is all a single secret. And similarly, it is written: 'and the flaming sword which turned every way', for there are angels sent to the world who turn a number of shades, sometimes female, sometimes male."

Zohar I 232a; ibid. 237a

The androgynous angel is the cherubim, who preceded creation and, after man's banishment from the Garden of Eden, were placed to guard the way of the tree of life. This is the angel charged with the redemption of the world and the safeguarding of mankind. This is the angel who enables the existence of blessings in the entire world. The two verses in Exodus cited by the *Zohar* do not refer to two different angels, but to a single angel who is sometimes male and sometimes female. The cherubim's bi-sexuality is related to the manner in which blessings are drawn into this world, and to the morality of its inhabitants. The androgynous angel is also the angel described in *Genesis* as "the flaming sword which turned every way" — from male to female and vice versa, in accordance with the need to bring blessings upon the world, and in keeping with the moral conduct of mankind.

The midrash concerning Adam's androgynous creation, male and female in a single body, is a cornerstone of the midrashic, mishnaic and talmudic wisdom of love. This "wisdom of love" is in fact a structured and consistent system founded upon two main principles: First — analysis of biblical sources and faithfulness of the Rabbis to the harmonious message of love characteristic of biblical literature;[26] and second — a realistic approach, well-rooted in everyday life, stemming from reality itself, reflected first and foremost in *halakhah*, in the commandment to "be fruitful and multiply", in the commandment of *onah* (sex for the sake of pleasure), and in the laws that maintain concord between marriage partners.[27] The androgyne midrash intensified the rabbinic conviction that complete man, "the crowning glory of creation", comprises both male and female. Since the physical separation into two distinct human beings — man and woman — they cannot be whole unless they are together. The pinnacle of this wholeness lies not in marriage per se, but in the coupling of the two partners — the physical expression of a spiritual wholeness, both on a human plane and in higher spheres.

The idea that human wholeness can be achieved only within a couple, and that a man is perceived as incomplete without a woman, was undoubtedly a revolution in prevailing thought and culture. This principle laid the foundation for the slow process of rejection of the polygamous family, and

---

26   See N Rothenberg 2000, pp. 25-50.
27   *Ibid.*, pp. 74-84.

the move toward a monogamous marriage structure more in keeping with the androgyne myth — a myth that contributed to the development of egalitarian views on relations between men and women.

Chapter Four

IN THE KABBALAH: AN ETERNAL/DIVINE, SPIRITUAL AND HUMAN ANDROGYNE

The Jewish, midrashic reworking of the mythological story of ancient, androgynous man, developed and progressed in the Kabbalah, reaching new heights. In the early midrashim cited above, we saw the joining of male and female at the time of man's creation as an androgyne. In other words, the androgyne appears contemporaneously with creation. According to the prevailing kabbalistic view in the *Zohar* however, bi-sexual union preceded creation, and is encompassed within divinity itself. The physical world is merely a reflection of the divine world, that is, the real world. Therefore, anything that can be described as presently existing or having existed in the physical world, exists to an infinitely greater degree in the divine world. Moreover, the key to understanding the physical world lies in understanding the divine world. It can therefore be said that from a kabbalistic perspective, any discussion of the human condition must begin by describing the divine and discussing the "divine condition".

The *sefirot* system enables the kabbalistic midrashist to discuss the divine world. He need not be satisfied merely with knowledge of divine reality, but can enter the sacred depths, plunging into the realm of the *ein sof*. We will discuss *sefirot* theosophy as it pertains to bi-sexual union. God would appear to be neither male nor female, encompassing and transcending rather, both essences. There are male *sefirot* and female *sefirot*, but in kabbalah such distinctions are never absolute, and neither male nor female essences are entirely absent in any of the ten *sefirot*.

Love, desire and coupling in divinity, in the world of the *sefirot*, are the source of all existence, a blueprint for creation, and the unification of all worlds. At the very pinnacle of the *sefirot* structure are *Hokhmah* (Wisdom) and *Binah* (Understanding),[28] described as a couple, and also called Father and Mother. The idea of a couple does not imply plurality within the divinity. On the contrary, it expresses God's unity in the profoundest of ways. These "Father and Mother" — Hokhmah and Binah — are united in a perfect, eternal union; a perpetual coupling that cannot be parted. The mystical

---

[28] *Ensof* (Infinity) or the *sefirah Keter* (Crown) are beyond the scope of the present discussion.

language of the Kabbalah thus enables one to express the concept of God's unity with an intensity that cannot be found in the cognitive structures of rational discourse. The message of unity resonates with those parts of human consciousness that contemplate the eternal coupling.

From the union of *Hokhmah* and *Binah* — "Father and Mother" — all the other *sefirot* were created/born. At first, they were inside *Binah*, like a foetus in its mother's womb, and then they emanated from *Binah*, which gave birth to them. Kabbalah identifies the mystery of birth with the mystery of emanation. Following the birth, the "Father and Mother" — the supreme couple, *Hokhmah* and *Binah* — continue to serve as a source for the lower *sefirot* that draw upon them, and a constant paradigm for their "behaviour". The enduring, unceasing and infinite love of *Hokhmah* and *Binah*, serves as an example and an inspiration. Their perpetual coupling is a paragon of love at its highest, toward which all aspire, whether they are capable of attaining it or not. The love of *Hokhmah* and *Binah* arouses the love of the lower *sefirot* for one another, and creates a harmonious coupling among them as well. The coupling of the lower *sefirot* however is not like that of *Hokhmah* and *Binah*, since their union is not constant; sometimes they separate and depart from one another, and sometimes they reunite:

> "For the first [letter] 'heh' (of the YHVH name of God) [Mother] is not called 'bride', and the last [letter] 'heh' is called 'bride' at certain times, for there are many times at which the male does not join with her but departs from her. Of such times it is written: 'Also thou shalt not approach unto a woman . . . as long as she is put apart for her uncleanness'. When the woman is purified and the male seeks to join with her, then she is called 'bride', as a true bride she approaches. This Mother however, the desire of the two [Mother and Father] never ends, together they go forth, together they remain, neither separating from one another nor departing from one another."
>
> *Zohar, Idra Zuta, III 290b*

The description of the perpetual joining, the constant union of the higher *sefirot Hokhmah* and *Binah*, conveys the message of unity in its pure state, the indivisible union of male and female. Perpetual joining is the sublime yet unattainable pinnacle. It is therefore a source of inspiration, a goal to which to aspire, for those couples that are separate but can reunite "at certain times", during which they can, through their union, express the unity of the ineffable name.

The divine androgyne depicted in their perpetual joining, in the eternal union of the *sefirot Hokhmah* and *Binah* called "Father and Mother", is not destined to be divided. The ingrained desire for union between male and female does not stem from the platonic memory of two that were once one, but from their desire to emulate "Father and Mother" in their perpetual joining and indivisible unity. The divine world is founded upon unity, represented by the bi-sexual unity of the higher *sefirot* that are never separated from one another: "together they go forth, together they remain, neither separating from one another nor departing from one another".

Indivisible bi-sexual unity does not exist beyond its manifestation in the *sefirot Hokhmah* and *Binah*, and does not recur among the other *sefirot*. However, when the other *sefirot* join with one another in "occasional desire" or "at certain times", it re-appears in the fruit of their love, i.e. in the souls that are born. From the joining of the *sefirot Tiferet* (Beauty) and *Malkhut* (Kingdom) — also portrayed as the joining of all the *sefirot* with *Malkhut*, or as the joining of *Melekh* and *Matronita*, but most often noted in the *Zohar* as the joining of God, or the "male aspect of the Creator", and the *Shekhinah*, or the "female aspect of the Creator" — the souls are created within the *Shekhinah*, are born from her, and descend to the world.

All of the souls that are the fruit of the joining of God and the *Shekhinah* are *bi-sexual*,[29] male and female united:

> "Come and see: All of the souls of the world, which are the fruit of God's actions, are all one in a single mystery, and when they descend to the world, they all separate into male and female form, and those male and female are joined together (within a single soul created in the *Shekhinah*). Come and see: The female's desire for the male makes life, and the male's desire for the female and his cleaving to her send life forth . . . When the souls go forth, they go forth male and female together, then upon their descent, they separate, one to one side and the other to the other side, and God joins them together later. And joining is not entrusted to any but God alone, who knows how to join them together in a fitting manner."
>
> *Zohar* I, 85b

The Jewish-midrashic reworking of the myth of androgynous ancient man, reaches its highest level of development in the Kabbalah. The subject is no longer a mythological figure from the dawn of creation, divided in two, each part henceforth longing to return to the whole from whence it came. The androgyne is not a legacy of the past, an ancient myth, but the past, present and future in divinity and in human souls: in "all of the souls of the world, which

---

29   This is the prevailing view throughout the *Zohar*. In the *Hekhalot* tracts, part II, 246a, it is written however, that male and female souls are each created complete in their own right, descending separately from the *Shekhinah* to the first *hekhal*, where male and female unite "and fly from this *hekhal*, separating [when they become] human beings". Note however, that the differences between the *Hekhalot* tracts and the *Zohar* with regard to human souls have no bearing upon the presence of the androgyne *per se* in the world of souls, in pre-corporeal human existence. These differences pertain rather to the afterlife and other matters concerning the soul. The androgyne myth, as noted, is equally embraced by both systems.

are the fruit of God's actions", i.e. the fruit of God's union with his *Shekhinah*. The *Zohar* even provides the mystical explanation for the bi-sexuality of souls: The desire of the female aspect of the Divine (*Shekhinah*) for the male aspect of the Divine (God), "makes life", i.e. bestows the female essence upon the soul. Similarly, the desire of the male (God) for the female (*Shekhinah*) — desire that causes him to cleave to her, unite with her — makes life and bestows the male essence upon the soul. Desire for the female is the male expression, and desire for the male the female expression. The androgyne is thus not an ancient mythological figure, but is recreated in the *Shekhinah* from her joining with God. The soul is divided in two upon its descent into the physical world, the world of division, manifesting itself in the corporeal forms of male and female: The soul-part including life — the male essence — will emerge from the womb in the body of a male child; and the soul-part including life — the female essence — will emerge from the womb in the body of a female child. Memory of the androgyne is not a distant, primordial remembrance in the minds of men and women who are attracted to one another, but rather a recollection of man's complete spiritual existence, the bi-sexual soul that preceded his/her divided corporeal existence.

The mystical explanation of the androgyne's creation in its spiritual manifestation as a bi-sexual soul affects the kabbalistic midrashic interpretation of the story of Adam's creation. Accounts of bi-sexual souls descending from the heavens and being divided into male and female before being placed within human bodies, do not apply to Adam. The bi-sexual soul was placed undivided within Adam's androgynous body, thus creating male and female in a single body:

> "Rabbi Abba said: This verse must be examined. For it is written 'So God created man in His own image, in the image of God created He him'. Since it says 'in His own image', what is (why the repetition) 'in the image of God created He him'? Rather, [there were] surely two levels (essences), the entirety of which [were] male and female. One for male and one for female, and there were therefore surly two faces. And the end of the verse supports [this], since it is written 'male and female created He them', entire on two sides."

> *Ibid.* III, 117a

The midrashim cited earlier introduced the androgyne myth, associating it with Adam, and basing it upon the verse 'male and female created He them' (*Genesis* 5), or upon the verse 'Thou hast beset me behind and before' (*Psalms* 139). These early midrashim focused on the physical form of the androgyne: "He created him double-faced, and sawed him [in two], giving him two backs, one back facing one direction and one back facing the other"; "Adam had two faces"; "he was created double-faced, and [God] sawed him [in half] and he became two- backed, a back for the male and a back for the female"; "They were created double-faced. Thus behind Adam was the form of Eve"; etc. Midrashic exegesis thus concerns physical appearance, i.e. Adam's body comprised both male and female forms.

Contrary to the earlier midrashim, kabbalistic midrashic interpretation addresses the metaphysical, the spiritual, the meaning within the unified creation of male and female. Rabbi Abba proposes that we begin our enquiry not from the Bible's reference to Adam's male and female creation, but from another concept, one that appears repeatedly in the creation story in Genesis: "the image of God". This is the concept that characterises man's creation, and not the strange double-faced appearance of Adam's body. In stressing and reiterating the concept "image of God", the verse alludes to Adam's essence, or more precisely, to the two essences that constitute the different facets of the single man: the male essence and the female essence. "In his own image" and "in the image of God", one for male and one for female, since Adam was "entire on two sides", i.e. his spiritual entirety, his identity, was expressed in both of these essences.

This interpretation is on the *remez* level of interpretation. The author of this midrash however, further supports his assertion with the simple meaning (*peshat*) of the verse, which states explicitly: "male and female created he them".[30]

The androgyne myth appears again in the *Zohar*, in the midrashim on the letters of the Hebrew alphabet, under the letter '*tzadi*' ('צ), which came before God and claimed that it should be used to create the world and to begin the Torah (instead of the letter '*bet*'):

> "The letter 'צ' entered and said before Him: Master of the world, may it please you to create the world with me, for the righteous ('*tzadikim*') are written with me, and you who are called righteous are inscribed with me, as it is written (Ps 11:7) 'For the righteous Lord loveth righteousness', and it is fitting that the world be created with me. *Tzadi*, '*tzadi*' you are, and '*tzadik*' (righteous) you are called, but you must be hidden and you should not be revealed so to the world. Why? [The *tzadi*] is a [letter] '*nun*' (נ). Came the [letter] '*yod*' (י) from the name of the sacred covenant (the ineffable name), rode upon it and united with it. And this is the mystery: When God created Adam, he created him double-faced, and therefore the '*yod*' faced backward, thus: צ; and not face to face, thus: צ. God said to her: Recant, for I am destined to saw you [in two] and make you face to face . . .".
>
> *Ibid.* I, 2b

---

30   In Rabbinic tradition, there are four levels of biblical hermeneutics (represented by the acronym *PaRDe"S* — the "esoteric orchard"): *peshat* — plain meaning; *remez* — inference; *derash* — interpretation; and *sod* — esoteric significance.

Jewish tradition maintains that the world was created using the 22 letters of the Hebrew alphabet, with each letter leaving its mark upon the world. The above midrash is an excerpt from the competition, as it were, between the letters — each coming before God and asking to be first in creation, first to begin the Torah with which the world was created. In the end, the letter 'bet' (for *Bereshit*, or "In the beginning") is chosen. The '*tzadi*' goes before God and states its case, which is accepted in principle, but rejected on the grounds of a great mystery. The reason is that the '*tzadi*' should not be so revealed, since its form reflects the mystery of unity depicted in the androgyne myth. The mark left by the '*tzadi*' on creation is no less than the creation of Adam, since the form of the '*tzadi*' alludes to "he created him double-faced". The form of the '*tzadi*' alludes however, not only to the unity of the sexes, but to the unity of the ineffable "name of the sacred covenant", since the צ was a נ, and the letter י from the ineffable name came and rode upon the נ, uniting with it and creating the letter צ. The '*yud*' however, faces backward. The mystery of Adam's creation lies within the letter צ: When God created Adam, he created him double-faced, and therefore the י (which rides upon the נ) faces backward,[31] and the two letters — like Adam in the Garden of Eden — do not face one another. And God will saw the צ — Adam who was created androgynous — in two, in order to enable the two parts to join with one another face to face, like the unity of the ineffable name. Joining the letter י from the ineffable divine name with the letter נ, creating the letter צ — double-faced — was the first stage. Sawing it in two and making the parts face one another completes the ineffable name.

We have seen above that the Rabbis, in the early midrashim, interpreted the verses in Genesis 2 pertaining to man's creation — which seem to imply that man was created first, and woman was created from him — in a manner consistent with the egalitarian creation story in chapters one and five. The *Zohar* too stresses the coherency of the biblical narrative:

> "'And the Lord God said: 'It is not good that the man should be alone . . .'. Rabbi Aha said: Was He alone? For it is written 'male and female created He them', and we have learned: Adam was created double-faced. And here it says 'it is not good that man should be alone'? Rather that he did not use his femaleness and he did not have a helper facing him,[32] since she was at his side, and they were as one from behind, and man was thus alone. 'I will make him an '*ezer kenegdo*'. What does '*kenegdo*' mean? Facing him, to cleave to one another, face to face. What did God do? He

[31] According to the custom based upon the work of the 16th-century kabbalist, Rabbi Isaac Luria, the letter צ is therefore written in this fashion in the Torah scroll — arousing halakhic controversy. See *Hazon Ish*, OH 9; and *Teshuvot Ukhtavim Hazon Ish* (M. Greinman ed), Bnei Brak 5751 (1991), 6-11.

[32] *Kenegdo*, understood here to mean "facing him", is usually translated 'meet for him'.

sawed him [in two] and took the female from him . . . He made her as a bride and brought her to face him, face illuminating face. Rabbi Shimon said: This is certainly how man was alone, for he had no help from his female, because she was at his side. It is therefore written: 'I will make him a helper' and it is not written 'I will create him a helper', as it is written 'male and female created He them'. . . . And what is [the meaning of] 'I will make'? It means 'I will repair', for God took her from his side and repaired her and brought her before him. And thus man benefited from his wife and she was a helper unto him."

Ibid. III, 44b

The kabbalistic author's reading of the biblical narratives, like that of the earlier midrashists, is consistent. Midrash is particularly suited to smoothing over inconsistencies and resolving contradictions between different versions of the same story. Such is the case with the various accounts of man's creation, in *Genesis* 1, 2 and 5. According to the *Zohar* midrashim, Adam was created double-faced, male and female in a single body, in which his/her complete soul was placed, including both the male and female essences—the image of God—as they appear in the divinity itself. Male and female were joined at the side and appeared as one from behind, to the imaginary observer.[33] The verse "it is not good that the man should be alone" can therefore not be interpreted in the sense of "solitary", for man was never alone, but rather created double-faced and androgynous. Specifically in this state of unified soul within a joined male-female body however, Adam felt lonely and was in fact alone. They were attached in body, but lacked the ability to couple with one another. Their attachment could therefore not be compared to the perpetual union of *Hokhmah* and *Binah*, because they could not face one another and join together. Although they were indeed attached in a single body, they were far from being united, and man was terribly lonely without the ability to join together as a couple.

The purpose of the androgyne's separation into male and female was to enable them to join together: "What does 'kenegdo' mean? Facing him, to cleave to one another, face to face"; and "What did God do? He sawed him [in two] and took the female from him . . . He made her as a bride and brought her to face him . . .". The *Zohar* does not merely offer a laconic description of Adam's creation with two faces and subsequent separation into male and female, but reiterates the deficiency inherent to his previous state—that of male and female attached at the side, lacking the ability to unite with one another—and stresses the aim of their separation, that is to enable them to join together as a couple. The two final passages emphasise God's active involvement not only in the separation that enables union, but also in bringing the female as a bride

---

[33] The early midrashim refer to man and woman joined at the back. The *Zohar* describes the androgyne as man and woman joined at the side.

and placing her before the male in order to arouse his passion and cause him to desire the union. The purpose of the androgyne's separation into male and female is not merely technical — to enable physical union — but sublime divine design, affording such union teleological status. Conjugality is termed 'illumination', and God himself in all His glory, brings the woman as a bride, placing her before the man that "face illuminate face", in the act of union. The *Zohar* midrash, citing Rabbi Shimon, completes the consistent interpretation of *Genesis* 2, and strengthens the teleological status of the conjugal act. The creation of Adam appears explicitly only in *Genesis* 1:27: "So God created man in His own image, in the image of God created He him; male and female created He them". In chapter two, there is no account of man's creation, and the woman is not created, since they were created together, according to chapter one. In *Genesis* 2:18 we read: "It is not good that the man should be alone; I will make him a help meet-for/facing him".

The *Zohar*, quoting Rabbi Shimon emphasises: "It is therefore written: 'I will make him a helper' and it is not written 'I will create him a helper' . . . And what is [the meaning of] 'I will make'? It means 'I will repair'". The verse in chapter two thus refers to repairing rather than to creation. The concept of "repairing" (*tikun*) should not be understood in its narrow, modern sense, i.e. fixing something that is broken. The ability to perform a *tikun* is an extension of free choice — possible in the physical world, but not in the divine world, where the immanence of the divine abrogates choice. The concept of *tikun* — fundamental in Kabbalah — expresses the ultimate purpose of the physical world. *Tikun* does not require something broken in order to be applied. *Tikun* brings harmony to the world of multiplicity, difference and contrast, and thence to all worlds. In dividing the androgyne into male and female, God himself performed a *tikun* and ingrained the act of *tikun* in the ability and desire of man and woman to join together. It is not a "base" physical act, as it is viewed from a Stoic or Christian perspective, but a sublime expression of *tikun olam* ("repairing the world").

The kabbalistic approach to conjugality, as derived from its teachings regarding the soul, is uncompromising, arising from a hermetic spiritual model. Within this model, celibacy has no place, even in the most extreme cases:

> "One who refrains from procreation, it is as if he diminishes the image that comprises all images, and causes the waters of that river to cease their flow, and impairs all aspects of the sacred covenant . . . and his soul does not pass beyond the curtain (*pargod*) and is banished from that world."
>
> *Ibid.* I 13a

Since uniting with the other half of one's soul influences the upper worlds, and arouses desire, leading to harmonious unions within the divine order, one who refrains from conjugality in this world "diminishes the image that comprises all images", i.e. inflicts damage as it were, upon the divinity and upon overall unity, diminishing existence itself.[34] A man who fails to unite with a female partner in the physical world, disrupts the harmony between the celestial male and female, preventing their union and thereby impairing emanation (ha'atzalah), since new souls that would have been created had he taken a wife and united with her will not come into being. One who is celibate diminishes the overall divine harmony of the emanation system. He "impairs all aspects of the sacred covenant" between the divine male and female, severing their bond to the higher sefirot Hokhmah and Binah, and to the soul that has descended to this world. The soul's connection to the system from which it was emanated is thus broken, it is prevented from returning to its source, "and is banished from that world". Clearly in order to pass again beyond the "curtain", the half-soul must reunite in the physical world with its other half. By refraining from this union the half-soul fails to fulfil its purpose in this world, and cannot return to its source.

The celibate's failing is absolute, and only a conjugal union between male and female — two half-souls joining together in love — can accomplish man's purpose in the physical world, and return the soul to its divine source.

Kabbalistic exegesis as a whole, like most rabbinic sources, discusses only monogamous married relationships, with no reference to polygamy.[35] The point of departure is the belief that every soul created within the Shekhinah comprises both male and female essences. Androgynous Adam was divided into one man and one woman, who must reunite in conjugal harmony. The complete soul, comprising male and female, is divided in two upon its descent into this world, and every man and woman is thus only half a soul. According to this approach, simultaneous marriage to more than one partner is inconceivable.

The androgyne myth reaches the height of its development in the Kabbalah. It is more than the memory of a primordial physical experience — Adam, created double-faced and divided into male and female — that causes each part to seek to reunite with the other. It is a perpetual androgynous experience, flowing from the celestial world of divinity and the sefirot, and from the soul at the time of its creation, comprising the spiritual essence of the female soul and

---

[34]   Cf. BT, Yevamot 63b: "One who does not engage in procreation . . . Rabbi Yakov (var. Akiva) says: It is as if he diminishes the image, as it is written 'So God created man in his own image', followed by 'Be fruitful, and multiply'; and Tosefta Yevamot 8, 7: "Rabbi Akiva says: One who sheds blood effaces the image . . . Rabbi Elazar ben Azariah says: One who does not engage in procreation effaces the image . . .".

[35]   Tishbi (1957), p. 613 n 49. I refer to the conjugal ideal as presented in aggadic and philosophical sources. Halakhic sources on the other hand, do relate to a polygamous reality.

the spiritual essence of the male soul. Following in the footsteps of the earlier midrashim, the *Zohar* also adopts the androgyne myth, moulding and shaping it, suffusing it with the messages it wishes to convey.

The androgyne myth, in its far-reaching interpretation by the *Zohar*, in effect shatters gender divisions. The androgyne that expresses the unity of God in the divine world is divided so that it may reunite in the physical world. Coupling and conjugality are the mystery of unity, the mystery of birth and emanation, the mystery of harmonious perfection in divinity and in creation. Love, desire and coupling in divinity, in the world of the *sefirot*, are the source of all existence, a blueprint for creation, and the unification of all worlds. A man and woman who unite in pure love, in spirit and in body, unite all worlds in a harmonious union, in which there are no barriers or distinctions, no high or low, but only a great love. This love fills the entire universe.

Chapter Five

THE REBIRTH OF THE ANDROGYNE:
JUDAH ABRAVANEL CITES PLATO AND MOSES

There are periods in the history of human culture that are deleterious to the ancient myths. These are times at which rulers strive to extend their frontiers to the provinces of the spirit and the imagination; not content merely to hold sway over their subjects' bodies, they wish to enslave their souls as well. The great myths stand as a bulwark, defending the human spirit, while tyrants wage all-out war against them, seeking to eradicate, obliterate, or at the very least, banish them from the face of human culture. They try to replace them with pseudo-myths and subservient ethos, designed primarily to instil in the masses a sense of fear, uncertainty and guilt. The great myths serve no regime, since they do not yield or answer to those in power, but only to values of the greatest importance for all people throughout the ages. There are times and places in which rulers have refused to accept this, supplanting the myths with alternatives that have better served their purposes and helped to consolidate their absolute rule, until nothing remained free of their reign — neither thought, nor vision nor dream. Such regimes prevailed in much of Europe during the Middle Ages. It is thus no wonder that during the Renaissance so many artists, writers and musicians rediscovered the ancient myths: through them finding ways in which to relate once again to the imaginations and thoughts of their viewers, readers and listeners, inspiring new hopes and expectations. This short period in European history witnessed the rebirth of the great myths.

Judah Abravanel's *Dialoghi d'amore* well reflects this process.[36] The return to authentic discussion of topics that truly matter to people everywhere — one of the foremost of these being the topic of *love* — also necessarily constituted a return to the great myths, including of course, that of the androgyne.

A book of this kind was needed in order to pass from the abstract, conceptual discussion of love — in mediaeval works — to practical issues pertaining to real human couples. In this sense, the *Dialoghi d'amore* made an extremely significant contribution toward restoring love to human beings. At work here is an interesting process of "personification" — a concept usually used to denote the attribution of human qualities to abstractions (or non-human physical beings), or to represent such concepts or beings in human form. The *Dialoghi* released love from the chains of allegory, returning it to its human source and natural place between lovers.

The book's protagonists are a pair of lovers, Philo and Sophia, who discuss love. Philo wishes to consummate his desire and physically unite with his beloved, while Sophia fears that yielding to her own desires and those of her beloved, will cause their pure, spiritual love to disappear. Her main fear is that her beloved's love will wane once he has fulfilled his desire. Since she holds his love for her in great esteem, she wishes to make it eternal by pursuing it on a philosophical level. She persists in making a clear distinction between spiritual and even spiritual-emotional love, and physical love. Confrontation between the lovers would thus appear to be almost inevitable. The author however, does not allow this to happen: Sophia does not entirely reject physical love, and Philo's position is not steadfast. From Sophia's point of view, this constitutes significant progress. With gentle hints she draws Philo into continuing their philosophical discussion, while fostering his hope and expectation that his desire for physical consummation will in the end be fulfilled. Sophia understands and would seem to accept this desire of Philo's, but claims that before she herself makes physical love, she must be well-versed in the theory of love, and then perhaps . . . but only "perhaps", since it appears from her words that her desire would be satisfied with intellectual knowledge. Philo's love, if it is true, must first attend to her soul far more than to her body.

The third dialogue, which is the longest and forms the bulk of the book, is entitled "On the Origins of Love". Judah Abravanel attributes love to the desire of man and woman to be together, to unite with one another. To this end he cites both the androgyne myth, based on Aristophanes' discourse in Plato's *Symposium*; and the story of Adam's creation, as told in the Book of Genesis.

[36]   Don Judah Abravanel (1460-1521), eldest son of Don Isaac Abravanel, was a physician, poet, and one of the greatest philosophers of the Renaissance. Following the expulsion of Jews from Spain, he settled in Naples, where he became court physician to the Spanish viceroy. His book, *Dialoghi d'amore*, which will be discussed at greater length in Section III, was first published in Rome in 1535.

After discussing the various opinions on the origins of love, including those of the guests at Agathon's supper, Abravanel places Aristophanes' words in the mouth of Philo:

> "Sophia: I have heard that which the poets consider to be the progenitors of love, and now I would like to understand what the philosophers believe these to be.
>
> Philo: Plato also used the language of legend, and attributed the birth of love to another source. In the *Symposium*, he recounts in Aristophanes' name that love began in the following manner: In the beginning, the human race was of a third sex, not only men and women, but a different sex called androgynous, which was both male and female together . . . and this androgyne was great and very strong . . . Filled with pride for its prowess, it dared to challenge the gods, to vex and harry them . . . Jupiter therefore decided to cut the androgyne in two."

Dialoghi d'amore (Hebrew edition, M. Dorman ed.) pp. 405-406

Abravanel provides his readers with an account of the androgyne legend according to Plato. In part, his descriptions are highly detailed — like those provided by Plato himself — regarding the androgyne's dual organs for example, or the punishment inflicted by the father of the gods, Jupiter-Zeus, with the help of Apollo: "He (Zeus) spoke and cut men in two . . . and as he cut them one after another, he bade Apollo give the face and the half of the neck a turn . . .", followed by a description of the new human form, which enabled men and women to join together, and which created love between them. Abravanel however, does not merely repeat the story as it appears in the *Symposium*. He interprets, edits and emends it to suit his own views. Earlier, we attempted to determine whether, according to the Platonic text, it was only the androgynes or all of mankind that rebelled against the gods' concluding that only the androgynes were to blame. Abravanel spares his readers this incertitude, stating explicitly that the androgyne, which was great and strong and filled with pride for its prowess "dared to challenge the gods, to vex and harry them". What appears at first to be an interpretation of the Platonic text, is much more than that:

Plato's *Symposium*	Abravanel's *Dialoghi d'amore*
". . . for the original human nature was not like the present, but different. **The sexes were not two as they are now, but originally three in number**; there was man, woman, and the union of the two, having a name corresponding to this double nature, which had once a real existence, but is now lost, and the word "Androgynous" is only preserved as a term of reproach."	"In the beginning, **the human race was of a third sex**, not only men and women, but a different sex called androgynous, which was both male and female together."

Plato refers to three sexes: male, female and androgynous. Abravanel, with a masterful pen, changes the legend's "factual" background: "In the beginning, the human race was of a third sex". The androgyne was first and alone. Seemingly, it would have been Abravanel's right to change the story as he saw fit — but only seemingly. He presents the legend **in Plato's name**, and should therefore have remained faithful to the details that form the basis of the story, as well as to Aristophanes' subsequent conclusions. Abravanel consciously changed the story and took great care in choosing his words, attempting to conceal the change as much as possible: "In the beginning, the human race was of a third sex, not only men and women, but a different sex called androgynous . . . ". He was aware of the fact that the *Symposium* was well known in educated circles, and therefore cloaked the changes he had made to the story in literary language. Not three sexes, as in Plato's account, but rather the entire human race was of a third sex — followed immediately by "not only men and women, but a different sex called androgynous". What does "not only men and women" mean? The previous sentence clearly states that the entire human race was of a different, third sex! Rather, it was deliberately worded this way, so that readers familiar with the Platonic source would not notice the difference.

In this, Abravanel was following in the footsteps of the Midrash and the *Zohar*: adopting the androgyne myth, but reworking it in such a manner as to convey a different message from that of Plato's Aristophanes. As we shall see, he tried to adapt the legend to the story of Adam's creation in Genesis, but that is not the only reason for the change. There are two further elements in the Platonic source that Abravanel attempts to avoid. One pertains to the legitimacy of male and female homosexuality. The primordial existence of three genders — male, female and androgynous — and the division of all three following the rebellion against the gods explains, according to Aristophanes, not only why men and women are attracted to one another, but also why men and women are attracted to members of the same sex:

> "The women who are a section of the woman do not care for men, but have female attachments; the female companions are of this sort. But they who are a section of the male follow the male . . . they hang about men and embrace them . . . "
>
> Plato, *Symposium*, 191e-192a

Homosexuality was entirely unacceptable in Judah Abravanel's social and cultural environment — both Jewish and Christian. All references to homosexuality — appearing both in the story itself, as told by Aristophanes, and in its conclusions — are therefore omitted in the account Abravanel presents as Plato's. The story's "factual" basis however, would also have had to be changed: Not three sexes, as in Plato's account, but rather the entire human race was of a different sex, called androgynous.

The second element in the Platonic account that Abravanel sought to avoid was the inherently negative perception of the physical union between male and female. The rebellion against the gods in the *Symposium* is in effect an attack against transcendent ideals, on all that is good and sublime; and of the three genders, it was the androgyne that committed the sin of pride. Even after the punishment was inflicted and male and female were divided, the androgyne's descendants, in longing for one another, continue to bear that negative aspect within them:

> "Men who are a section of that double nature which was once called Androgynous are lovers of women; adulterers are generally of this breed, and also adulterous women who lust after men."
>
> *Ibid.* 191d-e

We have already discussed the influence the Platonic androgyne myth may have had upon the development of the doctrine of "original sin" in Pauline and patristic theology. Perceiving sin as being immanent in the body, in the flesh, is very close to seeing an inherent negativity in the physical union of man and woman. Abravanel of course seeks to avoid directly addressing this viewpoint, which would have meant directly addressing Church doctrine. He does not even wish to attribute it to Sophia, as he does elsewhere in the book when seeking to criticise Church views, subsequently making it the subject of debate between Sophia and her beloved. On other topics, when Abravanel criticises the Church, the reader is left to decide between Philo's position and that of Sophia. Although the author's opinion on a given question may not be stated explicitly, he succeeds in raising doubt and provoking thought and discussion. Not so in the present case: Abravanel seeks to reject outright the idea of original sin and the inherent negation of relations between men and women. He sees himself as successor to the midrashists who adopted the androgyne myth, but edited and reworked it so that it would convey the opposite message to that expressed by Plato and especially by the Church, regarding physical relations between men and women. A small concession to the Platonic text would not be consistent with the message the author wishes to convey throughout the book.

The adaptation of the Platonic narrative to fit the Abravanelian message grows even stronger toward the end of Philo's account to Sophia of Aristophanes' discourse. Abravanel takes the liberty of practically ignoring the fact that the division of the androgyne was a punishment for having rebelled against the gods. He turns the division from a punishment into a reward, again changing and adapting the myth to the creation story in Genesis, and to the midrashic legends: The androgyne was not divided as a punishment, but in order to enable man and woman to reunite with one another. These emendations were entirely intentional, and the author attempted to disguise them with slight additions and subtle phrasing:

"Thenceforth love was born among people, renewing their nature as of old: making the two one, and thus repairing the sin that caused the one to be made two. In every person, love is thus male and female, for each is half a person and not a whole, and each therefore longs to reunite with its other half. According to this legend, human love was born of the splitting of man, and its parents were the two halves, the male and the female, that love one another in order to become one again."

Dialoghi d'amore p. 406

Not only is there no sin in the coupling of male and female, but it serves to "repair" sin. Love between the sexes repairs the sin that caused the one to be split in two: pride and rebellion against the gods — attacking transcendent ideals, the good and the sublime. Aristophanes warns that humankind may sin again and once again be punished: "And if we are not obedient to the gods, there is a danger that we shall be split up again" (Plato, *ibid.193a*). According to Plato, revering the gods in general, and obeying Eros in particular, has the power to bring love to perfection: "each one returning to his primeval nature . . . his original true love . . . ". Plato does not refer to repairing sin, but rather cautions against it, proposing a way in which one may avoid sinning again: revere the gods, and Eros above all. It is difficult to understand how, according to Abravanel, love repairs "the sin that caused the one to be made two", by "making the two one". In fact however, there is no mention of love between the androgyne's two parts. At most, the androgyne was possessed of self-love, if that is how we understand pride and arrogance. The androgyne was filled with a sense of pride in its own prowess — the cause of its rebellion against the gods. Human love was born of its splitting — mankind's splitting — and love makes the two one again. It is thus the birth of love that repairs the sin; and complete reparation — becoming one again — repairs the consequences of the sin as well, because it restores man to wholeness. Abravanel, who was an eclectic philosopher, was influenced by the Kabbalah, from which it is safe to assume that he draws the concept of "repairing" (*tikun*) with regard to the splitting of the androgyne into male and female, and the possibility of their reuniting in love. The author is thus duly cautious in his criticism of the doctrine of original sin: love and coupling repair original sin, and are by no means the sin itself.

For Abravanel however, neither the telling of the androgyne legend, citing Aristophanes, nor the cautious criticism of the doctrine of original sin were ends in their own right. The legend placed in the mouth of Philo indeed makes a great impression upon his beloved Sophia. She herself however, senses that Philo's intention lies elsewhere:

49

"Sophia: This legend is most beautiful, and it cannot but contain some weighty
philosophical lesson, especially if it is Plato who wrote it in his *Symposium*,
citing Aristophanes. Tell me then, Philo, what does it signify?

Philo: The legend was passed down by authors more ancient than the Greeks, and
its source lies in that which the Scriptures of Moses relate concerning the
creation of the first human parents — Adam and Eve.

Sophia: I have never heard that Moses told this legend.

Philo: Indeed, he did not tell the legend explicitly and in detail, but set it forth in
essence, and Plato took it from him, enhanced and embellished it in the
Greek fashion, thereby offering a distorted version of the Hebrew source.

Ibid. pp. 406-407

The author of the *Dialoghi* thus reaches the goal toward which he had been
striving: A discussion of the source of love and its significance according to
the Bible. An explicit and unmitigated discussion of the Bible would have
placed him in direct conflict with those whose exclusive province it was to
interpret the Bible: representatives of the Church. He thus chooses the safer
and, truth be told, more interesting path. Rather than focusing on interpreting
the Bible, he focuses on interpreting Plato. This path is in keeping with
the general character of the book: a discussion of love per se rather than
an interpretation of canonical scriptures or open controversy with the views
of other religious groups vis-à-vis the Bible. Judah Abravanel, the physician
and the philosopher, does not enter into religious discussion in the capacity
of a cleric (Jewish in his case) engaging other clerics, Christian and Jewish
alike. He chooses another, more universal plane, on which to examine the
phenomenon and essence of love, a plane that *also* allows him to discuss
religion and Scripture. It is clear however that interpreting Plato does not lead
him to the Bible by chance. It is rather the Bible he wished and intended to
address in the first place.

We have already discussed the fact that Plato's text is not cited faithfully,
but modified so as to conform to the story of Adam's creation in Genesis.
These changes make it easier for Abravanel to claim later on that it is Plato
who took the androgyne legend from *Genesis*, "enhanced and embellished it in
the Greek fashion". Abravanel's age was marked by ongoing debate regarding
the sources of culture. Alongside the prevailing view in Abravanel's cultural
environment, that Judaism and the Bible in the sense of the "Old Testament"
were the cradle of religions and civilisations in general, ancient Greek culture
was also considered to be a fundamental source of inspiration. This was true
not only of the cognitive structures of Aristotelian philosophy that dominated
the Middle Ages (actually on the wane in Abravanel's day),[37] but also of a return

---

[37] Primarily in European culture. In Jewish culture and especially rabbinic thought, such
structures persisted until the eighteenth century.

to Plato, Homer, ancient drama and mythology. Abravanel does not present the two ancient cultures as being in conflict, but as complementing one another. He uses both as sources of inspiration, but finds the time and place in which to confer primacy upon Moses and the Bible — a determination undoubtedly welcomed by both Christian and Jewish readers.

Abravanel was aware not only that Moses "did not tell the legend explicitly and in detail", as he concedes, but also — contrary to his claim — that he did not even "set it forth in essence". He therefore closely and extensively examines all of the verses in *Genesis* 1, 2 and 5 pertaining to Adam's creation, addressing the contradiction between the creation story in chapter two — whereby Adam was first created male and was alone until Eve was created from his rib — and the account in the other two sources that implies that man and woman were created together. He rejects interpretations on the level of the verses' simple meaning (*peshat*) that attempt to downplay the contradiction by explaining that chapter two is merely an elaboration upon the story in chapter one. According to Abravanel, the only possible explanation is that Adam was initially created androgynous. He interprets the pertinent verses accordingly, and in support of his assertion, cites the words of "the ancient Hebrew exegetes who wrote in the Aramaic tongue: 'God created Adam double-faced'". Abravanel stresses *Genesis* 5:2: "and called their name Adam, in the day when they were created":

> "For Adam alone comprised both. A single body was called Adam, for the female was not called Eve until she was separated from the male, from Adam. It is from this that Plato and the Greeks took their primordial androgyne, half male and half female."
>
> *Dialoghi d'amore* 409

Going to considerable literary lengths, the author seeks to extract from the terse words of the Torah, as many details as possible that might serve as a basis for the androgyne legend. The verses in *Genesis* in fact support the notion that male and female were created at the same time. It is only the reference to a common name that implies that they shared "a single body".

Regarding the appearance of the androgynous Adam, Abravanel adopts the midrashic descriptions of male and female attached at the back. That leaves only the manner in which they were split. *Genesis* 2:18 reads: "It is not good that the man should be alone; I will make him a help meet-for/facing him". This state of reverse attachment between male and female is not good, and must be remedied by separating the female from the male in such a way as to enable her to face him. The purpose of this separation is to enable "man and woman to unite in marriage and coitus, becoming once again a single body and a single person" (*Dialoghi, ibid.*). This is the basis for the story of the splitting of the androgyne into two separate parts, and the idea of the birth of love, reflected in "the inclination of each of the two halves to reunite with the other, in order to become a single whole body" (*ibid.*).

The "factual" basis for the androgyne legend, according to Abravanel, thus lies in the first chapters of Genesis, which he claims to be the source of Plato's account in the *Symposium*.

In one thing, the Book of Genesis differs fundamentally from the Platonic version of the legend; in the reason for the splitting of the androgyne:

> " . . . And that is the difference you will find between Moses and Plato. The former determines that the separation was for man's benefit (for he says: 'It is not good that the man should be alone; I will make him a help meet-for/facing him'), and after the separation he tells of the sin committed by Adam and Eve, who ate from the tree of the knowledge of good and evil, for which each of them was given a unique punishment; whereas Plato says that man first sinned, when he was still male and female attached, and for this sin was divided in two.
>
> Sophia: I am pleased to hear that Plato drank from the waters of the holy Torah. What is the source of this difference, Plato claiming that man was separated for having first sinned; contrary to the story in the Torah, whereby the separation was for man's benefit and succour, and preceded the sin?
>
> Philo: If you examine the matter closely, you will see that the difference is not so great, and that Plato, more than seeking to contradict the holy story, wishes to interpret it."

Ibid. p. 410

Man's sin, rebellion, is not a central theme in the *Dialoghi d'amore*. The book seeks to address the questions: How was love born? Why are men and women attracted to one another, and why do they long to unite with one another in love? The Adam-androgyne myth provides a remarkable, moving and exciting opportunity to discuss these questions. Sin is irrelevant, and Abravanel consequently emphasises the superiority of the "original" version, the Torah's, over that of Plato. Moses established that Adam's separation was for the benefit of man and woman, to endow them with love and the ability to reunite with one another in that love — this by the creator's design. In Plato's account, love is the haphazard result of the punishment inflicted upon the androgynes' for having rebelled against the gods. The splitting of the androgynes **explains** the advent of love, but was not effected with the specific intention of bestowing it upon mankind.

Abravanel strives to portray his interpretation of the biblical narrative and Plato's *Symposium* — or rather his version of Aristophanes' discourse in the *Symposium* — as being fully congruous. He develops a far-reaching allegorical interpretation of all that the male essence (mind) and the female essence (body, matter) represent, explaining both the story of Adam's creation in Genesis, and the Platonic androgyne legend in this vein. He does so at great length, becoming entangled, in the process, in a number of contradictions arising primarily from the eclectic nature of his philosophy. It is not our intention here to review or analyse this part of the *Dialoghi*. We shall merely note the fascinating progression from detailed presentation of Aristophanes' discourse and the androgyne legend; to detailed presentation of the biblical stories of Adam's creation; interpretation of the first chapters of the Book of Genesis; presentation of the differences between the Torah and Plato; exegesis and allegorical interpretation of the story of Adam's creation in Genesis; and identical allegorical re-interpretation of the androgyne legend in the *Symposium*.

In the *Dialoghi d'amore*, Judah Abravanel proposes a harmonious approach to relations between the sexes as an alternative to the dichotomous approach that had prevailed until his time — thereby joining the renascent neo-Platonic school, which placed natural harmony revolving around love, at its core.[38] The androgyne myth in its unified biblical-Platonic form is an appropriate medium through which to convey his messages, not least because it would have resonated with the spirit of the age. Sophia is struck by the beauty of the legend, and embraces the supposed connection between Plato's work and the holy Torah. Philo would undoubtedly have wished her to adopt the principle of renewed union between man and woman striving to return to androgynous wholeness. Sophia however, is not prepared to cut short the intellectual journey they have embarked upon together, and steers the discussion to the origins of universal love. The androgyne myth provided answers to questions regarding the birth of love, but failed to bring the lovers' intellectual journey to an end.

Chapter Six

SUMMARY: THE POWER OF MYTHS

What is the power of myths three thousand and more years old, upon which ancient cultures were founded? How did they survive the devastation, collapse and change beyond recognition of entire cultures, to rise from the ashes — like the legendary phoenix[39] — their glory restored and their golden feathers more

---

[38] On Abravanel's cultural milieu in Italy, and his mystical neo-Platonic approach, see Dorman, in the introduction to *Sihot al HaAhava* (Heb.), 1983, pp. 50-58; 156-165.

[39] In Egyptian mythology, a legendary bird sacrificed periodically upon the altar in Heliopolis, and reborn from its own ashes; in Greek mythology, this was said to occur every five hundred years. *Cf. Bereshit Rabbah* 19, on the verse (Job 29:18): "'I shall die

resplendent than ever? We shall leave such questions to scholars studying the great myths as formative phenomena — complex and multifactorial — limiting our remarks to one simple and basic assertion: These myths draw their tenacity and power of renewal from human nature, from shared aspirations and dreams that, incredibly, have remained unchanged for thousands of years. Love, honour, kindness, justice, faith, courage, the acquisition of knowledge-wisdom . . . have we forgotten something? Joy, friendship, peace, perfection . . . the list is far from exhaustive, but reflects that which was important to people millennia, centuries, or decades ago, and continue to be so to this day. Then — as far back as "then" might be — and now, these are the goals people strive to attain, adhering to them once they have been attained, and experiencing them in the profundity of their human existence. To this simple and basic assertion, let us add one small but important comment: The aspirations, dreams and desires noted above have retained their full force due to the fact that even if one can claim that such a thing as human progress exists (a matter of great controversy), it does not apply here. In other words, the human race is no wiser, more just, respectful or loving than it ever was. Apparently, neither the accumulation of knowledge, technological advancement, nor increased life expectancy, affects the state of kindness, peace and love in the world. Such matters have thus remained extremely important to people, and that is what sustains the great myths.

In this section, we have attempted to demonstrate that the legend of the androgyne — an ancient bi-sexual creature, male and female in a single body — offers an appropriate response to a number of important questions. The term "appropriate response" in the context of legends that explain natural phenomena, inter-personal processes or historical events, requires further clarification. Most people thoroughly enjoy such legends. As a group of tourists visits a grotto, staring at the crashing waves and listening to them roar, they know that the grotto was created by the physical forces of erosion and gravity. The enchanting legend their guide tells them however, about the nymph whose tears melted the rock, freeing her lover who had been imprisoned within, brings a smile to their faces — a smile, not of derision, but of enjoyment in hearing the legend, a kind of deep pleasure, touching a part of the psyche that suffers no erosion and is not subject to the law of gravity. It is a smile of happiness elicited by the legend, causing them to push the children forward, toward the guide, that they might stop their squabbling and savour the happiness afforded by the story-legend. It is also a smile of embarrassment, because they do not know how to relate to the legend in light of the scientific knowledge they acquired

in my nest and I shall multiply my days as the sand' –There is a bird and its name is sand . . . It lives a thousand years, at the end of which fire issues from its nest and burns it, and it remains there as an egg, and regenerates its limbs and lives."

at school. Is the legend an alternative to physics as an explanation of natural phenomena? Did people invent legends because they were primitive, because they lacked the rational tools to explain natural phenomena? Does Newton mark the beginning of the crusade against legends, and modern science its end, precluding the invention of any new legends?

It is of course the authors of the notion that legend and physics provide mutually exclusive explanations of natural phenomena who are primitive.[40] As long as they consider themselves advanced or superior because of their viewpoint, they will remain trapped in their inherent backwardness. Physics and legends do not afford mutually exclusive explanations of natural pheno-mena, because they appertain to different planes of knowledge. Alternative explanations can be found on each of these planes, but not between them. The appropriate response provided by legends stands on its own, and has no alternative on the cognitive plane.

It is not enough that a legend provide answers, as momentous as the questions may be, for it to command the power of a myth. In order to do so it must not only answers questions, but also resonate with human hopes and dreams. Questions pertaining to the secret of attraction between men and women, and to the essence of love, go beyond the mere acquisition of knowledge, and are inextricably linked to man's deepest yearnings. The Adam-androgyne legend has the power of myth because it strikes a chord with the ultimate and most profound aspiration in the context of man-woman relations: the desire for perpetual coupling, indivisible union.

The androgyne myth is an ancient one, going back no less than three thousand years, to the cradle of human civilisation. Like other ancient and formative myths, the androgyne story knows no boundaries: re-appearing in many different and far-flung places, among different peoples, in different languages, in various periods and contexts. Like other great myths, we must assume that it is not the product of any single culture, but was created simultaneously by people of different cultures with virtually no direct contact between them. We have not discussed the fascinating issues pertaining to the legend's origins, choosing rather to discuss that which originated from it: love. Nor have we discussed its appearance in such remote cultures as those of Buddhism, ancient China, South America, etc. The androgyne myth made

---

40   See Paul Ricoeur, *The Symbolism of Evil*, Boston, 1969, p. 5; I. Greenwald *"Nokhehuto Habilti Nimna'at shel Hamitos — Masat Petiha"*, in H. Pedayah (ed.), 1996, esp. p. 2. See also Z. Harvey, *"Mitos Batar Mikra'i Uvatar Filosofi"*, in H. Pedayah, *ibid.* pp112-113, who explains the words of David Friedrich Strauss on the standing of ancient mythology; J. Dan, 1997, pp. 155-178; S. Rosenberg, *"Mitos Hamitosim"*, in *Mada'ei Hayahadut* 38, 5758 (1998), pp. 145-281; Y. Liebes, *"Mitos Ve'ortodoksia — Teshuvah LeShalom Rosenberg"*, *ibid.* pp. 181-187; and I. Greenwald, *"Hamitos Bametzi'ut Hahakaratit, Hahistorit Vehamehkarit"*, *ibid.* pp. 187-210.

a lasting impression upon all of these cultures, but we have chosen to take a closer look at its appearance in two neighbouring cultures in constant dialogue with one another,[41] in the sense of "the beauty of Japheth [resides] in the tents of Shem".[42] The main elements of the androgyne legend in its Greek source are: the existence of this composite being; rebellion against the gods; punishment — splitting in two; male and female thenceforth seeking to reunite.

We have postulated that the perception of an inherent negativity in the physical coupling of male and female — associated, according to the legend, with the rebellion against the gods, against all that is good and sublime — influenced the development of the doctrine of original sin in the theology of Paul, Augustine and their successors. In this sense, the androgyne myth can be seen as a cultural crossroads between Judaism and Christianity. The myth was adopted by the Rabbis, and as we have seen, appears repeatedly. The messages it conveys however, changed, and consequently a number of elements in the "factual" fabric of the story were revised as well. According to the Rabbis, not only is there no inherent negativity in the physical coupling of man and woman, but the androgyne itself was a weak creature that did not rebel against God or attack the good and the sublime. The splitting in two was not a punishment, but a "reparation" in order to enable physical contact in a different way: not involuntarily attached at the back or the side, but united in their volition and by the force of their love and desire.

It is in this that Judah Abravanel, author of the *Dialoghi d'amore* , sees the main difference between the Greek androgyne legend and the story of Adam's creation recounted in the Torah. According to the Greek version, the androgyne was split in two as a punishment, and the attraction between male and female is merely a consequence, a kind of by-product. In the Hebrew version, Adam is

---

[41] See S. Lieberman, 1963, p. 69: "The cultural impact of Hellenism upon the [Jewish] People was even greater than one might conclude based upon the historical information provided by the Talmud."

[42] This statement by the Rabbis regarding Greek language/culture is based on Gen 9:27: "God shall enlarge (*yaft*) Japheth (*Yefet*), and he shall dwell in the tents of Shem . . . ". According to Gen 10:2, Javan (the Hebrew name for Greece) was one of Japheth's sons. The word "*yaft*" (shall enlarge), although actually deriving from the root *peh-tav-heh*, is interpreted by the Rabbis as (also) stemming from the root *yod-peh-heh* (to beautify) — hence: "the beauty (*YaFiuTo*) of Japheth [resides] in the tents of Shem".

This is how the Rabbis justified Jewish receptiveness to foreign languages and cultures in general, and particularly to Greek-Hellenistic culture. See *Megilah* 9b; *Yerushalmi, ibid.* 1, 9; *Bereshit Rabbah* 36; *Devarim Rabbah* 1. *Yalkut Shimoni, Noah*, 247, 61 reads: "Rabbi Shimon ben Gamliel also says: It is permitted to write books in Greek, as it is written 'God shall enlarge Japeth [and he shall dwell in the tents of Shem]' — the words of Japheth shall be in the tents of Shem. And this is the meaning of 'the beauty of Japheth [resides] in the tents of Shem."

split not as a punishment, but due to the creator's desire to improve man. This improvement is expressed in the ability of male and female to approach one another, cling together and be one flesh. Adam was split in two, according to the Hebrew version, in order to create the mutual attraction between man and woman, and to enable them to couple with one another.

According to the various midrashim, all of humanity — in the figure of Adam — was once androgynous. The *Zohar* develops the concept of the androgyne beyond a purely human phenomenon, taking it from the physical to the divine world. The androgyne is considered neither negative nor perverted, nor is it "a term of reproach", as Aristophanes remarks, and Androgynous Adam, in the eyes of the Rabbis, is the crowning glory of creation. Moreover, the androgyne, according to the Kabbalah, is a divine and ethereal creature, and souls, before descending to the physical world, are also androgynous.

Jewish literature throughout the ages, beginning with the earliest midrashim, adopted the Greek Adam-androgyne myth, reworking it for the purposes of biblical exegesis, polemics against Essene and Nazarene celibacy, and to convey its message of conjugal harmony in the union between man and woman, body and soul.

Interest in the androgyne myth did not wane after the extensive treatment it received at the hands of Abravanel in the 16th century, and continues to engage writers, poets and artists to this day.[43] No further proof of the myth's immortality is needed.

---

[43]   See Liat Kaplan's poem "*Androginos*", in *Moznayim*, 72(3), 1997, p. 48; and Sharon As' poem "*He-androginos*", in the *Efes Shtayim* literary review, 3, 1995, p. 40.

From Dan Pagis' "*Hehamamah Hatropit*" (*Dan Pagis — Kol Hashirim*, Tel-Aviv 5752 (1992), p. 237): "MeShe,
  Mediterranean androgyne,
  MeShe,
  Uniquely engendered."
From Esther Ettinger's poem "*Sipur*" (in *Lifnei Hamusika*, Tel-Aviv 5746 (1986), p. 5):
  "And so it was: The slow sawing
  Or the quick laceration of a bandage removed
  And man and woman
  Parted back from back and the pain
  As if In the Beginning was separation."
Moshe Yitzhaki's poem "*Shuvo Shel He'androginos*" (in *Hashemesh Yavo Veyifneh*, Mahberet Shedemot 11, 1999) shows that this myth is indeed eternal. The poem is printed so that its letters describe the form of an androgyne. Here is an excerpt:
  "Two-faces in the darkness taste
  What some strive to redouble
  And are cut out from the start
  To find halves
  New matching."

The ancient figure of the androgyne is also the figure of complete man, comprising both sexes together called "Adam", thus also serving as a paradigm to which we must aspire. The androgyne legend provides an appropriate response to the great questions of love, touches upon questions of individual sexual identity, and is felt in the interaction between partners united in love. The androgynous myth's three-thousand-year journey has not yet ended, and probably never will. This legend touches the most delicate fibres in our beings — men and women alike — and penetrates to the core of our human existence.

SECTION II
A PROFILE OF THE SAGE OF LOVE

Chapter One
INTRODUCTION:
THE PHILOSOPHER AS SAGE OF LOVE

> "I profess to understand nothing but matters of love."
>
> Socrates, according to Plato's *Symposium*

Philosophy is the love of wisdom per se, and the wisdom-loving philosopher demonstrates love and passion for wisdom, for the acquisition of knowledge purely for its own sake, without intending to put it to any use whatsoever. Plato however (at the end of the fifth and beginning of the sixth book of *The Republic*), characterises the philosopher, not by his desire, love and passion for the acquisition of knowledge, but by his already having acquired it; not as one striving to acquire wisdom, but as one who is already sage, one who knows virtue. The wisdom of the sage of love can be seen in his knowledge of true reality, his understanding of ideals, his experience of the changing world and daily reality, in his perfect moral comportment as a soldier and a civilian. Some have thus understood the platonic interpretation of philosophy as "the wisdom of love", and the philosopher as a sage of love. Even if the title, according to this interpretation, would not apply to every thinker or philosopher, it should be applied to anyone whose scholarly and practical interest in love are at the centre of her/his thought and life. Such a sage is Rabbi Akiva[1] — first discovered

---

[1] I first heard this idea from my teacher, Prof. Ze'ev Harvey of Hebrew University, in a course on the concept of love. See also Rabbi A.I. Kook, "*Shir Hashirim*", in *Be'oro — Iyunim Bemishnato shel Harav Avraham Ytzhak Hakohen Kook ZT"L Uvedarkei Hora'atah* — first published in B.M. Levin (ed.), *Alumah*, Jerusalem 5696 (1936).

by virtue of a woman's love, he engaged in the philosophy of love and all its inter-personal manifestations in both his philosophical and halakhic teachings; "rescued" the *Song of Songs* from being suppressed; established "love thy fellow as thyself" as a great principle in the Torah; and departed this world in a supreme expression of love of God, with all his soul — even when it was taken from him.

Rabbi Akiva ben Joseph was one of the leading sages of the mishnaic period, if not the greatest among them. His legendary figure, leadership, halakhic method and thought, occupy a central place in the tanaitic and amoraic literature: in the Mishnah and the Talmuds, in halakhic and aggadic Midrash, as well as later Midrash, edited over a period of centuries. The image of Rabbi Akiva, as it appears in the sources, is that of a sage in both scholarship and deed, in Halakhah and Aggadah, in *peshat* and *derash*, *remez* and *sod*,[2] and above all in moral conduct able to withstand the difficult trials presented by all aspects of daily life. This is the image of the perfect sage, and the following *beraita* expresses, in the clearest possible fashion, the Talmud's attitude to Rabbi Akiva, as the perfect sage:

> "Four entered the (esoteric) Orchard, and they were: Ben Azai, Ben Zoma, *Aher* and Rabbi Akiva . . . Ben Azai glimpsed and died . . . Ben Zoma glimpsed and was harmed . . . *Aher* slashed among the plants, Rabbi Akiva emerged safely."
>
> BT, *Hagigah* 14b; *Tosefta Hagigah* 2, 2

The *Tosefta* version concludes: "Rabbi Akiva ascended and descended in safety": He was a perfect sage when he entered and a perfect sage when he emerged.

The giant figure of Rabbi Akiva first appears in a love story. The legends that describe his early years do not attribute any greatness or unusual qualities to him. It is Rachel,[3] daughter of the wealthy man for whom Akiva worked as a shepherd, who was the precipitator, the active force behind all that transpired.

The profile of the sage of love should therefore begin with the love of Rachel.

---

[2]   See Section I, n. 33.

[3]   I owe the idea of viewing Rachel as the driving force, and presenting the love story between Rachel and Rabbi Akiva from her perspective, to Professor Eliezer Schweid, who commented on my interpretation of the story in *Be'ikvot Ahavah*. I thank him for having shown me the correct way of reading these legends.

Chapter Two

THE LOVE OF RACHEL

> "Rabbi Akiva was the shepherd of Ben Kalba
> Savua. His daughter saw that he was modest and
> excellent. She said to him: If I become betrothed
> to you, will you go to the house of study? He
> replied: Yes. She secretly became betrothed to
> him and sent him off. Her father heard, cast her
> out of his house and disinherited her."
>
> BT, *Ketubot*, 62b

According to this legend, it was Rachel, the wellborn daughter of a wealthy man, who initiated contact with Akiva ben Joseph, a poor, common shepherd who was, according to tradition, a descendant of converts, who had "learned nothing" and was completely ignorant. Nevertheless, he attracts her attention. She recognises the potential in his personality, sees that he is "modest and excellent", and proposes that she become betrothed to him, on condition that he go to the house of study. "She secretly became betrothed to him and sent him off," hoping that he would study so that she could then present him to her father and they could marry. (Betrothal — called *kiddushin* or *erusin* — was generally conducted in the house of the bride's father, and effected a change in the woman's personal status, from single to "the wife of another". The betrothed girl would remain in her father's house after the betrothal, and when the groom would finish preparing [or building] their joint home, he would bring her to it and the wedding feast would then be held.) Rachel thus became betrothed to Akiva, created a commitment, and sent him off to study. The same source tells us that when Rabbi Akiva completed his long years of study and had 24, 000 students, his father-in-law came to him:

> "[When] her father heard that a great man had come to town, he said, I will go to him. He may release [me from] my vow. [When] he came to him, [Rabbi Akiva] said to him, had you not known that her husband would become a great man, would you still have disinherited her? He said to him, [not if he had studied] **even a single chapter, even a single law**. He said to him, I am he. He fell on his face, and kissed his feet, and gave him half of his fortune."
>
> *Ibid. 63a*

Rachel had planned that Akiva would go to the house of study, learn a little ("even a single chapter, a single law"), thereby becoming acceptable to her father retroactively, and then they could marry. Her father however, discovered that she had secretly become engaged to this ignoramus, threw her out of his house and vowed that he would not give her any assistance or property. Rachel was left with no choice, and married Akiva, although he had not yet fulfilled his part of the agreement, and had not yet gone to the house of study to learn Torah.[4]

The married couple was destined for a life of poverty, without a roof over their heads. Only in the winter did they find shelter in a barn:

> "In the winter they would sleep in a barn, and [Rabbi Akiva] would pick straw out of her hair. He said to her: Were it in my power, I would give you a 'Jerusalem of gold' [diadem]. Elijah came and appeared to them as a man, and he called from the threshold: give me a little straw, for my wife has given birth, and I have nothing on which to lay her down. Rabbi Akiva said to his wife: Behold this man does not even have straw. She said to him: Go, sit in the house of study."

> BT, *Nedarim* 50a

The relationship between Akiva and Rachel is that of a pair of lovers, and their romance is not dulled by the poverty in which they live. How moving the description of the loving man picking bits of straw out of his wife's hair and whispering in her ear: "were it in my power, I would give you a 'Jerusalem of gold' [diadem]". Rachel is not moved by words of love however, but by a seemingly trivial occurrence, in which she once again glimpses her husband's special personality, his modesty and his greatness. Poverty does not make Akiva despair and does not distort his principles and moral outlook. Not only does he not allow hardship to spoil romance. He does not even hesitate to share the little that he has with someone poorer than himself. This event affords Rachel the opportunity to lead him to her goal, and she answers her husband in a manner that seems to be beside the point, but which as far as she is concerned is the only point: this man she loves for his superior qualities must go to the house of study: "She said to him: Go to the house of study!"

---

[4]   See Shmuel Safrai, *Rabbi Akiva — Hayav Umishnato*, pp. 11-12. Safrai questions the tradition of Rabbi Akiva's marriage to the daughter of Kalba Savua from a chronological point of view, claiming that the latter was one of Jerusalem's wealthiest men prior to the destruction of the Temple, while Rabbi Akiva could not have been more than 15 years old at the time. The doubts Safrai raises, based on a comparison of Babylonian and Palestinian sources and chronological analysis, cannot be dismissed. Nevertheless, they do not completely undermine the traditional narrative. I am surprised that Safrai does not mention the reading "*devar dekalba savua*" ("of the son of Kalba Savua") in BT, *Nedarim* 50a and in the manuscripts, from which the name would appear to have been a family designation rather than that of a specific individual. The text in *Ketubot* also reads "Rabbi Akiva was the shepherd of Ben Kalba Savua", so that he may in fact have been the shepherd of the son of the wealthy Kalba Savua of Jerusalem rather than of Kalba Savua himself. Safrai, p. 68, translates "*Ben Kalba Savua*" — "*Kalba ben Savua*", and adds in n.1: "One of Jerusalem's wealthy citizens before the destruction of the Temple" (BT, *Gittin* 56a). It is true that the wealthy man himself is not called "Kalba Savua" in *Gittin*, but "Ben Kalba Savua". In some texts however, he is referred to merely as "Kalba Savua", eg. *Avot deRabbi Natan* 6. It is therefore possible that "the daughter of Ben Kalba Savua" (BT, *Ketubot* 62b) was the granddaughter of the head of the family during the Temple period.

"He went and sat in the house of study for twelve years. When he returned, twelve-thousand students came with him. He heard a sage say to her: How long will you continue your living widowhood. She said to him: Were he to listen to me, he would sit for another twelve years. He said: In that case, I have [her] permission. He returned and sat for another twelve years in the house of study."

BT, *Ketubot*, 62b

According to the talmudic account, Rachel lived for more than two decades alone and poor, a widow in her husband's lifetime, but with determination and the knowledge that it was her desire that her husband study Torah. Most readers of this legend see the lengthy separation as a severe blow to their relationship, and fail to accept the emphases of the story's author, whereby it was she who initiated this separation, lovingly and willingly. Rachel's love for Rabbi Akiva brings her to love the wisdom and the Torah study to which he devotes his life, until he returns to her after having fulfilled his love pledge in having studied Torah, not only having gone to the house of study, but having become a great sage and acquiring many students. He thus justified the expectations she had of him when she saw him for the first time and noticed the potential in his personality.

The man who began his married life without a home, and his love-life picking straw out of his beloved's hair, is now the greatest of the sages, respected by all, and extremely wealthy, but he does not forget his years of poverty and his loving whispers on winter nights in the barn. To his mind, his murmurings were a kind of vow, and now that he has the means, he keeps that vow:

"One day, when Rabbi Akiva's situation improved, and he made his wife shoes of gold and a 'city of gold' [diadem], his students said to him: Rabbi you have shamed us by what you have done for her. Rabbi Akiva said to them: She has suffered a great deal with me in the Torah."

Avot deRabbi Natan 6, 2

Great was the power of love at the beginning of their shared journey, in light of the initial difficulties experienced by the couple, especially when love itself was the cause of their difficulties. Love made up for all of the obstacles and adversities. The transition to a life of comfort however — a drastic change from poverty to extreme wealth — also puts love to the test, and Rabbi Akiva does not forget his romantic promises from their days in the miserable barn. Now, decades later, he buys his wife the jewels and gifts he promised her then, reiterating his love for her, courting her and expressing his gratitude. Rabbi Akiva is now the admired teacher of thousands, the most revered and esteemed sage of his generation,[5] and no longer the simple shepherd he was when he married. He is no longer in financial straits, if only because his father-in-law

---

[5] "Whose fame extends to the ends of the Earth", see BT, *Yevamot* 16a.

has given him half of his vast fortune, yet his students think it unbecoming of their elderly rabbi to foolishly give his wife such extravagant gifts. They, who were so proud of their teacher, are now ashamed of him, and do not hesitate to criticise him. The relationship between rabbi and students, as it appears in this story, is noteworthy. The students have no qualms about criticising their teacher for extravagant or immoral behaviour. A teacher's decorous and dignified comportment also reflects upon his disciples, and their reaction is: "you have shamed us, Rabbi". The students demanded that Rabbi Akiva, known for his concern for his students' honour,[6] live up to his reputation.[7] Rabbi Akiva does not share the promises he made to his wife twenty years previously with them, but explains that the honour of the Torah is not cheapened by his actions, since his wife is an integral part of the recognition he has won. His self-sacrifice for the sake of Torah study was first and foremost her self-sacrifice and her merit, and the privations she suffered during his long years of study were even greater than those that he had experienced.

In his explanation however, Rabbi Akiva does far more than merely repeat the known facts. The suffering in Torah that she shared with him did not lie in the difficulty of separation during the many years he spent in the house of study and she lived as a widow in her husband's lifetime. She did not regret that. On the contrary, as the talmudic legends stress, it was her desire: "Were he to listen to me, he would sit for another twelve years" (*Ketubot, ibid.*).[8] She suffered greatly with him in Torah however, because he did not immediately fulfil the condition that she, in her love, had made **prior** to their marriage: "If I become betrothed to you, will you go to the house of study?" He promised her that he would, but he did not keep his promise, and Rachel found herself cast out of the home of her wealthy father, and married to a poor ignoramus, who loved her very much and promised to buy her expensive jewels, but withheld the most precious jewel of all: he failed to go to the house of study. Akiva must certainly have had a reason to break the promise he had given her: he felt that he could not leave her alone with a child, in such a state of poverty, without his support. From her

---

[6]   See BT, *Eruvin* 54b. His student Rabbi Elazar ben Shamua said: "Let the honour of your student be as dear to you as your own" (*Avot* 4, 12), which would appear to be his master's teaching.

[7]   *Avot deRabbi Natan*, vers. 2, 12 reads: ". . . Until he had made a crown of gold for his wife. And until he had made golden slippers for his wife. His sons said to him: People are laughing at us." According to this version of the story, it is his sons who criticise his actions.

[8]   The version in *Nedarim* reads: Upon completion of the twelve years he went home. Behind the house he heard a wicked man say to his wife: Your father did well, [for] he [your husband] is beneath you, and what is more has left you in living widowhood for all these years. She said to him: Were he to listen to me, he would go for another twelve years. He said: Since she has given me permission, I will go back. He went back for another twelve years, and returned with twenty-four thousand pairs of students."

perspective however, their economic hardship in no way justified his remaining with her. The fact that he had not gone to study was a source of great distress to her, and the fact that she had the man she loved by her side was no comfort to her. She seizes upon the appearance of Elijah in the form of a poor man whose wife was in labour and lacked even straw to lie on. Akiva uses the opportunity to comfort her in their poverty and distress, pointing out that some are in even greater straits, and Rachel replies: "Go to the house of study!" I can handle our hardships. They are not the most difficult, as there are those whose lot is worse. There is therefore no need for you to stay. Go to the house of study!

This is the great distress that Rabbi Akiva inflicted upon his wife Rachel — the fact that he did not go immediately after their betrothal to study Torah, and postponed fulfilling the promise he had given by a few years. Only when their son got older, and the time came to bring him to a teacher that he might learn to read and write, did he overcome his embarrassment and begin to study with his son:

> "He and his son went and sat before the teacher of children. He said to him: Rabbi, teach me Torah. Rabbi Akiva held the top of the slate and his son wrote the *alef-bet* at the top of the slate and he learned it. *Alef* [to] *tav* and he learned it. The book of *Leviticus* and he learned it. He continued learning until he had learned the entire Torah."
>
> *Avot deRabbi Natan ibid.*

In the eyes of many readers of the tales of Rabbi Akiva, the fact that he "left" his beloved wife for decades is incompatible with his legendary character as whole. This element of his biography would appear to be difficult to reconcile with the title "sage of love" and his many sayings on the subject of love. The natural place for lovers is by each other's sides, and Rabbi Akiva's prolonged absence tarnishes the obvious idyllic image. Talmudic legend also cites an anonymous sage who wonders how long she will continue her living widowhood (*Ketubot, ibid.*), and according to another version of the story,[9] her husband's absence results in her harassment by a wicked man who does not desist even when Rabbi Akiva returns at the head of a multitude of students. This is the source of the mistaken tendency to interpret Rabbi Akiva's words, "she has suffered a lot with me in the Torah", as a kind of justification of his long absence. It was not the separation however, the longing or the loneliness throughout the many years in which he applied himself to Torah study with endless devotion, that caused Rachel grief, but in fact the long period in which he failed to fulfil his promise to go and study. The source of this legend, in *Avot deRabbi Natan*, describes the depths of Akiva's ignorance — complete illiteracy: "His son wrote the *alef-bet* at the top of the slate and he learned it. *Alef* [to] *tav* and he learned it." How much Rachel

---

[9]   BT, *Nedarim, ibid.*, see previous note.

suffered, having to live with a man who didn't even know the *alef-bet*. Finally, he learns to read and write together with his son, and begins to study Torah as well: "the book of Leviticus and he learned it" — the first book of the Torah taught to children — continuing to learn until he had learned the entire Torah. Only then was he worthy of complying with her request/demand that he go to the house of study — that of Rabbi Eliezer and Rabbi Yehoshua. Rabbi Akiva expressed this in the words "she has suffered with me" — the suffering she endured until I went to study Torah was on my account. She is therefore all the more deserving of credit for all I have achieved. That is also the message that arises from the following:

> "A tale of Rabbi Akiva, who made his wife a 'city of gold' [diadem]. [The Patriarch] Raban Gamliel's wife became angry and jealous of her. She came and told her husband. He said to her: 'would you have done for me what she has done — selling her hair and giving him [the proceeds] that he might study Torah?'"
>
> JT, *Shabbat* 6, 7

The suffering that she endured with him in the Torah is thus not the suffering of separation as many mistakenly believe, but the suffering of a life of poverty and sacrifice, and above all, as we have seen, the great sorrow over the time that passed until he went to study Torah.

Rachel presents a more complex vision of love than merely living side by side for richer or for poorer. Love, to Rachel, is a driving force and the source of creativity and growth. "If I become betrothed to you, will you go to the house of study?" She does not love the illiterate shepherd as he is. Her love for him is aroused by her recognition of his character and his potential, taking it upon herself to help him realise that potential. Her love is not stagnant but evolving, and comes to fruition in Rabbi Akiva's accomplishments, in his becoming the greatest sage of his generation. Rabbi Akiva's return at the head of his students is the climax of this love story. The following are two versions of the story's ending, as they appear in the Talmud:

Ketubot 62b	Nedarim 50a
"When he returned, twenty-four thousand students came with him. His wife heard and went to greet him. Her neighbours said to her: borrow clothing and dress yourself. She said to them: 'a righteous man knoweth the spirit of his beast' (*Prov* 12:10). When she came before him, she prostrated herself and began to kiss his feet, and his students pushed her [away]. He said to them: leave her. What is mine and yours is hers."	He went away for another twelve years, and returned with twenty-four thousand pairs of students. Everyone went out to greet him, and she too went to greet him. The wicked man said to her: and where are you going? She said to him: 'a righteous man knoweth the spirit of his beast' (*Prov* 12:10). She went to appear before him and the rabbis began to push her. He said to them: leave her alone. What is mine and yours is hers."

According to the version in *Ketubot*, Rachel's neighbours try to convince her to borrow pretty clothes and dress up in honour of her husband's return. We know that Rabbi Akiva attached importance to external appearance and even the use of cosmetics — believing them to contribute to marital harmony — a fact that is reflected in his halakhic rulings.[10] Her behaviour, according to this account, is completely self-abasing: she prostrates herself and kisses his feet. His students, who see a strange woman dressed in rags kissing their rabbi's feet, push her aside.

The version in *Nedarim* features the same wicked man who twelve years earlier, justified her father's decision to disinherit her over that good-for-nothing of a husband, who had of course abandoned her, making her a living widow. He continues to torment her: "and where are you going?" Your husband left you when he was a nobody. Do you really think he will notice you after all these years, especially now, when he is a great sage and you are still the same miserable creature? Regarding the meeting between them, this version is far less dramatic: "she went to appear before him and the rabbis began to push her", seeking to prevent her from joining those who were being received by the great Rabbi.

What is disturbing here however is not the extent to which she humbled herself before him — whether she prostrated herself or merely sought to be received by him — but rather the way in which she appears to compare herself to a beast: "a righteous man knoweth the spirit of his beast". One need not possess a heightened awareness or feminist sensibilities to wonder at the use of this expression (taken from the book of *Proverbs*), which in fact disturbed talmudic commentators throughout the ages. The many comments on Rachel's use of this phrase show the extent of discomfort aroused by this apparent comparison. Some explain that having heard that a great man had come to town and not knowing whether it was Rabbi Akiva or not, she went to greet him anyway, remarking that a righteous man would not humiliate someone, even a poor woman like herself. Others reject this reading entirely, claiming that the text should read: "a righteous man knoweth the cause of the poor" (*Shitah Mekubetzet, loc. cit.*). Yet others explain that the expression's imagery is well suited to Rabbi Akiva, who was a shepherd in his youth (*Maharsha loc. cit.*). Rachel remembered how she recognised his potential when he was still a shepherd tending her father's flocks. Her words may also be an allusion to Rabbi Akiva's statement that "poverty becomes a daughter of Jacob like a red ribbon on the head of a white horse" (Midrash, *Vayikra Rabbah* 35, 6). Moreover,

---

[10] For example, he allowed a woman in a state of menstrual impurity to use kohl and rouge so that she might not become unattractive to her husband, and permitted divorce even when there was no cause other than the husband's having found a more beautiful woman. See below.

the Jewish People is compared to a handsome beast, and the comparison is not perceived as being derogatory.[11] In any case, the many comments elicited by the use of this phrase indicate that scholars and readers throughout the generations have been uncomfortable with the comparison made by Rachel herself, or ascribed to her by the author of the legend.

A look at *Proverbs* 12, from which the phrase is taken, allows us to understand the phrase in its original context. The chapter compares the path of the righteous to that of the wicked: the former love correction and knowledge while the latter hate reproof and are deceitful and ignorant. The righteous are diligent and unashamed of their poverty, while the wicked waste their time in the company of idlers like themselves. Rachel goes to meet her husband, who is — in keeping with the opening verse in *Proverbs* 12 — a lover of correction and knowledge. She — who was the first to recognise his moral qualities, that he was "modest and excellent", brought him to love knowledge, in the belief that love of morality (correction) and love of knowledge are one and the same — is called (in 12:4) "a virtuous woman", who is "a crown to her husband". Although she is poor and dressed in rags, there is no shame in that (12:9): "Better is he that is lightly esteemed, and hath a servant, than he that playeth the man of rank, and lacketh bread" — one who does not despise labour of any kind and is servant to himself is better than one who is so filled with pride that he refrains from work and thereby suffers privation. Rachel has nothing to be ashamed of: "a righteous man knoweth the spirit of his beast" — its desires and needs — and provides for them.[12] Rachel's needs are not physical, and are in fact satisfied only by Rabbi Akiva's going to study. She goes to greet him knowing that he knows her spirit — the spirit that caused him to study and acquire knowledge, the spirit that was the source of his greatness. The comparison to a beast is therefore not degrading. It is meant to convey the idea that honour or shame depends upon the way in which one perceives oneself. The righteous man knows even the spirit of his beast, and that knowledge is not beneath his dignity, but rather a manifestation of his righteousness. How much greater is Rabbi Akiva's knowledge of her own spirit, of her longing all of those years for him to study Torah.

In a similar vein, one might interpret "the spirit of his beast" in the text as referring not to her, but to the beast within himself. "The righteous man who knows" is thus juxtaposed with "the spirit of his beast". The concept of "the righteous man who knows" expresses recognition of the value of Torah study,

---

[11]   See also "I have compared thee, O my love, to a company of horses in Pharaoh's chariots" (*Song of Songs* 1:9).

[12]   This interpretation of Proverbs 12 was inspired by Mordechai Zer-Kavod's commentary in *Da'at Mikra*, Mossad Harav Kook. See also Naftali Hertz Tur-Sinai's original commentary in *Peshuto Shel Mikra*: "The righteous man knows spirit in his intensity of emotion" ("*Yodea tzadik nefesh behemiyato*") — indeed a fitting interpretation of this legend.

and "the spirit of his beast" the need, the longing to study Torah, for without the Torah, all that remains is the beast without the spirit. The unique character of the righteous man lies in this knowledge, in recognising that the beast's spirit must be sustained, that the spiritual needs of "the beast" — Torah study — must be satisfied. Knowing "the spirit of the beast" is thus the essence of all that has passed between Rachel and Rabbi Akiva: what began as her knowledge alone has become his/their shared knowledge. She does not need to borrow clothes and dress up for him, because that is not the basis of their relationship. According to the version in *Nedarim*, in response to the wicked man's question, "and where are you going?" she says "a righteous man knows the spirit of his beast". This has been my goal ever since I married him, for all these years, to get him to know this. Now that he does, I am going to greet him. She goes to greet him with the knowledge that her great sacrifice has not been in vain, that her work has been rewarded, and that he has been worthy of her love.

It is Rachel's love that made Rabbi Akiva a wise man, one of the greatest and most influential figures in all areas of Jewish culture in his and in subsequent generations. And when she came before him, she prostrated herself and kissed his feet. His students began to push her away, and he said to them: leave her, what is mine and what is yours — is hers. All of my Torah, and thus all of your Torah, belongs to my wife Rachel, because it emanates from her love. As Rashi explains: "The Torah that I have studied and that you have studied — is **by her hand**". It is she, through her love, who insisted that I study Torah, that I persevere, and that I go on to teach you. What is mine and what is yours — is **hers**: the wisdom and Torah of the sage of love is the result of his love for a woman, belongs to that woman.

Rachel's love brought Rabbi Akiva's wisdom to fruition, making his Torah and that of his students for all generations hers. The sage of love is a woman's creation, and a woman's love begot his wisdom.

Chapter Three

THE SAGE OF LOVE "RESCUES" THE *SONG OF SONGS*

There are a number of ways in which to develop a philosophy or unifying approach. Some seek commonality in the phenomena they observe and when they believe they have collected sufficient data, offer a comprehensive explanation. Others first set a goal, and then go about looking for evidence to support it, deciding upon their approach before conducting research — having perhaps studied and observed, but not yet corroborated. It is in this second way that Rabbi Akiva's wisdom of love developed. He established love — his point of departure — as his overall objective, governing the positions he took on the things he observed, the ideas he considered, the sources he chose to interpret, and the decisions he made regarding events in his own life. Rabbi Akiva's wisdom of love can be seen throughout his work, in his halakhic rulings no less than in matters of scholarship and morality. It is often difficult to make a clear distinction between Halakhah and Aggadah in his teachings. His ruling concerning the status of the *Song of Songs* is a clear example of this, as analysis of the well-known debate in the Mishnah regarding the status of this book will show:

> "All holy scripture makes the hands impure. The *Song of Songs* and *Ecclesiastes* make the hands impure. Rabbi Yehudah says: *Song of Songs* makes the hands impure, and *Ecclesiastes* is [a matter of] dispute. Rabbi Yose says: *Ecclesiastes* does not make the hands impure, and *Song of Songs* is [a matter of] dispute. Rabbi Shimon says: [Regarding] *Ecclesiastes, Beit Shamai* are lenient and *Beit Hillel* are stringent. Rabbi Shimon ben Azai said: I received from seventy-two sages on the day that Rabbi Elazar ben Azariah ascended to the patriarchate that *Song of Songs* and *Ecclesiastes* make the hands impure.
> Rabbi Akiva said: Heaven forbid! [There is] not a man in Israel who disputes [the fact] that the *Song of Songs* makes the hands impure, for the entire world was never so worthy as on the day on which the *Song of Songs* was given to Israel, since all of scripture is holy, and the *Song of Songs* is holy of holies! And if there was a dispute, it was only with regard to *Ecclesiastes*."

Mishnah, Yadayim 3, 5

The Rabbis decreed that all works of holy scripture make the hands impure, i.e. anyone who touches them with bare hands will become impure. It was common practice at the time to store priestly tithes together with Torah scrolls, since both articles were considered holy. However, rodents found in the foodstuffs of the tithes would also gnaw at the scrolls. The rabbis therefore decreed: first, that the scriptures would make foodstuffs with which they came in contact unfit for the priestly tithe; and second, that the hands of anyone who touches the scrolls would also become impure, so that touching the scrolls and then the tithes would make the tithes unfit.[13] They thus hoped to prevent the two items from being stored together, thereby preventing holy scriptures from being gnawed by rodents.

This would appear to be a practical halakhic decision in the area of ritual purity, designed to preserve precious books. Between the lines however, we discover another, broader discussion, regarding the canonical status of certain books. The fundamental questions therefore go well beyond the specific field of ritual purity, extending to the process of the canonisation of the Bible.

---

[13]   Maimonides, in his Commentary on the Mishnah writes: "Later, they made a broad decree that hands attain the second degree of impurity and make priestly tithes unfit." See *Zavim* 5, 9.

It is worth noting that the concept of "canonisation", as it is commonly used in reference to the books included in, or excluded from the Bible, is essentially anachronistic. Books that are considered canonical "attained" that status over the course of centuries. The Rabbis argued not over what should be included in the canon, but over the simple, practical question of whether a book should be disseminated among Jewish communities throughout the world—thereby preserving it for future generations, due to the need for many copies of the manuscript. Should there be no public need to make many copies of the text, it would in the natural course of events, without specific intention, be lost over time. A book established as holy scripture, stood an infinitely better chance of survival—both because it was copied many times over—for each and every community—and because it was then carefully safeguarded, as demonstrated by the mishnah above.

The *Mishnah* begins with a general injunction: "all holy scripture makes the hands impure"; and immediately repeats the same *halakhah* with regard to two specific books: "the *Song of Songs* and *Ecclesiastes* make the hands impure". These books are indeed holy scripture, but because there was a dispute concerning their status, the *mishnah* emphasises the fact that the dispute was resolved, and that the Rabbis' decree applies to these books as well. It appears from the remainder of the *mishnah*, that there were a number of other traditions concerning *Song of Songs* and *Ecclesiastes*: that neither book is holy scripture and therefore does not make the hands impure; that *Ecclesiastes* is not scripture, but the *Song of Songs* does make the hands impure; and vice versa. Ben Azai attests to the fact that the status of both books was a matter of dispute, but that these disputes had been laid to rest on the day of Rabbi Elazar ben Azariah's appointment as head of the yeshivah[14] at Yavneh. Many *halakhot* were restored on that day, and no legal dispute remained unresolved. According to Ben Azai's account, this was also the case with the *Song of Songs* and *Ecclesiastes*. Rabbi Akiva however, not only takes a clear stand in favour of the *Song of Song*'s sacred status, but dismisses the possibility that it could ever have been in doubt: "Heaven forbid! [There is] not a man in Israel who disputes [the fact] that the *Song of Songs* makes the hands impure, for the entire world was never so worthy as on the day on which the *Song of Songs* was given to Israel, since all of scripture is holy, and the *Song of Songs* is holy of holies! And if there was a dispute, it was only with regard to *Ecclesiastes*".

Judging by the *Mishnah* in *Yadayim* however, it appears that Rabbi Akiva's position was not accepted: "Rabbi Yohanan ben Yeshuah, son of Rabbi Akiva's father-in-law said: as asserted by Ben Azai, so [the matter] was disputed and so [it was] concluded". In other words, the status of both books was disputed, and not only that of *Ecclesiastes*. The fact that there was indeed a debate regarding

14   President of the Sanhedrin, appointed after Raban Gamliel was removed for having offended Rabbi Yehoshua. See BT, *Berakhot* 27b.

the status of these books, and that the opinion that they are both holy scripture prevailed at one time, is confirmed by another source:

"At first it was said: *Proverbs, Song of Songs* and *Ecclesiastes* were suppressed, for it was said that they were proverbs and not scripture and they were suppressed, until the members of Great Assembly came and interpreted them."

Avot deRabbi Natan 1, 4

According to this source, not only was there a dispute regarding these books, but they were even banned. It is unclear what interpretations were offered by the members of the Great Assembly, but the debate would appear to have continued for many years, until it was resolved by the Sanhedrin under the presidency of Rabbi Elazar ben Azariah. Nevertheless, it is the words of Rabbi Akiva that are remembered and quoted most often, becoming firmly established in historical memory as having determined the status of *Song of Songs*: "for the entire world was never so worthy as on the day on which the *Song of Songs* was given to Israel, since all of scripture is holy, and the *Song of Songs* is holy of holies!"

Although the canonical status of the Holy Scriptures, including *Ecclesiastes* and *Song of Songs*, was determined by the Sanhedrin headed by Rabbi Elazar ben Azariah,[15] the rescue of *Song of Songs*, and its establishment as part of the canon is attributed to Rabbi Akiva. We can assume that he took part in these early debates, or some of them, or that the matter was at least brought to his attention, and to his mind there were perhaps a number of approaches, but no real debate among the Rabbis regarding the status of the *Song of Songs*. As noted above, the *mishnah* explicitly rejects Rabbi Akiva's opinion on this matter. Both *Song of Songs* and *Ecclesiastes* had been in dispute, and Rabbi Akiva himself had taken part in that dispute.

What was the dispute all about? According to the primary sources, it appears to have been a theological debate:

"Rabbi Shimon ben Menasya says: *Song of Songs* makes the hands impure because it was inspired by the holy spirit, *Ecclesiates* does not make the hands impure because it is merely the wisdom of Solomon. They said to him: Is that all he wrote? For it is written [*1 Kings* 4:32]: 'and he spake three thousand proverbs, and his songs were a thousand and five', and it is written [*Proverbs* 30:6]: 'add thou not unto his words.'"

Tosefta Yadayim 2, 5

[15] Rabbi Akiva was himself a member of the Sanhedrin at the time, and was even considered as a successor to Raban Gamliel, before Rabbi Elazar ben Azariah was chosen. His lineage, as a descendant of converts however, prevented his appointment. See *Berakhot ibid.*: ". . . Let us remove him [from the presidency]. With whom shall we replace him? Shall we replace him with Rabbi Yehoshua? He is a party to the affair. Shall we replace him with Akiva — the merit of his forebears. They examined Rabbi Elazar ben Azariah who is a sage and a wealthy man and tenth [generation descendant] of Ezra.

Rabbi Shomon ben Menasya's opinion is not accepted, but the debate itself would appear to be of a theological nature, regarding the question of whether the book was prophetically inspired or merely the product of the author's "human" wisdom. That is also how the commentators explain Rabbi Akiva's statement in the Mishnah — "the *Song of Songs* is holy of holies", i.e. it is of deep theological value.[16] The debate between the Rabbis regarding the canonical status of one book or another however stems first and foremost from the book's content, from what it states explicitly, and not the various interpretations associated with it. The Rabbis sought to determine whether the book merited public reading, and the extent to which its content contributed to the community's intellectual, spiritual and cultural discourse, whether it was worthy of being a "source of knowledge". The debate concerns the book itself, what it contains and what it lacks. The Rabbis' discussions are on this plane and this plane alone, and do not address external factors such as the question of whether a book was composed in a spirit of prophecy or was merely the product of human wisdom. The theological questions should be seen as nothing more than supporting arguments in the campaign over the fate of a book that, due to its content, was the subject of controversy among the Rabbis. One need not look very far to discover that the *Song of Songs* differs fundamentally from every other text in the Prophets and Writings. It lacks religious or nationalist content, and God's name does not appear in it.[17] It is rather, a poem in praise of human love between man and woman. Contrary to the books of the Prophets that clearly use human love as a metaphor for divine love and a means of conveying religious and spiritual messages, *Song of Songs* refers to human love per se and leaves no room to think that it might be allegorical. Allegorical interpretations throughout the generations have been imposed upon the text rather than emanating from it. The subject of the Rabbis' debate was thus love itself. Those who supported the status of *Song of Songs* as scripture — Rabbi Akiva foremost among them — did so not because of any esoteric significance

---

16   See Rashi on *Song of Songs* 1:1: "For it is full of fear of God and acceptance of the yoke of his kingship"; and *Melekhet Shelomo*: "For sacred matters and secrets are intimated therein".

17   Some argue that God's name appears in the word/s "shalhevet-yah" ("a most vehement flame/a very flame of God"). *Song of Songs* 8:6 reads: ". . . for love is strong as death; jealousy is cruel as the grave: the flashes thereof are flashes of fire, a most vehement flame/a very flame of God (*shalhevetyah*)." See Ibn Ezra, who notes that it is a matter of dispute among the Massoretes whether *shalhevetyah* should be written as one or two words. According to the commentators, the word means "a great flame", and as in the word *merhavyah*, the suffix *-yah* is simply augmentative. See *Minhat Shai* on *Exodus* 16:16; and see also BT, *Pesahim 117a*: and BT, *Shevuot* 35b: "Every 'Solomon' (*Shelomo* in Hebrew) in the *Song of Songs* is holy", i.e. implies "King to whom peace belongs" (*melekh shehashalom shelo*). The discussion here refers to the book's plain meaning, before any clear decision had been reached regarding its holiness.

or inferences hidden within the text, of which the majority of readers would not be aware in any case, but because they believed that love is the most sublime manifestation of the human experience. They believed in the ideal of human love as the greatest expression of the bond between man and God. The love of the Jewish People for God, of man for God, is not a different kind of love, but the same love that exists between man and woman. Moreover the love between human partners is true love. There is no other kind. It is not a parable for something loftier or different. It is the real thing. It is therefore no coincidence that the one to rescue the *Song of Songs* from oblivion was none other than Rabbi Akiva, the sage of love.

The subject of the song is the love between the beloved (*dod*) and his love (*ra'yah*). The commentators, without saying so explicitly, relate the book's content to the life of Rabbi Akiva. Some (e.g. Rashi in the introduction to his commentary on *Song of* Songs) explained that the verses are spoken "in the words of a woman suffering living widowhood who longs for her husband and fondly remembers her beloved . . . Her beloved shares her suffering and recalls the kindness of her youth, her beauty and her talents, by which he became bound to her with intense love . . . she is yet his wife and he her man, and he is destined to return to her." Rashi refers to a "living widow" — a woman who lives apart from her husband — whose longing for her husband, as well as his longing for her and his promise to return, is expressed in the song. Did Rabbi Akiva read the *Song of Songs* in a similar fashion, seeing in it an expression of his longing for his wife and her longing for him during the two decades of their separation? Or was Rashi's commentary inspired by the life story of Rabbi Akiva, the song's "rescuer".

Other commentators assert that the song's beloved (*dod*) is a shepherd, and his love (*ra'ayah*) the daughter of a wealthy family. Her family is unaware of her love for the shepherd whom she met in the vineyards: "a very small girl whose breasts had not yet grown was guarding the vineyard when she saw a shepherd passing, and desire was aroused in both their hearts" (Ibn Ezra, introduction to his commentary on *Song of Songs*). Rabbi Akiva would not have had to delve very deeply to discover his wife Rachel, the daughter of a wealthy man,[18] who saw him herding her father's sheep, recognised his qualities, and secretly became betrothed to him.

Rabbi Akiva's wisdom of love is profoundly reflected in his position on the *Song of Songs*. He makes no attempt to change its content or ascribe far-fetched allegorical meanings to it. The goal is to make love between man and woman holy, or in Rabbi Akiva's words: "holy of holies". It is in this light that the following should be understood:

---

[18] Kalba Savua is so called because all who entered his home left satiated (*savu'a*).

"Rabbi Akiva says: 'He who sings the *Song of Songs* with quavering voice in the banquet halls and makes it a [profane] song, has no share in the next world."

Tosefta Sanhedrin 12, 5

Rabbi Akiva's approach to love is profound and serious, as to something sacred, and that is why he rejects behaviour that debases love. What would the fate of the *Song of Songs* have been had the opinion of those who opposed its inclusion in Holy Scripture been accepted? It would have passed from the synagogue and the hall of study to the banquet hall, where it would have become a profane song, sung with quavers and trills. We can assume that its magnificent verses were already sung at pleasure parties and banquet halls: some even believe the book itself to be a collection of wedding songs. Rabbi Akiva's struggle to bring the *Song of Songs* into the realm of the sacred and to have love recognised as the most sublime expression of humanity, is conducted on two fronts: opposite the rabbis who sought to detract from the book's merit by rejecting it outright or by asserting that it was "a matter of dispute"; and opposite the masses, who sought to profane this love song, by turning love into licence.[19] In his opposition to promiscuity and licentiousness, Rabbi Akiva was no different from the other rabbis. The difference between them lay in the fact that the others feared that texts such as the *Song of Songs* would increase licentiousness, whereas Rabbi Akiva believed that a harmonious view of human love — one that rejects both puritanism and licentiousness — would strengthen true love and repudiate debauchery and vulgarisation.

The insight that love between man and woman is the source of wisdom, conferring upon it the highest possible level of sanctity — the status of "holy of holies" — is the cornerstone of moral life, as expressed by Rabbi Akiva in the following statement:

"Had the Torah not been given, the *Song of Songs* would have been worthy to guide the world."

Agadat Shir Hashirim p. 5

There are no laws or commandments in the *Song of Songs* as exist in the Torah, but the book provides the guiding principles for moral behaviour. Had the Torah — that commands the path of moral conduct in great detail — not been given; the *Song of Songs* — from which the principles of human morality can be inferred — would have been a suitable guide for the world. Such an assertion cannot be made by those who distinguish between a sublime spiritual world and a base physical world — associating love between the sexes with the latter category. It requires a change in attitude toward such love, ascribing purity

---

[19]   See *Avot* 3, 13: "Rabbi Akiva says: Jesting and frivolity lead a man to sexual misconduct."

and sanctity to physical as well as emotional and spiritual love, as a supreme expression of humanity. Love between a man and a woman is the harmonious essence of all harmony. Its violation is the source of all prohibited, improper action, and its preservation the source of all moral conduct. The key to guiding the world thus lies in the *Song of Songs*, and had the Torah not been given, it would have been a worthy guide.

The sage of love "rescued" the *Song of Songs*, and by virtue of his position, human culture retained one of its deepest and most magnificent works of love poetry, a work that has always been a source of inspiration for poets and other artists. Rabbi Akiva's intention however, was to build a hierarchy of holiness, with love between man and woman, as depicted in the *Song of Songs*, at its highest level. All other levels of holiness flow from this holy of holies, draw upon it, and are defined in relation to it.

Chapter Four

PRACTICE AND THEORY IN THE WISDOM OF LOVE

In his halakhic and philosophical approach to the *Song of Songs*, Rabbi Akiva stands out as the sage of love; so too in a series of halakhic rulings. His lenient position regarding adornment and the use of cosmetics by women in a state of menstrual impurity clearly reflects this approach:

> "'And of her that is afflicted in her seclusion (menstrual impurity)' [*Leviticus* 15:33] — The first sages would say 'afflicted in her seclusion' — she may not paint her eyes or her face until she immerses herself in water. Until Rabbi Akiva came and taught: She will lose her attraction and he will seek to divorce her. How do I fulfil [the verse] 'afflicted in her seclusion'? She will remain impure until she immerses herself in water."

Sifra, Metzora

There would appear to be a disagreement regarding the interpretation of a phrase appearing in the last verse of the Torah portion of *Metzora* (*Leviticus* 14-15): "And of her that is afflicted in her seclusion and of him that hath an issue, of the man, and of the woman, and of him that lieth with her that is unclean" (*Leviticus* 15:33). The first sages understood that a woman in a state of menstrual impurity must be in her seclusion, and she must therefore not beautify herself, use cosmetics to make herself attractive to her husband, lest he become aroused and commit a grave sin. Rabbi Akiva interprets the phrase afflicted in her seclusion to mean that she must remain in her state of impurity until she immerses herself in water — i.e. in the *mikveh* (ritual bath) — with no need for further restrictions.

The debate between Rabbi Akiva and the first sages however, goes well beyond the interpretation of a biblical phrase. It is a debate over the respective weight that should be given to different values. From the perspective of the first sages, the prohibition against having sexual intercourse with a woman in a state of menstrual impurity requires the imposition of further safeguards, because the libido cannot be trusted.[20] They therefore prohibit the use of cosmetics during a woman's days of impurity so as not to arouse her husband's desire for her. Rabbi Akiva on the other hand, weighs the danger that the husband might sin, against the chance that he might cease to be attracted to his wife if she neglects her appearance for two weeks of every month, thereby undermining marital harmony and eventually leading to divorce. In Rabbi Akiva's eyes, the value of maintaining harmony within the marriage and sustaining the constant attraction between husband and wife justifies even the risk that the husband might commit the grave sin of "lying with her that is unclean".

Beyond the debate itself, Rabbi Akiva's ruling is clearly audacious and shows great determination. Even today, it is unusual for rabbis to overturn the halakhic decisions of previous generations, certainly with regard to fundamental issues, unaffected by changing circumstances. Moreover, Rabbi Akiva's time was marked by a process of recollection aimed at restoring *halakhot* established by the first sages in the days of the Temple — a process in which Rabbi Akiva himself played an active role. The first sages, citing the biblical verse, established that a woman may not beautify herself when in a state of impurity. "Until Rabbi Akiva came and taught . . . " — i.e. until Rabbi Akiva came and revoked the halakhic ruling of the first sages, and established a new *halakhah,* contrary to their opinion. According to this halakhah, a woman may adorn herself even in a state of menstrual impurity, and it is her prerogative to care for her appearance and not allow herself to become unattractive, because the constant attraction between marriage partners plays an important role in maintaining the harmony in their relationship.

Overturning the halakhic ruling of the first sages for the sake of the principle of harmony between marriage partners is not a chance occurrence, but a reflection of the halakhic approach of the sage of love — evident in many of the *halakhot* attributed to Rabbi Akiva, some of which will be discussed in this chapter.

Rabbi Akiva's unequivocal position regarding spots of menstrual blood is presented in the following mishnah:

"A woman once came before Rabbi Akiva. She said to him: I saw a spot. He said to her: Perhaps you had been injured. She said to him: Yes, and it [the wound] had healed. He said to her: Perhaps it could have been scratched and bled? She said

---

[20] See BT, *Ketubot* 13b, and the remarks of Rashi and the other commentators there.

to him: yes. And Rabbi Akiva declared her pure. He saw his students looking at one another [in puzzlement]. He said to them: Why are you puzzled by this? For the Rabbis did not say this to be more stringent, but to be more lenient, as it is written [*Leviticus* 15:19]: 'And if a woman have an issue, and her issue in her flesh be blood' — blood and not a spot."

Mishnah, Nidah 8, 3

The Mishnah tells the story of a woman who came to Rabbi Akiva and told him that she had seen a spot of blood inconsistent with her regular cycle, and asked him whether she was pure or whether she had to observe the days of impurity required for menstrual blood. From the facts presented in the *mishnah*, the spot that the woman had seen was clearly blood. Rabbi Akiva however, sought to determine the source of the blood, asking whether she had been injured recently and whether the stain might not have been blood from that injury. She replied that she had been injured, but that her wound had healed. Rabbi Akiva then asked whether the wound might not have reopened and bled. The woman answered that it was possible. "And Rabbi Akiva declared her pure!" — he ruled that if the presence of the blood spot could be explained by the wound the woman had received, that should be favoured over the possibility that it was menstrual blood. In reality, there was no reason to determine that the spot was from the healed wound rather than menstrual blood. The former was only a possibility, but Rabbi Akiva decided in favour of that possibility. He immediately noticed that his students were exchanging puzzled glances, and had to explain that according to the Torah the spot that the woman had seen did not make her impure and that only menstruation could make her impure. The Rabbis decreed however, that a woman who sees a spot should consult with a halakhic authority, that lenience might be exercised: that a way might be found to attribute the spot to a source other than menstrual blood, that she might be declared pure and permissible to her husband.

In this *halakhah* as well, we see Rabbi Akiva's approach and his understanding of the complexity of marital harmony and the possible effects of a stringent attitude to the laws of menstrual purity. Irresponsible expansion of the purity laws can result in a constant obsession with the woman's state of ritual purity becoming the main focus of a relationship, and make it far too easy to declare menstrual impurity unnecessarily. He therefore clearly establishes the law regarding such spots, and the meaning of the rabbinical decree on the matter : "For the Rabbis did not say this to be more stringent, but to be more lenient". Needless to say, Rabbi Akiva did not take the laws of ritual purity lightly.[21] He merely weighed them against the great moral value of preserving

---

[21]   See for example his stringent position in a dispute in the Mishnah regarding a man or a woman afflicted with "an issue" who did not check themselves daily, as required, but only on the first and seventh days: "Rabbi Akiva says: Only the seventh day is

harmony between man and wife. He therefore set boundaries for the laws of menstrual impurity, precluding any further expansion that might undermine the harmony between marriage partners. Observing the laws of ritual (family) purity need not isolate or humiliate a woman in a state of impurity, and its duration must not be extended beyond what is strictly required by law. Rabbi Akiva's words in the Talmud (*Rosh Hashanah* 26a) encapsulate his approach to the issue: "And Rabbi Akiva said: When I went to Galia (Galatia), menstruating women were called desolate". One could say that Rabbi Akiva rescued women from their desolation, or at least limited the possibility that they might be completely desolate.

Rabbi Akiva utterly rejected the possibility of remaining unmarried,[22] but demanded that marriage be treated seriously and responsibly, avoiding marriage for marriage's sake and especially incompatibility:

> "Rabbi Akiva says: He who marries a woman who is not suited to him violates five negative precepts: 'Thou shalt not take vengeance'; '[thou shalt not] bear any grudge'; 'thou shalt not hate thy brother in thy heart'; 'thou shalt love thy fellow as thyself'; and 'that thy brother may live with thee'. Due to his hatred toward her . . . he will allow procreation to pass from the world."
>
> *Avot deRabbi Natan 26, 4*

One must not marry without the compatibility that can lead to love, not only because of the likelihood that the marriage will fail, but also because it is prohibited to place oneself in circumstances that will lead to hating a fellow Jew. We must recall that it was Rabbi Akiva who said that "love thy fellow as thyself" is the Torah's greatest principle. What this means is that the precept has broad implications on many different planes. One of these is the plane of marriage, in which a situation might arise that runs counter to the categorical principle of "love thy fellow as thyself". Marrying without love and treating his future wife unfairly, will bring a husband to harbour animosity toward her. Furthermore, he violates a number of biblical precepts, such as the prohibition "thou shalt not hate thy brother in thy heart", possibly leading to verbal and physical

---

counted," and they must consequently count a further six "clean" days (BT, *Nidah* 10, 3). See also his stringent position in the matter of ritual baths: *Mikva'ot* 2, 2; and *Tosefta Mikva'ot* 1, 17-19.

22   See BT, *Yevamot* 63b regarding one who fails to marry. The opinions of Rabbi Eliezer, Rabbi Ya'akov (alt. reading: "Rabbi Akiva") and Ben Azai are cited: "Rabbi Ya'akov (Akiva) says: It is as if he diminishes the image [of God]. For it is written: 'in the image of God made He man', followed by 'be fruitful and multiply.'"
Regarding the alternative reading: The reading "Akiva" appears in parallel sources. See eg., the gloss on the page in *Yevamot*. Based on the citation of "in the image of God made He man", the similarity to *Avot* 3, 18, the chronological order of the *tanaim*, and the parallel sources, I believe that Rabbi Akiva is undoubtedly the author of these words.

violence — all as a result of his having married for reasons extraneous to marital harmony, compatibility and reciprocity.

Applying the rule of "love thy fellow as thyself" to married life and the laws that pertain to it, brought about the later development of further laws in the same context. The Babylonian Talmud states the following, citing amoraic sources:

> "Rabbi Yehudah said in the name of Rav: A man may not marry a woman until he has seen her, lest he find something repulsive in her and she become hateful to him, and the Torah said (*Leviticus* 19:18) 'Love thy fellow as thyself.'"
>
> BT, *Kidushin* 41a

Rabbi Akiva's ruling that a man may not marry a woman who is not suited to him, and other *halakhot* of this kind, established the proper manner in which to embark upon married life — based on prior acquaintance, suitability and appropriate grounds for true love to develop between the marriage partners.

The wisdom of love advocates the harmonious development of love between partners. It is not puritanism and guilt that prevent the licentiousness, hedonism and debasement expressed in "substitutes" for love, but a harmonious love life. It is therefore very desirable, according to Rabbi Akiva, to avoid postponing marriage, since the non-realisation of love within its proper framework can lead to immoral behaviour. One must therefore strive to marry at a young age, and parents must not delay the marriage of their children:

> "As it is stated [in the *beraita*]: 'Profane not thy daughter, to make her a harlot' (*Leviticus* 19:29) Rabbi Eliezer says: This is one who marries his daughter to an old man. Rabbi Akiva says: This is one who delays [the marriage of] his mature daughter."
>
> BT, *Sanhedrin* 76a

The above refers specifically to daughters, because the cost of marriage was born by the father of the bride. Many would therefore delay the their daughters' marriages — sometimes indefinitely — for financial reasons. Rabbi Akiva sharply condemns the practice and explains its ramifications. He also encouraged his students to find husbands for their daughters of marriageable age without delay:

> "Rabbi Hanania ben Hakhinai and Rabbi Shimon bar Yohai went to study Torah with Rabbi Akiva in Benei Brak. They remained there for thirteen years. Rabbi Shimon bar Yohai would send for news from home. Rabbi Hanina [sic] would not send for news from home. His wife sent to him, saying: Your daughter is grown. Come and find her a husband. Nevertheless, [he did not go.] Rabbi Akiva saw by the holy spirit and said to them: He who has a grown daughter should go and find her a husband."
>
> Midrash, *Vayikrah Rabbah* 21, 8

These two sages, Rabbi Hanania ben Hakhinai and Rabbi Shimon bar Yohai were away from their homes for thirteen years so that they could study Torah with Rabbi Akiva. Talmudic legend tells of a number of sages who were absent from their homes for the sake of Torah study, and some condemn this practice.[23] We must remember that Rabbi Akiva himself left his home for a very long time to study Torah. It appears however, that one may be absent yet take an active interest in domestic affairs, as did Rabbi Shimon bar Yohai, who "would send for news from home".

Rabbi Hanania ben Hakhinai on the other hand, cut himself off completely from his family throughout his years in the house of study, resulting, *inter alia*, in his neglecting the marriage of his grown daughter. Rabbi Akiva did not merely correct Rabbi Hanania ben Hakhinai, but established the general *halakhah* that one must not neglect the marriage of one's daughters — whose futures were almost entirely dependent on their fathers' actions.

Rabbi Akiva's approach to the marriage relationship as an expression of harmony and love, and his sensitivity to the need to nurture and safeguard love — also reflected in his halakhic rulings — is not only a necessary condition for sustaining marriage and the marriage bond, but is the very essence of that bond. It thus follows that if there is no longer any love between the partners, there is no point in maintaining the framework. Rabbi Akiva, who is stringent in matters of love, which he perceives to be the purpose of man's existence, is among the most lenient when it comes to divorce, as we can see in the following *mishnah*:

> "Beit Shamai say: A man may not divorce his wife unless he finds some unseemly thing in her, as it is written 'because he hath found some unseemly thing in her' (*Deuteronomy* 24:1).' And Beit Hillel say: Even if she has spoiled his food, as it is written 'because he hath found some unseemly thing in her'. Rabbi Akiva says: Even if he has found another fairer than she, as it is written 'if she find no favour in his eyes' (ibid.)."
>
> Mishnah, *Gitin* 9, 10

Both Beit Shamai and Beit Hillel assert that a man may divorce his wife if she has behaved wrongly, and if she is the cause of the discord between them. According to Halakhah, the power of divorce, although the exclusive province of the husband, cannot be governed by whim, but requires a specific context. Beit Shamai prohibit divorce altogether, except when the marriage is no longer viable, due to a fundamental breach. They refer specifically to cases in which the woman has committed adultery, or some sexual impropriety has been found

---

23   See BT, *Ketubot* 62b — A tale of Rav Rehumi and Yehudah son of Rabbi Hiya son-in-law of Rabbi Yanai. See also N. Rothenberg, *Be'ikvot Ha'ahavah*, pp. 60-67; 84-90.

in her, i.e. her behaviour has undermined the basis of their relationship. Beit Hillel also seek just cause for divorce in the woman's behaviour, e.g. she is not sufficiently forthcoming in caring for her husband's home, and refuses to comply with his wishes.[24] They disagree on how broad an interpretation one may ascribe to the verse "because he hath found some unseemly thing in her". Beit Shamai favour the verse's plain meaning, while Beit Hillel understand it in a broader sense. Contrary to Beit Shamai and Beit Hillel, Rabbi Akiva justifies divorce even in cases in which no fault can be found with the wife's behaviour, and the husband's desire to divorce her is unrelated to anything she has done — for example when he desires another, more beautiful woman, and his wife no longer pleases him, as it is written: "if she find no favour in his eyes" (*Deuteronomy* 24:1). If he no longer loves her, and there is no chance of the love between them being rekindled, the union must, in Rabbi Akiva's opinion, be dissolved by means of divorce. No moral judgement is passed on the fact the husband desires another woman. A harmonious and strong relationship would probably have prevented it, and Rabbi Akiva, in his halakhic rulings and moral assertions, repeatedly stresses the importance of nurturing the marriage relationship. He is, nevertheless, familiar with human nature and the often tortuous course it runs. He deals with the moral and halakhic ramifications of a man desiring another woman — prior to the circumstances discussed in the above *mishnah* — elsewhere. The question at this point is not how happened, but now that it has happened, how do we proceed. The essence of marriage, in Rabbi Akiva's eyes, is love and harmony. When these things are gone, the marriage has already been emptied of content and no longer serves its purpose, and should therefore be dissolved.

It is worth noting here that, according to Rabbi Akiva's philosophy of love, passivity in a marriage relationship is, in the end, a recipe for divorce. Although he is lenient with regard to divorce relative to Beit Shamai and Beit Hillel, he does not treat it lightly, and developed an entire philosophy of love, aimed at creating and sustaining harmony between marriage partners. He sees the relationship's starting point in its being a marriage for the sake of love. Their lives after marriage are a partnership that must be deepened and nurtured through mutual attention and courtship, care for one's appearance, affection and respect, on a daily basis.

A series of halakhic rulings demonstrate Rabbi Akiva's great sensitivity to the predicament of deserted wives (*agunot*). He who permitted divorce due to the disappearance of harmony from a marriage, spared no halakhic effort in releasing deserted wives from the bonds of matrimony, thereby preventing them from sinning and giving them the opportunity to remarry. The best known example of this is Rabbi Akiva's role in establishing that a woman

---

[24]   See Rabbi Menahem Hame'iri's commentary *Beit Habehirah*, on *Gittin ibid.*

may remarry based on the testimony of a single witness[25] to her husband's death abroad:

> "Rabbi Akiva testified in the name of Nehemiah of Bet-Deli that a woman may be married based on [the testimony of] a single witness."
>
> Mishnah, *Eduyot* 8, 5

Rabbi Akiva was not the first to establish this *halakhah*, whereby a woman whose husband has gone abroad and a single witness comes and testifies to his death, is permitted to remarry. In *Eduyot*, this testimony is attributed to Rabbi Yehudah ben Bava (ibid. 6, 1), who attests to having heard it from his teachers. Rabbi Yehudah ben Bava's direct testimony is thus preferable to, and carries greater weight than that of Rabbi Akiva, who cites Nehemiah of Bet-Deli who in turn heard it from his teachers. However — as described elsewhere in the Mishnah, toward the end of *Yevamot* — it was Rabbi Akiva's testimony in the end that determined the *halakhah*: Rabbi Akiva recounts that when he went to Nehardea (in Baylonia) to proclaim the leap year, he met Nehemiah of Bet-Deli, who asked him whether it was true that in *Eretz Yisrael* a woman was not allowed to remarry based on the testimony of a single witness, because the testimony of Rabbi Yehudah ben Bava — itself the testimony of a single witness without corroboration from another source — had not been accepted. Rabbi Akiva confirms this, and Nehemiah asks him to tell the sages of *Eretz Yisrael* in his name that he himself cannot come from Babylonia to *Eretz Yisrael* to testify before them, due to the dangers such a journey would entail, but that he had heard from Raban Gamliel the Elder that a woman is permitted to marry based on the testimony of a single witness. Upon his return, Rabbi Akiva conveyed the message to Raban Gamliel the Patriarch (who was the grandson of Raban Gamliel the Elder). As they were speaking, Raban Gamliel himself recalled that his grandfather, Raban Gamliel the Elder, had permitted the wives of those killed at Tel-Arza to remarry, based on the testimony of a single witness. It was this corroborating testimony conveyed by Rabbi Akiva that brought about the change in the *halakhah* — inasmuch as this position was now sustained by two witnesses — and the revolutionary ruling that women may remarry based on the testimony of a single witness.

Elsewhere, the halakhic ruling in this matter is attributed to Rabbi Akiva alone:

> "'One witness shall not rise up against a man for any iniquity, or for any sin' (*Deuteronomy* 19:15) — for any iniquity or for any sin he shall not rise, he shall rise for the benefit of a woman. From this Rabbi Akiva said: A woman may be permitted to [re]marry based on the testimony of a single witness."
>
> *Midrash Tanaim* on *Deuteronomy* (Hoffman), 19:15

---

25   In Jewish law, two witnesses are generally required.

The Mishnah in *Yevamot*, tells another story of Rabbi Akiva, in which he takes a far-reaching position regarding the release of a *yevamah* who performed the *halitzah* ceremony in private, i.e. not before a court of three:[26]

> "A woman who performed the *halitzah* ceremony before two or three [people], and one was discovered to be a relative or [otherwise] unfit, the *halitzah* is invalid. Rabbi Shimon and Rabbi Yohanan Ha-Sandlar approved it. A woman once performed *halitzah* in private in prison and the incident was brought before Rabbi Akiva and he approved it."
>
> Mishnah, *Yevamot* 12, 5

According to the Talmud in *Yevamot* (105b),[27] the incident occurred at home rather than in prison, but the question was posed to Rabbi Akiva when he was in prison. The *mishnah* should thus read: "A woman once performed *halitzah* in private and the incident was brought before Rabbi Akiva [who was] in prison, and he approved it." Presenting halakhic questions to Rabbi Akiva in prison would have been no trifling matter, for Torah study had been the cause of his incarceration, and any connection to Torah would have been extremely dangerous both for him and for those who had come to seek his opinion. The Jerusalem Talmud recounts that Rabbi Yohanan Ha-Sandlar, pretending to be a street vendor, passed by the prison and called out his question as he cried his wares: "Who wants needles? Who wants hooks? **Performed *halitzah* in private, what's [the law]?** Rabbi Akiva looked out his prison window and asked the vendor whether he had spindles (*kushin*), surreptitiously adding: "It is valid (*kasher*)", i.e. the action is valid and the woman is free to marry.

These halakhic rulings demonstrate how the sage of love does not merely conceive abstract ideas, but applies his principles to daily life through his legal decisions.

Rabbi Akiva explains the biblical precept concerning a woman suspected of adultery (*sotah*) in a similar vein. The Torah suspends the grave prohibition against erasing the divine name (the Tetragrammaton) in order to achieve peace between a jealous husband and his wife, by removing the husband's suspicion and restoring trust between them:

> "Rabbi Akiva said: Know how great is the power of peace, that the Holy One blessed be he said: when a man is jealous of his wife, let the Name written in holiness be erased into water in order to make peace between a wife and her husband."
>
> Midrash, *Devarim Rabbah* 5, 15

---

[26] According to the law of levirate marriage, a man must marry his childless brother's widow — the *yevamah*. He may be released from this obligation, by means of the *halitzah* ceremony.

[27] See later in BT, *Yevamot* 108b on the danger posing halakhic questions to Rabbi Akiva in prison entailed.

The chapter concerning marital jealousy and the ordeal of the bitter waters can be read with various emphases and from diverse perspectives. Rabbi Akiva perceives the background story of the ordeal as a problem for which the Torah provides a solution. The source of the problem is a husband who is overcome by a spirit of jealousy and suspects, or knows for certain that his wife has been unfaithful to him with another man. He has lost all trust in her, and where such trust is lacking the relationship cannot survive, let alone deepen and grow. It is therefore essential that trust be restored unequivocally. The assumption is that the woman will come through the ordeal safely, and the bitter waters will have no effect. The convincing part of the ceremony lies in the preparation of the waters the woman is given to drink. The divine name, written in holiness on a piece of parchment, is blotted into the water, and that is what gives the entire ceremony its drastic effect, the ability to allay the jealous husband's suspicions.[28] Rabbi Akiva gives expression to a widely held belief among the Rabbis that peace in the home — the basic human social unit — is the basis for peace throughout the world. In order to achieve this peace, important values — like the holiness of the ineffable and inviolable name of God — are set aside.

Rabbi Akiva's philosophy of love and his principles regarding peace in the home were not meant for Jews alone. The Midrash shows that non-Jews also admired Rabbi Akiva's wisdom, as a sage in general and a sage of love in particular:

---

[28] See *Sotah* 9, 9 and 47b: "With the proliferation of adulterers, the bitter waters ceased". Contrary to BT, *Avodah Zarah* 10a, which teaches that capital punishment was discontinued due to the proliferation of murderers, the reason given for the discontinuation of the bitter water ceremony is not the proliferation of 'adulteresses', but rather adulterers. According to the explanation offered in the Mishnah and the Gemara, the ceremony served a purpose as long as men were faithful to their wives and the waters possessed the ability to restore their trust in them. Once adulterers proliferated however, the ceremony became pointless: "Rabbi Elazar said: The Prophet said to Israel: If you mind yourselves, the waters will test your wives, and if not, the waters will not test your wives" (*ibid.*). The Midrash, *Sifre, Bamidbar*, attributes the statement to Rabbi Akiva: "And Rabbi Akiva says: The verse comes to say that she will die . . . Why does it say 'then shall the man be guiltless from iniquity'? When the man is guiltless from iniquity, this woman shall bear her iniquity — and not [when he has misbehaved] as in the case of which it is written (Hosea 4:14) 'I will not punish your daughters when they commit whoredom, nor your brides when they commit adultery: for themselves are separated with whores, and they sacrifice with harlots: therefore the people that doth not understand shall fall'. He said to them: Since you pursue harlotry, the water will not test your wives. That is why it is written: 'then shall the man be guiltless from iniquity' — of that iniquity."
According to the Mishnah, it was Raban Yohanan ben Zakai who abolished the ceremony of the bitter waters, and by the time of Rabbi Akiva, it had not been in practice for decades. Rabbi Akiva's position was therefore solely hermeneutical, lacking any practical ramification.

"The king of the Arabs asked Rabbi Akiva: I am a Cushite and my wife is a Cushite, and she has borne me a white child, shall I kill her for her infidelity to me? . . . He said to him: Are the forms of your house black or white? He said to him: White. He said to him: When you lay with her she looked upon the forms and bore [a child] like them. And if you wonder at this, learn from the sheep of Jacob, they conceived [while looking] upon the rods, as it is written (*Genesis* 30:39): 'And the flocks conceived before the rods'. . . . And the king of the Arabs thanked Rabbi Akiva and praised him."

Midrash Tanhuma, Nasso 7

Rabbi Akiva, in his wisdom, understood that the king's jealousy had been aroused when he saw that his wife had given birth to a white child, but that he was not entirely convinced of his suspicions. As with the husband who is visited by a spirit of jealousy, here too it is the jealousy itself that must be addressed — in this case by means of an explanation that set the king's mind at rest with regard to the white child.

It was very important to Rabbi Akiva that people view marriage as a challenge for which sacrifices must be made, and a goal on the road to attaining happiness — expressed for example in the following maxim:

"Who is wealthy? . . . Rabbi Akiva says: He who has a wife who is beautiful in [her] deeds."

BT, *Shabbat* 25b

Such adages help define man's aspirations, emphasising the things that are both important and attainable. The wealth to which people aspire is usually unattainable, since one is never satisfied with what one has. It is better to set goals that can be achieved in one's lifetime. In pursuing economic wealth a person directs attention outward, beyond the home, while in that very home lies true wealth. Rabbi Akiva may be speaking from personal experience. The following can also be understood in the same spirit:

"Rabbi Akiva says: What shall a man do that his sons might be wealthy and live? Let him fulfil the desires of heaven and the desires of his wife . . . These are the desires of his wife: Rabbi Eliezer says: Let him seduce her when they lie together. Rabbi Yehudah says: Let him give her joy as they lie together in [fulfilment of] a commandment, as it is written (*Ecclesiastes* 8:5): 'Whoso keepeth the commandment shall know no evil thing.'"

Mishnah, *Kallah* 1, 21

Rabbi Akiva cites two sources from which one who seeks a lasting future for himself and his family may learn appropriate behaviour: the desires of heaven and the desires of his wife. The comparison between the two cannot be ignored; an indication of the great value Rabbi Akiva placed upon harmony between husband and wife. No less important however, is the manner in which Rabbi Akiva's philosophy of harmonious love continues to be developed by his disciples/interpreters, in this case Rabbi Eliezer and Rabbi Yehudah. The manner in which they understand Rabbi Akiva is important in determining the way in which we interpret his words. The great importance he ascribed to sexual compatibility between husband and wife is also evident in sources attributed to him directly. That is the light in which we should view his words to Rabbi Shimon bar Yohai in prison: "You should not cook in a pot in which another has cooked" (*Pesahim* 112a), i.e. he did not recommend the he marry a divorced woman whose husband was still alive, although it is important to note that Rabbi Akiva was merely offering Rabbi Shimon bar Yohai his advice, and not a binding halakhic ruling. It is said elsewhere of a divorced man who marries a divorced woman that they have "four opinions in bed" — as if four people are present in the couple's marriage bed, because they think both of themselves and their previous partners. Problems may arise both in the case of a widow and that of a divorcee, since "all limbs are not equal" — or as Rashi explains: "The sexual performance of the [second husband] may not be as good as that of the first, and she may treat him with disdain". What is striking about these words is the fact that they place women's feelings and desires at the centre of the marriage relationship, and emphasise the importance of sex in a harmonious relationship.

To Rabbi Akiva, harmony in marriage was a great blessing, and he did not hesitate to associate it with divine involvement:

> "Rabbi Akiva taught: If a man and a woman are blessed — the *Shekhinah* [dwells] in their midst. If they are not blessed — they are consumed by fire."
>
> BT, *Sotah* 17a

According to this approach, God's role[29] does not end once a couple is matched, and a good relationship between the partners cannot be taken for granted, but is a "blessing" for which the couple should be grateful and in which they should see the involvement of the Divine Presence. Rabbi Akiva may even identify love itself and the harmony between marriage partners with the *Shekhinah*. The commandment to marry is of course very important, but as central as it might be, it depends upon the existence a loving relationship, a true and profound bond that goes well beyond the association created by the official framework of marriage per se. Great danger lies in a loveless marriage, and the purpose of

---

[29] See Midrash, *Bereshit Rabbah* 68; *Vayikra Rabbah* 8; *Bamidbar Rabbah* 4 and cf. BT, *Sotah* 2a: Forty days before a child is conceived, a heavenly voice declares 'the daughter of so-and-so to so-and-so." See also *Zohar* I 85b, on the descent of souls to the world: "As they descend, they separate, one to one side and one to the other side, and God pairs them later. And pairing is given to none but God alone, for He knows their pairing to join them suitably."

married life cannot be achieved in such a relationship, which can be harmful to the partners and have the opposite effect.

Making harmony the focus of married life and attributing it to divine involvement and presence in the couple's midst, demands that the reverse situation, the opposite of the ideal to which Rabbi Akiva aspires, also be addressed. The lack of harmony, the *Shekhinah*'s absence, is characterised sharply: "they are consumed by fire!" Such a life is unworthy, and as we have seen above, should be avoided — not only because there is a good chance that a loveless marriage will fail, but because the hatred to which it will give rise will bring the partners to commit grave sins.

Rabbi Akiva's belief that man, woman and God combine to form a single, perfect whole, can be summarised in his words to Rabbi Yishmael in the Midrash:

> "Henceforth 'in our image after our likeness' — man shall not be without woman, and woman shall not be without man, and the two shall not be without the *Shekhinah*."
>
> Midrash, *Bereshit Rabbah* 22, 2

This *Midrash* is interesting and unusual in its emphasis on reciprocity. Most traditional sources on the importance of marriage are directed solely at men: the shortcomings of bachelorhood, the rewards a man can expect if he marries, his poor prospects if he does not marry. In these words, Rabbi Akiva stresses the importance of both partners: "man shall not be without woman," and immediately "and woman shall not be without man". The perfection of each depends upon their being together. If their union is deep and sincere however, their dyad becomes triad: "and the two shall not be without the *Shekhinah*". Some explain that when the *Shekhinah* is absent, "the two" — i.e. their togetherness as a couple — ceases to exist; whereas the *Shekhinah*'s presence sustains it. Others understand the phrase to mean that the presence of the *Shekhinah* depends upon "the two": if they are together in every sense, they cannot be without the *Shekhinah*: "and a three-fold cord is not quickly broken".

Chapter Five

THE SAGE AND TEMPTATION

Generally speaking, the political philosopher is not expected to prove himself as a statesman; we do not necessarily look for the works of a philosopher of art and aesthetics in a museum; and we do not expect the philosopher of science to devote his life to laboratory experiments. This is not the case however, when it comes to the sage of love — and particularly to one such as Rabbi Akiva, who comes from the love of Rachel. We examine and re-examine every detail, every intimation we are given regarding his relationship with his wife, and rightly wonder at the many years they lived apart. We look upon the aggregate of his philosophical and halakhic opinions and ask ourselves whether we should simply make do with the words that constitute a theoretical system and afford him the title sage of love, or should we not be satisfied merely with theoretical philosopher, but examine his actions as well.

Aggadic literature enables us to see Rabbi Akiva not only in the context of his relationship with his beloved, wife of his youth, but also in terms of his relations with other women — usually not love relations, but the basic passion felt by a man toward a woman, especially one who arouses his desire. Through these sources, we will address a number of important questions.

Has a sage of love in general, and a man of Rabbi Akiva's stature in particular, already overcome his desires, or perhaps "he who is greater than his fellow has greater desires" (BT, *Sukah* 52a)? Does the philosophy of love Rabbi Akiva developed help him resist temptation and delay gratification? Is there a connection between a harmonious love-life and one's ability to contend with casual pleasures, and formulate practical moral guidelines?

According to the prevailing view in the Talmud, the most difficult temptation is that associated with sexual desire. The general assumption is that an ordinary man is incapable of controlling his sexual desires, and will not resist temptation when it presents itself, except with the greatest difficulty. This is also the conventional theme of the temptations offered to man by Providence, and such was the test with which Rabbi Akiva was confronted:

> "Rabbi Akiva would ridicule sinners (since he would say that sin is easily avoided). One day Satan appeared to him in the form of a woman at the top of a palm tree. He took hold of the tree and began to climb.[30] When he had climbed halfway it departed (his desire or Satan).[31] He (Satan) said (to Rabbi Akiva): Had it not been declared in heaven 'beware of Rabbi Akiva and his Torah' I would have valued your life at two *maʾot* (I would have made your life worthless because you would have sinned)."

> BT, *Kidushin* 81a

The life of a Rabbi who teaches and studies Torah day and night, often distances him from the daily ordeal of resisting his various desires, and sexual desire in particular. Consequently, many great sages we are told would ridicule sinners and call them weak, for their inability to overcome their desires. The Talmud in *Kidushin* tells us of a few such sages who, for their condescension, were

---

30   In this context, it is impossible not to mention the verse (*Song of Songs* 7:9): "I said, I will go up to the palm tree, I will take hold of the boughs thereof". I thank Dafna Schreiber for having brought it to my attention.

31   In various sources, Satan and the Evil Inclination are equated with one another. See BT, *Bava Batra* 16a: "Resh Lakish said: Satan, the Evil Inclination and the Angel of Death are one and the same".

presented by Providence with temptations they would not ordinarily have encountered in their daily lives. They were thus taught a lesson regarding the great difficulty of controlling one's desires. The legend above also belongs to this genre. It tells of Rabbi Akiva, who would ridicule sinners and tell them that transgressions are easily avoided. As a result, a woman appeared to him atop a palm tree, arousing his desire to the point that he began to climb the tree. Only after he had climbed halfway, did his exertions cause his desire to leave him. The text can be interpreted to mean that Satan gave in and left him alone, but often — in this and other sources — no distinction is made between Satan and the desire to sin. The goal of the trial was not to cause Rabbi Akiva to sin, but to impress upon him the power of the evil inclination and the difficulties involved in exercising self-control and avoiding sin. We learn this from Satan's words to Rabbi Akiva: "Had it not been declared in heaven 'beware of Rabbi Akiva and his Torah'," I would have made you stumble and sin, making your life worthless — in the sense of "one who loses everything in an instant". The "private lesson" Rabbi Akiva is given by Providence, enables him to experience first hand the power of lust, the force of the evil inclination and the tremendous resources upon which one must draw to control one's desires, to resist temptation and avoid sin.

This unusual trial, beyond the natural course of events, may have helped Rabbi Akiva contend with subsequent temptations in the form of beautiful, flesh-and-blood women, who aroused his desire.

Various missions on behalf of the Palestinian Jewish community — proclaiming the leap year, raising funds for the poor,[32] or pleading the community's cause before the authorities in Rome against the harsh treatment meted out by the procurator in Palestine — took Rabbi Akiva to Babylonia, Rome and elsewhere. On a number of these journeys, Rabbi Akiva faced great temptations, as in the following story:

> "Do not wonder at Rabbi Zadok, for Rabbi Akiva was greater than him. When he went to Rome, he was informed upon to a certain official, who sent him two beautiful women, washed, anointed and adorned like brides, and they pressed themselves upon him throughout the night. The one saying 'come to me', and the other saying 'come to me', and he sat between them, spitting, and turned to neither. In the morning they left and went to see the official, and said to him: We would rather die than be given to this man. He sent for him. He said to him: Why did you not do with these women what men are wont to do with women? Are they not beautiful? Are they not human like you? Did he who created you not create them as well? He said to him: What could I do? Their smell was to me like the meat of forbidden and unclean animals and creeping things."
>
> *Avot deRabbi Natan* 16, 2

---

[32] Rabbi Akiva was considered the "champion of the poor". See *Ma'aser Sheni* 5, 9; BT, *Kidushin* 27a; JT, *Pesahim*, the end of chapter 4 and the end of *Kallah*; BT, *Arakhin* 28a; and BT, *Bava Batra* 10a.

What is the point of this legend, and what lesson is it trying to teach? As far as the Roman official was concerned, Rabbi Akiva was a public figure, a political leader of the Jews, like any other leader coming to argue his people's case before the authorities. His visits to Rome involved petitioning its rulers to ease pressure upon the Jews of Palestine. Other sources mention journeys undertaken for the sake of raising money for the poor. The official, a representative of the authorities, sends Rabbi Akiva two beautiful women, a common gesture of hospitality toward important guests the Roman government wished to entertain. The legend notes however, that the women were sent in response to an informer's report, in order to blacken Rabbi Akiva's name and sabotage his mission. How could this possibly have undermined his efforts however, considering the cultural norms of the day in Rome? Would the Roman leaders have thought less of the representative of the Jews of Palestine were he to have spent the night with a couple of beautiful Roman women? When the official questions Rabbi Akiva: "Why did you not do with these women what men are wont to do with women?" he explains that he was revolted by their smell, which was "like the meat of forbidden and unclean animals and creeping things". Did he not fear that the official, who undoubtedly ate such things, would be offended by this answer? The subject of the legend would thus appear to be, not Rabbi Akiva's standing in Rome and his image in Roman eyes, but his moral image, standing and spiritual leadership among the Jews. The author therefore directs his message at Jews, especially men entertaining thoughts of sin and conjuring up visions of casual and non-committal pleasures with foreign women.

The legend depicts Rabbi Akiva's moral conduct in the immoral and corrupt environment of Rome; remaining pure in the company of people who eat unclean animals and creeping things, and most importantly: overcoming his desires, controlling his lust and withstanding the temptation presented by the two beautiful women who spent an entire night doing all they could to seduce him. In Rabbi Akiva's opinion, the physical bond between man and woman is an essential part of love and marital harmony, and must not be used only to satisfy desire. It was not the smell of forbidden and unclean animals and creeping things that repelled Rabbi Akiva, who noticed their beauty and was even affected by it, but the moral compulsion to overcome temptation and avoid being drawn after lust that stands on its own, without any connection to true love. Rabbi Akiva was not indifferent to their beauty, and needed some action to distract him and help him overcome temptation: "he sat between them, spitting, and turned to neither". His remark regarding the smell of their flesh (which was, as noted above, certainly not made to the official, who would have been accustomed to eating such things) is not a reply to the question "why did you not do with these women what men are wont to do with women?" but the sage's words to himself, as a way of contending with his desire, and the author's advice to his readers, that they too might resist temptation. Rabbi Akiva manages to see through the women's arousing beauty, to their tawdriness, and this is reflected in his metaphorical reference to the smell of forbidden and unclean meat and creeping things.

The sage of love resists temptation, albeit with no little effort, and does not give in to loveless lust.

In a different story, Rabbi Akiva is tempted by another beautiful woman (also a Roman), but this time, for some reason, he is not disturbed by the stench of forbidden and unclean meat and creeping things:

> "Rabbi Akiva would defeat Turnus Rufus[33] in [discussions of] scripture before Caesar, and taunt him. Once he returned home with a scowl upon his face. His wife said to him: Why do you scowl? He said to her: Because of Rabbi Akiva, who taunts me daily. She said to him: Their God hates lewdness. Give me your permission, and I will cause him to sin; for she was extremely beautiful. He gave her permission, she adorned herself, went to Rabbi Akiva and exposed her thigh before him. Rabbi Akiva spat, laughed and wept. She said to him: What are these three things? He said to her: Two I will explain, and the third I will not explain. I spat — because you came from a fetid drop. I wept — for this beauty that will decay in the earth. And the reason for his laughter he did not explain. And the reason he laughed was that he saw by the holy spirit that she was destined to convert and marry him, and he did not want to tell her. She said to him: Does repentance exist? He said to her: Yes. She went and converted and married him, and brought him a great deal of wealth."

> Ran and Rashi on BT, Nedarim 50b
> Based on BT, Avodah Zarah 20a

The encounter with Turnus Rufus' wife is difficult for Rabbi Akiva, who cannot remain indifferent to her beauty — that affects him to that point that he bursts into tears "for this beauty that will decay in the earth". It is interesting that the act of spitting appears here, as in the previous legend, but here it is explained not as an attempt at distraction, but an expression of disgust. The disgust might be at Turnus Rufus' wife's origins: conceived in impurity from the seed of a gentile. The expression "fetid drop" however, usually signifies sperm. Its use here therefore, should be understood as conveying appreciation for her present beauty that belies the origin of all human beings: a "fetid drop".[34] According to this interpretation, her beauty is a thing of the present that stands in sharp contrast to its beginnings as a fetid drop and its end in decay. Rabbi Akiva's success in resisting temptation in this legend is not that heroic, since he foretells that she will convert and marry him. What is required of him is patience and the ability to renounce immediate gratification, knowing that she will one day

---

[33] That is what Tineius Rufus, Roman governor of Judea at the time of the Rebellion, is called in the Talmud. Known for his brutality, his name was intentionally distorted to Turnus, which means tyrant.

[34] See Avot 3, 1.

be his. Unlike in the previous legend, he shows an interest in the woman, and in his way expresses appreciation of her beauty. She is aware of the fact that she has made an impression on him, and wonders at his self-restraint, which apparently inspires in her a sense of respect for him and for the moral position he represents. The sage of love is rewarded for his restraint in a commensurate fashion: as in a typical love story, they marry, and what was not taken in sin is given lawfully.

For readers who are wondering whether this means that he took a second wife during Rachel's lifetime, his second marriage would appear to have taken place after her death. According to legend, Rabbi Akiva lived 120 years: 40 as a shepherd, 40 studying and 40 teaching.[35] There is no evidence that Rachel was as long-lived, so that Turnus Rufus' wife married him when he was already very old, a short time before his execution at the hands of the Romans. The rivalry between Turnus Rufus and Rabbi Akiva thus passed from the public to the personal level. The cruel Roman governor executed not only the national leader who travelled to Rome to seek the repeal of his decrees and gave his support to the rebel Bar-Koziva; not only the revered teacher who risked his life for the sake of Torah study, teaching large crowds and acquiring a vast number of students; but one who put him to personal shame, taking his wife from him.[36]

Rabbi Akiva' life story however, is not the subject of the present discussion. We do not presume to know and tell readers what really happened to the figures mentioned in the legends. Our interest lies in the figure of Rabbi Akiva as it appears in the aggadic sources — for the most part, composed decades and even centuries after his death. We have thus focused not on the "events" depicted, but on the messages they convey, and what they can teach us about the figure of Rabbi Akiva as a paragon.

These are the messages the legends' authors wish to convey to readers: The sage of love is a man of powerful desires (as noted above: "he who is greater than his fellow has greater desires"), but also of great vigilance and ability to uphold his moral principles. For that reason he, rather than a shallow puritan, is capable of withstanding the greatest temptations. In the broader context of Rabbi Akiva's philosophy of love, these legends, which focus on practical experiences, complement the sage's theoretical assertions. One who believes in love as the

---

35 "Rabbi Akiva was ignorant for forty years, and studied for forty years, and served Israel for forty years." In Midrash, *Bereshit Rabbah* 100, 10: "Rabbi Akiva studied Torah at the age of forty, and served the sages for forty years, and served Israel for forty years."

36 This may be the source of the need to explain his death. *Semahot* 8 reads as follows: "When Rabbi Akiva was killed in Caesarea, the news came to Rabbi Yehudah ben Bava and Rabbi Hanina ben Teradion. They stood and put on sackcloth, and said: Here us Jewish brothers: Rabbi Akiva was not killed for theft or for having studied Torah with all his might. Rabbi Akiva was killed as a sign (i.e. as a warning that worse days would come)."

greatest expression of man's humanity cannot bear the tawdriness of immediate and incomplete gratification. Philosophy and theoretical musings were not enough for the sage of love, who also withstood temptation and successfully contended with the practical trials he faced.

Chapter Six
LOVE THY FELLOW AS THE BASIS OF HUMAN SOCIALISATION

Inquiries into the concept of love in human thought and culture devote a great deal of attention to the question: Are the different kinds of love — love between man and woman; love between friends; love of mankind; parental love; love of God — different in essence, or do they have something in common beyond the term they all share?[37]

The sage of love's philosophy takes a unifying approach. It sees in love the source of all that is good, and recognises love in all positive phenomena. According to Rabbi Akiva, love does not create a distinct "domain" and is not in itself a distinct domain. Love is the source and the explanation of all phenomena of positive human behaviour, upon which interaction between people in all spheres of human relations must therefore be based.

It is in keeping with this approach that Rabbi Akiva determined his position in the famous dispute with Ben Azai:

"'Love thy fellow as thyself' (*Leviticus* 19:18) — Rabbi Akiva says: This is a great principle in the Torah. Ben Azai says: 'This is the book of the generations of *Adam*' (*Genesis* 5:1) is a greater principle than that."

Sifra, Kedoshim 2

Rabbi Akiva and Ben Azai were attempting to determine the categorical imperative from which all morality can be inferred. Ben Azai's claim rests upon the creation of man in God's image: "This is the book of the generations of *Adam*. In the day that God created man, in the likeness of God made He him" (*Gen. ibid.*). According to this principle, all human beings were created equal, and humanity — of which each and every individual human being is a part — embodies the image of God. Each part of humanity therefore has its own worth, just as every limb in the body has a place and value of its own. Ben Azai further developed this idea in the following *mishnah*:

---

[37]   Hunt 1993, pp. 3-7; Gasset 1991, pp. 13-16.

"Do not despise any man and do not dismiss any thing. For there is no man without a time and no thing without a place."

Avot 4, 3

Ben Azai thus resolves the great dilemma of the principle of equality: the fact that in reality men are not equal in any sense — not ability, not in behaviour, and not in the contribution or disturbance they offer society and their surroundings. Nor are the limbs of the body equal, but since none can be eliminated without "diminishing [God's] image", the principle of equality is upheld inasmuch as each has its proper place. They are equal in their right to exist, and every person is responsible for the existence of her/his fellow. The idea that man was created in God's image is, in Ben Azai's opinion, a greater moral/social principle than the commandment to love one's fellow.[38] According to Ben Azai, the categorical imperative is a rational law from which responsibility for one's fellow man derives. It is thus written in the Talmud (*Berakhot* 6b): "The entire world was created only for the sake of fellowship" — i.e. it is a categorical imperative from which all moral behaviour stems.

Rabbi Akiva's criticism of Ben Azai's approach derives first and foremost from the fear that it is not practicable and therefore unsuited as a practical basis for morality. The debate regarding the "great[est] principle in the Torah" is not an abstract philosophical discussion, but a practical discourse on human nature, and it is in this context that Rabbi Akiva claims that rational knowledge is not enough to create a sense of mutual responsibility and commitment to one another. Moreover, he is sceptical regarding the rationality of this sublime principle, since absolute equality goes against reason. One always takes precedence over one's fellow man, and one's responsibility to oneself comes before one's responsibility toward others. The following debate in the Midrash demonstrates the profound difference between the two approaches on a practical moral level:

> "'That thy brother may live with thee' — Ben Peturei taught: Two are walking in the desert, and only one has a jug of water. If he drinks it, he will reach an inhabited place, and if thy both drink, they will both die. Ben Peturei taught: They should both drink and die, as it is written 'that thy brother may live with thee'. Rabbi Akiva said to him: 'that thy brother may live with thee'– your life takes precedence over that of your fellow."

Sifra, Behar 5

---

[38] The version in Midrash, ***Bereshit Rabbah*** 24 presents Rabbi Akiva's opinion as "a greater principle than that": "Ben Azai says: 'This is the book of the generations of ***Adam***' (***Genesis*** 5:1) is a great principle in the Torah. Rabbi Akiva says: 'Love thy fellow as thyself' (***Leviticus*** 19:18) is a greater principle than that."

Ben Azai's principle of equality between all who are created in God's image is represented in this debate by Ben Peturei, who rules that both men have equal right to live and therefore equal right to the water, regardless of the fact that the water is presently in the possession of one of them. The principle of equality is the categorical imperative from which the laws of morality derive. Ben Peturei therefore rejects the principle of ownership and dismisses the fact that the water belongs to only one of the two. Rabbi Akiva does not believe that the principle of equality is practicable, and therefore qualifies the responsibility one has for one's fellow, making it conditional upon first fulfilling one's responsibility toward oneself: "your life takes precedence over that of your fellow" — in the sense that your duty toward another begins from the point at which you have favoured and ensured your own life.

From this we can understand the deep meaning of the principle "love thy fellow as thyself" according to Rabbi Akiva. One cannot love one's fellow man unless one first loves oneself. According to Ben Azai, the principle of equality that stems from man's creation in God's image precludes the individual's independent existence, projecting it to the totality of the divine image. From this derive the rational moral principles, including one's responsibility for each and every human being by virtue of her/his humanity. Rabbi Akiva restricts this principle in two stages: first, love thy fellow as thyself — love of yourself takes precedence over love of another, and is a precondition for its existence; second, love thy fellow — specifically your fellow and not just any one. Boundless, unreserved love is limited to one's immediate surroundings — family, friends, fellow townspeople, members of one's people — and is not shown toward all human beings per se. Limiting one's love of man to a smaller circle of people is a practical necessity. Rabbi Akiva's criticism of Ben Azai's categorical principle is, once again, that it is impracticable. In his opinion, moral behaviour cannot proceed solely from a rational tenet, even when that is accepted as a sublime principle founded upon a clear intellectual premise. One cannot exercise responsibility toward another if one is not first at peace with oneself. Just as love of one's fellow depends upon love of oneself, so moral responsibility toward humanity as a whole — with an emotional as well as a rational basis — depends first upon love for one's own people. Rabbi Akiva believes that universal moral values can be developed and practised, but only by a gradual process, layer upon layer. One must begin from the most basic principle, as expressed by Hillel the Elder: "What is hateful to you do not unto your fellow".[39] Before you can perceive something as being hateful to you, which you can then be required not to do unto another, you must first have a basic sense of self worth. Here too,

---

[39]   BT, *Shabbat* 31a, and *Targum Yehonatan* on the verse "love thy fellow as thyself". The verse itself does not refer only to refraining from doing harm to others, but to doing good as well. See *Maharsha, loc. cit.*

the basis is not purely rational, but rests upon feelings — toward oneself and consequently toward one's fellow. Henceforth: "the rest is commentary — go and learn", i.e. the principle of mutual responsibility can be expanded and applied to a broad range of areas, such as saving the life or property of another, charity, kindness, etc. A system of moral practice thus arises, on a social and national, as well as a personal level. At this point, it is possible to demand that one exercise responsibility toward all of mankind — every human being created in the image of God — as Rabbi Akiva himself explains:

> "He [Rabbi Akiva] would say: Beloved is man for he was created in the image of God; He was accorded great love, being created in God's image, as it is written: 'for in the image of God made He man' (*Genesis* 9:6). Beloved are Israel for they were called children of God; They were accorded great love, being called God's children, as it is written (*Deuteronomy* 14:1) 'Ye are the children of the Lord your God'. . . "

Mishnah, Avot 3, 14

The phrase "beloved are Israel who were called children of God" qualifies the *mishnah's* previous assertion — "beloved is man who was created in the image of God" — making it clear that the first statement should be construed as referring to every human being, whether of Israel or the nations. The text is thus not susceptible to emendation or limitation, as in the case of another adage: "he who saves a single life, it is as if he has saved the entire world". The saying first appears in the Mishnah, and subsequently, several times in the Gemara (in both Babylonian and Jerusalem Talmuds) and the Midrash. It is sometimes inclusive — "he who saves a single life," any life; and sometimes exclusive — "he who saves a single Jewish life". Maimonides,[40] who wished to re-establish the statement's original meaning and prevent its exclusive interpretation, changed the Talmudic text to read: "he who saves a single life in the world".[41]

In this *Mishnah* in *Avot*, Rabbi Akiva establishes the principle that all men were created in God's image, whence arises the mutual responsibility expressed in the words "beloved" and "great love". When we wrong one another, we do so less from hatred than from self-absorption and ignorance of the other's existence. Responsibility for one's fellow man does not derive solely from the principle of equality mandated by creation in God's image, but from being encouraged to develop a positive attitude toward him. It is not merely a matter of rational solidarity, but of real empathy toward all human beings, be they of Israel or of the nations. One can only develop a sense of responsibility toward

---

[40] Maimonides *Hilkhot Sanhedrin* 12, 3. See also *Hilkhot Rotzeah Ushmirat Hanefesh* 1, 16.

[41] See BT, *Sanhedrin* 4, 5. The word *miyisrael* (of Israel, Jewish) does not appear in the Munich Ms. or other talmudic manuscripts. This is also the reading in the JT, *Sanhedrin* 4, 22a; *Pirkei deRabbi Eliezer* 47; and *Eliahu Rabbah* 11. It does appear however, in BT, *Bava Batra* 11a; BT, *Sanhedrin* 37a; *Avot deRabbi Natan* vers. 2, 6. In the last source, the word *miyisrael* (of Israel) clearly contradicts the meaning of the text.

one's fellow man based on awareness of the other's existence, if one has already developed love toward those in one's immediate circle: friends and compatriots. Such love can only be felt by one who has attained basic recognition of his/her own worth.[42] The process that leads up to the principle of equality based on the premise that all men were created in God's image is thus a gradual one: first "love thy fellow as thyself", and only then "beloved is man for he was created in the image of God".

Threats to the practical application of the moral process, according to Rabbi Akiva, proceed from two sources: 1) lack of self-esteem that prevents one from loving others; and 2) egotism and narcissism that entail ignoring others' existence.

Rabbi Akiva thus established as the categorical imperative, something capable of addressing these two threats: "Love thy fellow as thyself . . . this is a great principle in the Torah". Against lack of self-esteem: "as thyself" — one must first love oneself and thereby discover, first and foremost, self-responsibility. The great principle as a whole however, comes to counter egotism: "love thy fellow".

One manifestation of the great principle, as understood by Rabbi Akiva, was the great love he showed toward his students. The following excerpt concerns his views on teaching:

> "Rabbi Akiva says: Where is it written that one must repeat [a lesson] until one's student has learned it? It is written: 'and teach thou it the children of Israel' (*Deuteronomy* 31:19). And where is it written until he knows [the lesson] thoroughly? It is written: 'put it in their mouths' (*ibid.*). And where is it written that one must explain [the lesson's] meaning? It is written: 'these are the ordinances which thou shalt set before them (*Exodus* 21:1)."

> BT, *Eruvin* 54b

Successful teaching requires great dedication, contingent upon a teacher's great love for his student. One who wishes to teach must possess not only patience — the ability to bear with a student until the lesson has been understood — but total dedication, of a kind that can only be motivated by love. It is the teacher's responsibility to ensure that the student achieves three things:

— "Until he has learned the lesson" — comprehension.

— "Until he knows the lesson thoroughly" — proficiency and recall.

— "One must explain [the lesson's] meaning" — complex grasp of the material.

Some interpret the last phrase to mean bringing various opinions and interpretations to the student's attention. A loving teacher does not keep knowledge from his students, particularly when it does not coincide with his own

---

42   See Erich Fromm, *The Art of Loving*, Harper Perennial, 2000, pp. 23-30.

opinion. One can also understand the phrase to mean "show kindness" — one who loves another shows kindness toward them, and a teacher should accord a student no less.

The teacher-student relationship however, is not limited to academic activities, for the students also constitute the teacher's social milieu, and as such provide ample ground for the fulfilment of the social precepts — the commandments governing man's behaviour toward man — as illustrated in the following story:

> "A student of Rabbi Akiva's once fell ill. The scholars did not go to visit him, but Rabbi Akiva went to visit him, and because he had honoured him and sprinkled the floor [of his room] with water, he lived. He said to him: Rabbi, you have restored me to life. Rabbi Akiva went out, and taught: He who does not visit the sick, it is as if he has spilt blood."
>
> BT, *Nedarim* 40a

Rabbi Akiva here exemplifies his own approach to the commandment to visit the sick and the performance of acts of kindness. He goes to visit his student who has fallen ill, but has not received visits from the scholars (his friends, and presumably students of Rabbi Akiva). Rabbi Akiva tends to the patient, cares for him, washes his room, and by virtue of these actions he recovers. The incident brings Rabbi Akiva to reflect unequivocally on the value of visiting the sick in general. We see Rabbi Akiva as one who is not content merely to preach, but puts his beliefs into practice, implementing the great principle of "love thy fellow as thyself" in the precepts that arise from it.

Rabbi Akiva's philosophy is not merely theoretical, but rests upon a pattern of personal example, so that theory and behaviour together form the source from which his approach may be learned. One of his friends attests to his behaviour, from which we can gain insight into his understanding of mutual responsibility and his willingness to receive reproof:

> "And Rabbi Yohanan ben Nuri said: Let heaven and earth be my witness that Rabbi Akiva was often chastised on my account, for I would complain to Raban Gamliel, and of course he loved me all the more, fulfilling the verse (*Proverbs* 9:8): 'Reprove not a scorner, lest he hate thee; rebuke a wise man, and he will love thee.'"
>
> BT, *Arakhin* 16b

Rabbi Yohanan ben Nuri's complaints to Raban Gamliel the Patriarch, about Rabbi Akiva, caused the latter to be chastised on numerous occasions. Rabbi Akiva did not shun his friend or condemn his "unfriendly" behaviour, but responded with love. Not only was their friendship not harmed, it actually deepened. In his comportment, Rabbi Akiva teaches another lesson on the meaning of loving one's fellow: the mutual responsibility that arises from "love thy fellow as thyself" entails not ignoring his mistakes and sins. From this responsibility stems the commandment: "thou shalt surely reprove thy neighbour, and not bear sin because of him" (*Leviticus* 19:17). The laws of reproof teach us whom, how and when to reprove. The book of *Proverbs* cautions that it is pointless to reprove a scorner, and one should avoid doing so because it increases hatred. One should reprove the wise man, who wishes to be reproved that he might better his ways, and love those who reprove him. The responsibility that stems from "love thy fellow as thyself", from which the commandment to reprove in turn derives, obligates both reprover and reproved. Reproof that comes from love increases love among friends and arouses the love of the one who is reproved.

The commandment "love thy fellow as thyself" comprises the duty to avoid doing others ill, as well as the duty to do them good. The following incident teaches us how Rabbi Akiva respected all Jews:

> "This is the rule. Rabbi Akiva said: Even the poor of Israel should be considered free men[43] who have fallen on hard times, since they are the descendants of Abraham, Isaac and Jacob. A man once removed a woman's head-covering in public. He came before Rabbi Akiva, who ordered him to pay the woman 400 *zuzim*. He said to him: Rabbi, give me time. And he gave him time. The man waited for her at the entrance to her courtyard, and broke a jug containing an *issar* (a small amount) of oil in her face. She removed her head-covering and wiped [her face], placing her hand upon her head. He brought witnesses to see, and came before Rabbi Akiva. He said to him: To a woman such as this I must give 400 *zuzim*? He said to him: You have said nothing. One who harms himself, although he is not permitted to do so — is not accountable. Others who harm him, are accountable . . . "

> Mishnah, *Bava Kama* 8, 6

This *mishnah* discusses torts that have not inflicted pain or caused great damage, and the specific fines that the Rabbis established for them. The first speaker establishes a maximum fine — to be paid to the most respectable victims — recommending that the fine decrease in direct proportion to the victim's respectability as determined by the judges. Rabbi Akiva disagrees with this opinion, asserting the principle of equality. He therefore rules that all Jews — respectable or not — are equal in the awarding of damages.

We have noted that according to Rabbi Akiva's approach, a fitting attitude to others is based upon recognition of their existence and the prohibition against ignoring them. The obligation to recognise others' existence needs to be defined, and this *mishnah* provides quantifiable definitions of non-ignorance.

---

[43] This idea, presented by Rabbi Akiva, can be compared to the concept of *libertus* in Roman law. See Smith (1875), *A Dictionary of Greek and Roman Antiquities*, as well as primary Roman legal sources.

These definitions have legal significance in cases of violent behaviour toward others, or their public humiliation. The source of the definition regarding recognition of others' existence lies therefore, not in the others per se, in the way they appreciate or fail to appreciate their own worth, but in one's obligation toward one's fellow man. In this definition, Rabbi Akiva remains faithful to the process whereby love of one's fellow develops: love of oneself, one's own presence gives rise to the presence of others, which in turn gives rise to responsibility toward others. This responsibility is independent of the other's identity, standing or sense of self-worth. Here, Rabbi Akiva establishes another important principle in the love of one's fellow. We have said that such love is contingent upon self-appreciation and basic recognition of one's own worth. And what of the other? Are we commanded to love others when they do not appreciate themselves? When others have no respect for themselves or even harm themselves, are we required to exercise greater responsibility toward them than they do toward themselves? Rabbi Akiva rules that our obligations to others are absolute, and do not depend upon the way in which they view themselves. "Love thy neighbour" depends upon "as thyself" — love of self and self-preservation first — not upon "as himself". It is therefore unrelated to the other's love of herself/himself, but stands alone, as a categorical obligation toward one's fellow man.

The view that "love thy fellow" is the categorical imperative from which all moral obligations derive also has bearing upon the relationship between commandments that govern man's relationship with his fellow man, and those that are exclusively between man and God:

> "Rabbi Akiva says: The Bible says in one place (*Exodus* 34:7) 'He will clear', and in another 'He will not clear' (*ibid.*). How can the two be reconciled? Rather: in matters between you and Him — 'He will clear'; in matters between you and your fellow — 'He will not clear.'"
>
> Midrash, *Bamidbar Rabbah* 11, 7

From this we learn the well-known principle that for purposes of reward and punishment and repentance, sins between man and his fellow are worse than sins between man and God. For the latter, God forgives one who repents; whereas the former require that one appease one's fellow before one can be cleansed of sin. This teaching of Rabbi Akiva's developed further in the talmudic literature, and the centrality and great importance of commandments "between man and his fellow" relative to commandments "between man and God" went on to become a fundamental principle in the halakhic and philosophical works of all subsequent generations:

A famous passage in the Talmud raises serious doubts regarding the extent to which Rabbi Akiva's students practised his philosophy however:

"It was said that Rabbi Akiva had twelve thousand pairs of students from Gevat to Antipa[t]ris, and all died in a single period because they did not show respect to one another. And the world was desolate until Rabbi Akiva came to the Rabbis in the south and taught them. Rabbi Meir and Rabbi Yehudah and Rabbi Yose and Rabbi Shimon and Rabbi Elazar ben Shamo'a, and they [re-]established the Torah at that time."

BT, Yevamot 62b

The Talmud in *Yevamot* discusses the type of plague that brought about their deaths, but offers no further explanation regarding the mutual respect that Rabbi Akiva's students were lacking. Other sources state that they were punished because they "behaved begrudgingly toward one another".[44] How was this begrudging behaviour manifested? Perhaps they ignored the *mishnah*'s admonition: "let your fellow's honour be as dear to you as your own"; and what is more: "and the honour of your fellow be like reverence for your teacher, and reverence for your teacher be like reverence of heaven"?[45] In any event, it is clear that they behaved improperly toward one another, thereby desecrating God's name and bringing terrible tragedy upon themselves. What significance does this have however, with regard to their rabbi's teachings?

These sources strengthen the claim we have made that Rabbi Akiva did not merely make a theoretical study of the categorical imperative, but developed his system of love for one's fellow from a clearly realistic standpoint, taking into consideration the experiences of daily life. His students, as we have seen in other halakhic contexts, were his main source of inspiration. One could say that Rabbi Akiva's rulings were a response and a warning, arising from the failed interpersonal relations he observed among his students.

A closer look at the context of the talmudic discussion offers a possible explanation of the fact that his students did not implement his teachings:

"Rabbi Akiva says: He who studied Torah in his youth, will study Torah in his old age; he who had students in his youth, will have students in his old age."

Ibid.

Torah study is not meant to occupy a specific period in the life of a rabbi who wishes to study and teach, and it goes without saying that one must toil before one can reap the benefits. A teacher cannot rely in his old age upon what he studied in his youth or upon the students he had then, but must continue to study and to teach. The Talmud explains Rabbi Akiva's words as stemming from the fact that his first students had died in a plague, "and the world was desolate until Rabbi Akiva came to the Rabbis in the south and taught them". It was they

---

[44]   BT, *Yoma* 86a; Midrash, *Bereshit Rabbah* 61.
[45]   *Avot* 2, 8; *ibid.* 4, 13. See also *Sefer Hatashbetz* vol 1, 178.

who continued his Torah, further developed it, and earned it a central place among the teachings of the *tanaim*; and it was in this later Torah that he taught to the rabbis of the south, that Rabbi Akiva developed his "love thy fellow" approach.

Rabbi Akiva established "love thy fellow" as the basis of socialisation, and studying his philosophy in these contexts has given us new insight into the phenomenon. Rabbi Akiva's approach is not based upon understanding interests and power struggles, or analysing the nature of man as a social animal. It is based upon an attempt to understand the essence of love, how to love and how to develop love. The ability to love another depends upon one's first loving oneself. From loving oneself, one can proceed in two possible directions. One can allow the ego to take control of the man — such love tends to burn itself out; or one can love others, exercising responsibility toward them, performing act of kindness for them — such inter-personal relations eventually develop into love for all human beings created in God's image. "Love thy fellow" strengthens "thyself", and love of oneself provides a solid basis, a mainstay, for love of others. Socialisation based upon "love thy fellow" is in fact a system of love ties between people and themselves that sustain and strengthen one another. A better understanding of the philosophy of the sage of love thus helps us to better understand the concept of love itself.

Chapter Seven
OPTIMISM OUT OF LOVE

Upon examining the sources describing the events of Rabbi Akiva's life, one cannot help but notice the sharp contrast between the hardships he experienced — both individually and as a member of the Jewish community in Roman Palestine[46] — and his optimistic, accepting, grateful and even joyous behaviour. We stand awestruck before a fundamental and deep-seated approach,[47] reflected in the manner in which he relates to the severe blows he suffers one after another. We first come upon Akiva's optimism in relation to the state of poverty in which he lived with Rachel immediately following their marriage and before he had begun to study Torah. Picking the straw out of his wife's hair, he promises her that better times will come and that her hair will some day be adorned with a "city of gold" rather than straw, and tries to comfort

---

[46] In *Avot deRabbi Natan*, 40, 11: "One who sees Rabbi Akiva in a dream should fear misfortune".

[47] Rabbi Akiva's approach to suffering has been analysed and described by E. Urbach. See Urbach *Hazal: Pirkei Emunot Vedeot* pp. 354-370, 384-392, 454-464.

her, pointing out that some are poorer than they, lacking even straw. These difficulties however, pale in comparison to the tragedy of his sons' deaths:

> "One may not desist from Torah study for [the sake of] the dead, until the soul has departed. When Shimon, the son of Rabbi Akiva was ill, he did not leave the study hall, but sent messengers [to inquire] after him. The first came and said to him: he is very ill. He said to them [his students]: ask [questions pertaining to your studies]. The second came and said to him: he has grown worse. He returned them to Torah study. The third came and said to him: he is dying. He said to them: ask [questions pertaining to your studies]. The fourth came and said to him: he is spent. He arose, removed his *tefilin* and tore his clothes, and said to them: hear, Jewish brothers, until now we were obligated to study Torah, now you and I must honour the dead."
>
> Mishnah, *Semahot* 8, 13

Rabbi Akiva's behaviour in this story appears inhuman. Shimon, Rabbi Akiva's son, falls ill, and he does not deviate from his normal routine of Torah study and teaching—letting messengers' reports on his son's condition suffice. The first messenger reports that his son's illness is very grave. The students, it would seem, expected their teacher to cancel or suspend the lesson in the hall of study, but Rabbi Akiva encourages them to ask questions on the subject they had been studying. The students here represent the reasonable human approach: their teacher's son is ill, it must be difficult for the father to study Torah, to concentrate on his lessons, and perhaps he would like to go and help care for his son. Rabbi Akiva on the other hand, represents the ideal of accepting and coping with the hardest facts of life in the best possible way. When the second messenger comes and tells the Rabbi that his son's condition has worsened, once again he returns his students to their studies. When the third messenger reports that the son his dying, again he encourages them to ask questions about the material they had been learning. Only when the fourth messenger brings the terrible news of Shimon's death, does Rabbi Akiva stop studying, remove his *tefilin*, tear his clothes and say: "hear, Jewish brothers, until now we were obligated to study Torah, now you and I must honour the dead".

The obligation of Torah study stands above all else, and cannot be set aside for the sake of fulfilling other very important precepts. Honouring the dead however, supersedes even Torah study. The Mishnah seeks to establish the limits of this rule, and determines that "one may not desist from Torah study for [the sake of] the dead, until the soul has departed". The story of Rabbi Akiva and his son Shimon is cited in support of the halakhic ruling, but also provides an opportunity to learn from Rabbi Akiva's attitude and comportment at the time of his greatest calamity. Even at this most difficult and terrible hour, he remains true to his moral principles. His son's illness and death put his principles and their practical application to the test. He draws his strength from his belief in these values and their inherent truth, flowing in turn from his devotion and love of God. Passing events — including unbearable trials for those of impoverished moral principles, or those who have not attained the level of lovers of God — are in the eyes of Rabbi Akiva, opportunities to reaffirm his belief system and strengthen hope and optimism.

In the story, Rabbi Akiva's students appear to be more shaken than their teacher, and it is he who must return them to their studies following the arrival of each of the first three messengers. The students determine their attitude to reality based on emotion, whereas Rabbi Akiva's approach and corresponding actions — as difficult as reality may be — stem from his values. Often, this value system entails inner clashes, and Rabbi Akiva's students receive a practical lesson in what to do when a conflict arises between values. Up to a point (perhaps excessive in the eyes of the students), the value of Torah study outweighs all other values. Eventually however, even Torah study is superseded by another value — in this case, honouring the dead. As a result of his optimism and his approach to the misfortune that befalls him, all who seek to comfort and sustain him are themselves comforted and sustained — and in that Rabbi Akiva finds comfort:

> "A great multitude assembled in honour of Rabbi Akiva's son. He said to them: Bring me a bench from the graves. They brought him a bench from the graves and he sat on it and said: Hear, Jewish brethren. It is not that I am wise — there are here wiser than I. And it is not that I am rich — there are here richer than I. The people of the south know Rabbi Akiva, whence do the people of the Galilee know [him]? The men know Rabbi Akiva, whence do the women and children? Rather, I know that your reward is great, because you did not come to grieve, but to honour the Torah and fulfil a *mitzvah* — I would have been comforted were I burying seven sons, **and not that a man wants to bury his sons**, but I know that my son will enter the next world . . . "

> *Ibid.*

Here, Rabbi Akiva teaches us the source from which we can draw the strength to deal with our worst misfortunes. "And not that a man wants to bury his sons" — for those students and readers who were puzzled by his behaviour and sought the human side of Rabbi Akiva — he is a man like any other, and as such grieves that he must bury his son. The meaning is provided by the many who have flocked to the funeral — to whom Rabbi Akiva immediately ascribes the best of intentions: that they had come to honour the Torah and to fulfil the *mitzvah* of "true kindness".[48] This is a source of comfort and hope: that the death of his son does not imply a loss of meaning, but on the contrary offers greater meaning — particularly in such a large crowd.

---

[48] Kindness afforded to the dead is traditionally referred to as "true kindness", because one expects nothing in return. See Rashi, *Gen* 47, 29.

The meaning was also provided by the son himself, at whose death so many came to honour the Torah and fulfil a *mitzvah* — which merit gained him entry to the next world. At this point however, the grieving father must stress that he is not, God forbid, sanctifying death, and even moral benefit cannot mitigate the pain: "and not that a man wants to bury his sons". Nevertheless, no misfortune is without comfort. There can be meaning and consequently some comfort even in a tragedy such as this, and even in one seven times more terrible ("I would have been comforted were I burying seven sons").

Rabbi Akiva's optimism looks toward the future. He does not renounce the future in the face of adversity, as long as misfortune leads to moral triumph. When faced with the possibility of giving weight to the tragedy itself or ascribing meaning to moral principles and hope for the future, he chooses to harness misfortune to morality and hope for a better future, in this world and the next. This is his response to national and personal tragedy alike; to individual suffering as well as the anguish of the entire community.

Rabbi Akiva's approach and comportment stem from the fact that he worshiped God out of love. The Rabbis examine the behaviour of a number of biblical figures in the face of adversity, and compare Abraham to Job.[49] Contrary to Abraham, who worshiped God out of love, "Job did not worship God but for fear", according to Rabbi Yohanan ben Zakai (*Sotah* 5, 5). Rabbi Yehoshua ben Hyrcanus, who cites Rabbi Yohanan ben Zakai's opinion, disagrees, and asserts that Job worshiped God out of love. This position however, was not accepted by his student, Rabbi Akiva, who criticised Job severely, calling him one who "was afflicted and rebelled" (*Semahot* 8, 11). Even *midrashim* that mention Job in a favourable light, for having said "The Lord hath given and the Lord hath taken away. Blessed be the name of the Lord" fail to address the main issue. Job did not withstand his afflictions, and certainly did not imbue them with meaning or transform them into a message of optimism. His behaviour was thus the complete opposite of the behaviour and philosophy of Rabbi Akiva.

Rabbi Akiva's approach to misfortune and suffering rests first and foremost upon love:

> "And thou shalt love the Lord thy God with all thine heart, and with all thy soul, and with all thy might (*Deut* 6:5). Rabbi Akiva says: If it is written 'with all thy soul', is 'with all thy might' not obvious? Rather, [love God] in the portion he allots to you, whether good or ill."
>
> Sifre, Devarim 32

Man is obligated to love God whether he has been given a good reason to be thankful, or whether his allotted portion has been one of misfortune. According to Rabbi Akiva, the difference between a worshiper of God and an idolater is

---

[49]   Urbach, *op. cit.* p. 355 *et seq.*

manifest in their respective attitudes to suffering. People worship idols that they might serve them, and therefore "when they are visited by good [fortune], they respect their gods . . . and when they are visited by misfortune, they curse their gods" (*Mekhilta, Yitro* 10). A worshiper of God accepts with love both the good and the bad, and gives thanks to his god in times of prosperity and anguish alike. It is not God that is tested, but man and his moral principles. This is not enough for Rabbi Akiva however, and he calls upon his listeners to rejoice in suffering:

> "And what is more, a man should rejoice in suffering more than good [fortune], for even one who has been fortunate all his life, is not forgiven his sins. And what atones for one's sins? That is suffering."
>
> *Mekhilta, ibid.*

A fortunate life, in and of itself, lacks meaning, whereas suffering is inherently meaningful. Although one does not wish to suffer, there is a certain joy that is the sufferer's exclusive province — the joy of purification from sin. This is not, God forbid, masochism or an addiction to suffering, but a way of coping with misfortune by introducing another element to the constant contemplation, characteristic of those who suffer. All who suffer misfortune also experience a sense of guilt — usually groundless and unjustified. Although Rabbi Akiva uses the guilt that accompanies hardship, guiding his listeners toward release from it. Rather than agonising over the thought that had one not sinned, misfortune would never have struck, he stresses, as we will see below, that "there is not a righteous man upon earth that doeth good and sinneth not" (*Ecclesiastes* 7:20). Even the best of people must contend with the earthly reality of sin, for even the most saintly, the "righteous upon the earth", cannot escape life's complexity. One should therefore not regret past failures, but rejoice in their atonement. Rabbi Akiva's approach enables man to cope with misfortune, while maintaining internal serenity, despite the upheaval caused by adversity.

Rabbinical sources repeatedly emphasise the fact that Rabbi Akiva's approach was unique and was not shared by his peers:

> "Raba bar Bar Hana said: When Rabbi Eliezer fell ill his students came to visit him. He said to them: There is great wrath in the world. They began to cry, and Rabbi Akiva to laugh. They said to him: Why are you laughing? He said to them: Why are you crying? They said to him: A Torah scroll suffers, shall we not cry? He said to them: That is why I laugh. As long as I saw that my master's wine had not turned to vinegar, his flax was not stricken, his oil had not gone rancid, his honey had not soured, I said: Perhaps, God forbid, my master has received [all of] his reward [in this world]. Now that I see my master in sorrow, I am glad. He [Rabbi Eliezer] said to him: Akiva, is there any part of the Torah that I have neglected? He said to him: You have taught us Rabbi: 'for there is not a righteous man upon earth that doeth good and sinneth not."
>
> BT, *Sanhedrin* 101a

These words, spoken as the students gathered around their teacher's sickbed, place their different approaches to his condition in sharp relief — beginning with the patient himself, whose entire outlook is altered by the prism of his pain and suffering to the point that it is no longer his personal suffering, but a tragedy that befalls the entire world: "He said to them: There is great wrath in the world" — my affliction is an expression of God's anger with the world, and that is why I must endure this terrible suffering. The aggadic author portrays the figure of the righteous man suffering for the sins of his generation. The students are moved by their teacher's plight, and begin to cry at the terrible price he must pay for the misdeeds of the world. While they are crying, Rabbi Akiva laughs. They attribute Rabbi Eliezer's suffering to the sins of others and the injustice of the righteous man's lot. Rabbi Akiva, who believes that one must accept suffering with love, attributes his master's tribulations to God's love for the righteous, but also to the righteous man's own sins. "That is why I laugh", because I see my teacher — who is likened to a Torah scroll — suffering, and I know that this suffering is inflicted upon him for his own benefit, that he might attain the highest level in the next world. According to Rabbi Akiva's optimistic approach, hope must be long-lived. An immediate end to suffering and a peaceful death are not to be aspired to at this moment. There are times in life when one is interested in nothing less than eternity. The level one attains in the next world however, depends upon the transitory suffering one endures in this world.

In the *beraita* cited by the Talmud as another version of the sages' visit to Rabbi Eliezer's bedside, the latter, in his agony, accepts Rabbi Akiva's multi-dimensional approach, and that is what finally sets his mind at rest:

> "The rabbis taught: When Rabbi Eliezer fell ill, four sages came to visit him: Rabbi Tarfon, Rabbi Yehoshua, Rabbi Elazar ben Azariah and Rabbi Akiva. Rabbi Tarfon spoke and said: You are better for Israel than the rain, for the rain is [only] in this world, and my master is in this world and the next. Rabbi Yehoshua spoke and said: You are better for Israel than the sun, for the sun is [only] in this world, and my master is in this world and the next. Rabbi Elazar ben Azariah spoke and said: You are better for Israel than father and mother, for father and mother are [only] in this world, and my master is in this world and the next. Rabbi Akiva spoke and said: Beloved is suffering. He [Rabbi Eliezer] said to them: Hold me up, that I might hear the words of Akiva my student, who said that suffering is beloved . . . "

Ibid.

According to the first version of the story, Rabbi Eliezer was initially puzzled by Rabbi Akiva's remarks, interpreting them as criticism of his behaviour. Rabbi Akiva responds cautiously, quoting the verse from *Ecclesiastes*, and respectfully attributing its study to his teacher. From his answer we learn another fundamental lesson regarding misfortune. Man is never perfect, and cannot attain eternal life by virtue of good deeds and moral behaviour alone, for the goodness God showers upon his creations in this world can be considered sufficient reward. Suffering however, can tip the balance, and earn one her/his place in the world to come.

According to the version appearing in the *beraita*, Rabbi Tarfon, Rabbi Yehoshua and Rabbi Elazar ben Azariah attempt to take their teacher's mind off his illness, ease his suffering, and cheer him up with lavish praise, emphasising his standing and achievements that have benefited the entire Jewish People — to his credit in this world and the next. Rabbi Akiva's approach differs in that he does not try to distract Rabbi Eliezer from his suffering, but rather suggests that he relate to it differently — by recognising its benefits: beloved is suffering! Rabbi Eliezer, whose three other visitors have failed to distract him, wants to hear more about Rabbi Akiva's approach, in order to determine the feasibility of a change in attitude that might make suffering bearable, enabling him to accept it and understand its meaning.

The idea that suffering is specifically intended for the righteous — that they might merit a greater reward in the world to come — appears frequently in rabbinical literature, as in the following:

> "Rabbi Akiva says: . . . He is meticulous with the righteous, and exacts punishment for their few evil deeds in this world, giving them serenity and ample reward in the world to come. He bestows serenity upon the wicked and rewards their few meritorious acts in this word, in order to exact punishment in the next."
>
> Midrash, *Bereshit Rabbah*, 33, 1

One's attitude to suffering is a test of true moral and spiritual stature. It goes beyond the common theme of "why do the righteous suffer while the wicked prosper", although it is also frequently cited as an answer to that dilemma. Emphasising the transitory nature of suffering with respect to eternal life and serenity offers relief in dealing with adversity in this world. Moreover, Rabbi Akiva cautions the righteous — those who strive to live moral, worthy lives — not to expect to be rewarded in this world for their efforts. Those who are fortunate, and enjoy good, pleasant lives, should be concerned and examine their actions, lest they are not truly righteous. When a moral action is part of general moral behaviour rather than a random act, one should expect more suffering than serenity in this world. Not only does misfortune not serve as grounds for grievance against God, (as we have already learned from Rabbi Yohanan ben Zakai's criticism of Job, and Rabbi Akiva's even more scathing characterisation of Job as one who "was afflicted and rebelled"), but for the righteous person, it is a sign, attesting to God's immanent presence in the world. For the wicked, suffering is exactly the reverse:

"Rabbi Akiva said: 'Wherefore doth the wicked condemn God? He hath said in his heart, Thou wilt not require it' (*Ps* 10:13) — there is no judgement and there is no judge; but judgement there is and judge there is."

Ibid. 26, 6

The wicked person lives as if there were no judgement and no judge, nor anything that might elicit recognition of divine immanence, since s/he enjoys a tranquil existence in this world. Here too, belief in God's immanence is reiterated and emphasised — as both cause and consequence of suffering. Also reiterated is the principle that suffering is neither pointless nor meaningless. In accepting suffering one imbues it with meaning, to the point of turning the concept itself around, since suffering is certainly the opposite of "beloved", yet according to Rabbi Akiva: "beloved is suffering".

Rabbi Akiva learned his approach to suffering from one of his teachers, Nahum Gimzo. "Nahum Gim-zo was wont to say of everything that befell him: 'this too ("*gam zo*" in Hebrew) is for the best'" (BT, *Sanhedrin* 108b). Some say the name "Gim-zo" derives from this habit, although he was apparently a native of the town of Gimzo on the Judean plain. Rabbi Akiva studied with him for many years, and adopted his method of halakhic interpretation — as opposed to that of Rabbi Nehunia ben Hakanah, espoused by Rabbi Yishmael (BT, *Shevuot* 26a; BT, *Hagigah* 14b). Nahum's life was fraught with suffering. According to legend, he was blind, had lost both arms and legs, and was covered with boils. Nevertheless, he never gave in to despair. A well-known story about Rabbi Akiva and misfortunes that had a positive outcome, begins with his version of Nahum Gimzo's motto ("this too is for the best"):

"Rav said in the name of Rabbi Meir, and it is also said in the name of Rabbi Akiva: One should always be in the habit of saying 'all that God does is for the best.'"

BT, *Berakhot* 60b-61a

All of these statements stress the principle that one should embrace reality and behave accordingly, rather than inveigh against one's circumstances.

Rabbi Akiva did not merely keep his optimism and vitality to himself. His manner of viewing a given situation in all its complexity and finding its positive sides helped not only his teachers, but his students as well. His intercession in the renowned dispute between the Patriarch Raban Gamliel and his teacher Rabbi Yehoshua, regarding the blessing of the new moon, caused the latter to accept the Patriarch's decision. Another story is told of a student who came to the house of study in a very agitated state due to a bad dream he had dreamt, and Rabbi Akiva interpreted the dream in a positive light.[50] This story can serve

---

[50] JT, *Ma'aser Sheni* 4, 6.

as a metaphor for Rabbi Akiva's approach to adversity and suffering: they are little more than bad dreams, requiring only a shift in meaning — in order to understand their purpose and interpret them in a positive way, since "all that God does is for the best".

Rabbi Akiva's optimism, as noted above, is based upon belief in God's presence and involvement in the world. His is not a simplistic belief that detaches one from reality, but a complex method, the product of vast knowledge and deep contemplation. Rabbi Akiva was legendary for his ability to state the most profound ideas in simple language, capable of appealing to his thousands of students and the general public:

> "Rabbi Akiva says: . . . All is foreseen and freedom is granted; the world is judged with kindness and all in accordance with the preponderance of deeds."
>
> Mishnah, *Avot* 3, 15

The expression "all is foreseen" has engaged Jewish thinkers throughout the ages. Was Rabbi Akiva referring merely to divine immanence — in other words, God's awareness of all of man's actions (see commentary on the Mishnah by Rabbi Ovadiah of Bertinoro, *loc. cit.*) — or was he expressing a deterministic point of view, i.e. that all is preordained as a result of divine knowledge, but man is nevertheless granted free will (Rabbi Hasdai Crescas, *Or Hashem*)? Or perhaps, as Maimonides claimed, our inability to "know God" precludes understanding the concept of free will (*Introduction to Avot*, and *Mishneh Torah, Hilkhot Teshuvah* 5). Scholars usually associate the deterministic interpretation of Rabbi Akiva's words with the Middle Ages, and prefer a simpler reading of the *mishnah*. It is difficult to determine Rabbi Akiva's original intention however, since all of the commentaries — those that limit the meaning of the expression "all is foreseen" to divine immanence as well as those that infer "soft determinism" — are mediaeval, and we are no longer able to approach the *mishnah* except through the prism of these commentaries. The *Tosafot Yom Tov* on the Mishnah examines the syntax of Rabbi Akiva's statement: had he simply meant to say that all man's actions are manifest before God, the sentence would have read "freedom [of action] is granted, but [know that] all is foreseen", because man's actions would have been the subject of the observation. It was not Rabbi Akiva's intention however, to say something so obvious:

> "It was certainly his intention to remark that although all is foreseen, man still has the ability to choose, because freedom is granted."
>
> *Tosafot Yom Tov* on the Mishnah, *loc. cit.*

The emphasis that commentators throughout the ages have placed upon the relationship between divine knowledge and free choice in Rabbi Akiva's statement draws attention away from the fact that the expression "all is foreseen" also refers to events that are not the result of human choice. The hardships caused by severe illness, natural disaster, economic crisis, or war between military powers, should not be attributed to chance, but to divine providence. Even when suffering is very great, the knowledge that it is not the work of chance, without cause or meaning, but in fact the opposite, gives reason for optimism. "All" includes the situations people encounter in their lives, with which they must contend using the freedom of action they possesses. The knowledge that reality is preordained by God leads to acceptance, and to the optimistic belief that man has the ability to cope with all of the challenges s/he may face. Despite everything, "freedom is granted" and man can and must lead a dignified and moral life, be the circumstances of that life what they may.

Misfortune, as explained above, is not the result of chance but of intent — not ill intent, but the will of God, as he guides the world, which is positive, since "the world is judged with kindness". It is not only man's actions that are judged with compassion, but the entire world and all its phenomena: negative as well as positive.

Rabbi Akiva's optimism and his unique approach to life features prominently in legends describing the experiences of Rabbi Akiva and his friends in connection with the destruction of the Temple:

"Raban Gamliel and Rabbi Elazar ben Azariah and Rabbi Akiva were travelling on the road when they heard the din of the city of Rome from [the town of] Puteoli, at a distance of one hundred and twenty miles, and they began to cry and Rabbi Akiva to laugh. They said to him: Why do you laugh? He said to them: Why do you cry? They said to him: These heathen who bow down before images and offer incense to idols sit in safety and tranquillity while the footstool of our God lies burnt. Shall we not cry? He said to them: That is why I laugh. If that is [the condition of] those who transgress his will, all the more so those who do his will. Another time, they were going up to Jerusalem. When they reached Mount Scopus, they rent their clothing. When they reached the Temple Mount, they saw a fox come out of the Holy of Holies. They began to cry and Rabbi Akiva to laugh. They said to him: Why do you laugh? He said to them: Why do you cry? They said to him: Foxes now walk upon the place of which it is written 'and the stranger that cometh nigh shall be put to death'. Shall we not cry? He said to them: That is why I laugh. For it is written 'And I took unto me witnesses to record, Uriah the priest, and Zachariah the son of Jeberechiah.' What has Uriah to do with Zechariah? Uriah [lived at the time] of the First Temple, and Zechariah [at the time] of the second Temple? Rather, the verse linked the prophecy of Zechariah to the prophecy of Uriah. Regarding Uriah it is written 'therefore shall Zion for your sake be plowed as a field'. Regarding Zechariah it is written 'there shall yet old men and old women dwell in the streets of Jerusalem'. Until the prophecy of Uriah was fulfilled, I feared that the prophecy of Zechariah would not come to be. Now that the prophecy of Uriah has come to be, it is known that the prophecy of Zechariah will come to be. They said to him in these words: Akiva you have comforted us. Akiva you have comforted us."

BT, Makot 24a-b[51]

The peace and prosperity of Rome—the evil and hated empire—sadden and frustrate the rabbis. As they cry however, Rabbi Akiva laughs: "That is why I laugh. If that is [the condition of] those who transgress his will, all the more so those who do his will." In his profound faith, he cannot ascribe either of these elements—or the fact that he has been given the opportunity to observe them both—to chance. This opportunity can only have been afforded to him and to his friends that they might learn from it. The conclusions that Rabbi Akiva himself draws require a certain detachment from the situation at hand, as well as a broad and far-reaching vision, in order to entertain hope at the right time. God's will, as manifested in the prosperity of Rome, whose people are undeserving, is destined to express itself sevenfold in the prosperity those who worship God will enjoy.

The second example cited in this passage stresses the importance of far-reaching vision, of the time frame required by Rabbi Akiva's optimism, and the complexity of offering an interpretation in keeping with his approach to difficult and painful experiences. We can easily imagine the state of mind of Rabbi Akiva and his companions as they journey toward the Temple Mount. Coming from the north, they reach Mount Scopus, where they behold the Temple Mount in ruins and tear their clothes. They go on, slowly approaching the site of the destroyed Temple, flooded with difficult emotions and a deep sadness. When they finally reach the Temple Mount itself, they see the holy place in all its desolation, and a fox emerges from the site where the Holy of Holies once stood. They have witnessed the words of Jeremiah in the book of *Lamentations* (5:17-18) fulfilled: "For this our heart is faint; for these things our eyes are dim. Because of the mountain of Zion, which is desolate, the foxes walk upon it." Their eyes are indeed dim and their hearts faint, and they burst into tears. As they are weeping however, Rabbi Akiva laughs! What greater contrast could there be than the sight of one man rejoicing in the face of the others' terrible pain and sadness? While they are still reeling from the effect of what they have seen, Rabbi Akiva relates the situation to the sum total of his experience and understanding, resulting in an entirely different response on his part. Throughout their journey to Jerusalem, and particularly as they walked from Mount Scopus to the Temple Mount, Rabbi Akiva shared his friends' feelings. It was the fox emerging from the Holy of Holies however that made it clear to him that just as the prophecies of destruction were coming true before his eyes, so would the prophecies of comfort and future redemption come true.

---

[51]　See also *Sifre, Devarim* 43; *Eichah Rabati* 5, 18.

Rabbi Akiva's analysis, his approach to this difficult experience and his unique perspective are accepted by his friends: "Akiva you have comforted us. Akiva you have comforted us."

Rabbi Akiva's approach to misfortune and suffering can be summarised as follows:

1. "All is foreseen and freedom is granted": "Soft determinism" that enables one to accept reality without resentment and almost without recourse to avoidance or denial, making it possible to view difficult events in a positive light. Reality is a preordained result of divine knowledge and providence, and must therefore be accepted as is. The words of the Prophets and especially the comfort prophecies — as revelations of divine knowledge — can serve as a prism through which to view reality, discover signs of redemption, and interpret events optimistically. Soft determinism is expressed in the principle of free choice, i.e. although all is foreseen and predetermined, man is still given the freedom to choose between good and evil. Reality is given, and man is measured by her/his moral behaviour, which is neither given nor imposed, but solely the responsibility of the individual. "All is foreseen and freedom is granted" is one of the most ancient and wonderful expressions of the belief in both freedom and determinism, which together shape reality. This approach enables man to focus on the moral behaviour that stems from free choice and individual responsibility. Even immutable circumstances offer the opportunity to contend with them in one's own way, to choose the path of virtue, and cast every situation, as difficult as it might be, in a positive light.[52]

2. "The world is judged with kindness and all in accordance with the preponderance of deeds": Deterministic reality does not relieve man of the responsibility to account for her/his actions, since these are the result of free choice. Nevertheless, Rabbi Akiva's optimistic approach draws encouragement from two other articles of faith: first, that God judges man with kindness and compassion, i.e. with the quality of compassion rather than that of judgement, in the spirit of the verse "slow to anger and abundant in goodness (*Exodus* 34:6), and in *Psalms* (*Ps* 145:9) "The Lord is good to all"; and secondly that man is judged according to the extent of her/his commitment to doing the right thing, and the worthy acts s/he has performed. The fact that man must account for her/his actions is not a source of fear and despair but of hope and optimism, since good deeds will be rewarded. One has the ability to take action, to do good deeds, and on their strength, to merit a favourable judgement.

---

[52] See Y. Leibowitz, *Sihot Al Pirkei Avot Ve'al Harambam* pp. 100-114.

3. "All that God does is for the best": Since reality proceeds from divine knowledge and providence, and God acts only for the best, the negative phenomena we perceive — misfortune and suffering on both a personal and national level — are merely the result of subjective and incomplete understanding. A broader and more far-reaching analysis of reality would show that the temporary evil is but a phase or a part of a divine plan that is wholly good. The perceived misfortune is but one aspect of reality, and never the complete picture. Time and personal experience will demonstrate that the event, as difficult and hopeless as it may appear, has occurred only that relief and salvation might be effected at a later date. If personal experience is inadequate, reality should be analysed in the spirit of the prophecies or one's own positive insight, unrelated to the events themselves. And if all else fails, there is always the final option: "beloved is suffering".

4. "Beloved is suffering": Human perception, limited as it is, can view the misfortune and suffering that befall us in a negative light. Consummate faith and certainty that God acts only for the best must lead to understanding that suffering can only be a manifestation of divine goodness. Suffering affords the righteous an opportunity to atone for some of the sins that they have nevertheless committed in this world. It is an expression of God's love for the righteous, who accept it with love.

5. "They began to cry and Rabbi Akiva to laugh": The way in which one relates to a difficult, saddening and depressing experience, should go beyond the situation at hand. It's meaning should be examined in light of the words of the Prophets and used to create hope for the future.

The sage of love's optimistic approach comes from love, love of God and love of one's fellow man: love of God whatever lot he has meted out, and love of one's fellow man — for whom only an all-encompassing, positive and true perspective can provide the strength and encouragement to cope with difficult circumstances in the hope of a better future.

Chapter Eight
ULTIMATE LOVE

The passing of sages in general and the execution of the Ten Martyrs in particular feature prominently in talmudic and midrashic legend. Rabbi Akiva's death however, would seem to have left a greater impression in the rabbinical sources than the deaths of all of the other *tanaim* and *amoraim*. The legends about Rabbi Akiva's death contend with two main dilemmas. The first: horror at his cruel end, the manner in which this very old man — 120 years old according to legend[53] — was executed. The dilemma here pertains to the issue of theodicy, in the case of one who lived a long and full life and came to such a terrible end. The second dilemma concerns the meaning of the death of someone who strove so hard to give meaning to his life, and especially to the suffering and misfortune that befell him throughout it. Life is the ground upon which meaning is built, and when it comes to a close, is death meaningless?

According to legend, Adam was the first to see the lack of sense in Rabbi Akiva's death: "When he came to the generation of Rabbi Akiva, he rejoiced in his Torah and was saddened by his death" (*Avodah Zarah* 5a; *Sanhedrin* 38b). Another well-known legend that tells of Moses' encounter with Rabbi Akiva, greatly heightens the dilemma regarding his death:

> "Rabbi Yehudah said in the name of Rav: When Moses ascended to heaven, he found God sitting and tying crowns to the letters. He said to him: 'Master of the Universe, who requires this of you?' He said to him: 'There is a man who will live in a few generations and Akiva ben Joseph is his name, who will learn mounds and mounds of laws from each cusp . . . ' He [Moses] said to him: 'Master of the Universe, You have shown me the Torah; show me its reward!' He said to him: 'Look behind you'. He looked behind him and saw them weighing his flesh in the market. He said to him: 'Master of the Universe, is this the Torah and is this its reward?' He said to him: 'Silence! That is how I conceived it.'"

> BT, *Menahot* 29b

There is not even a pretext of theodicy in this text, just arbitrary and unthinking acceptance of God's decree. The bluntness of God's answer to Moses heightens the pointlessness of theodicy and strengthens the sense of injustice at the death of Rabbi Akiva. That is why it is Moses' resounding statement — "this is the Torah and this is its reward?!" — that remains in the reader's mind, rather than God's unequivocal and unacceptable response. Although God's answer is explained by some to mean "do not contemplate that which you cannot understand", we must remember that it was said to Moses, and not just any prophet or sage. One might conclude that if this is what was said to Moses, how much more so it must apply to everyone else. This is not however, the natural mindset that has brought readers to fix Moses' anguished question/cry "this is the Torah and this is its reward?!" in their minds.

---

[53] According to legend, Rabbi Akiva began studying at the age of forty, studied Torah for forty years, and served Israel for forty years. See Midrash, *Bereshit Rabbah* 100; *Avot deRabbi Natan* vers. 2, 12. Historians see in the number 120 a tradition deriving from Moses, and attributed to a number of prominent sages, including Rabbi Akiva. See eg. Shmuel Safrai, *op. cit.*, pp. 10-14. Even if the number 120 is apocryphal however, historians estimate that Rabbi Akiva was about 85 years old at the time of his death.

Rather surprisingly, one of the later midrashists placed words of theodicy at this horrifying death, in the mouth of Rabbi Akiva himself:

> "And then they brought out Rabbi Akiva ben Joseph, who learned from the crowns of the letters and discovered facets of the Torah as they were given to Moses in Sinai . . . And they combed his flesh with iron combs. And with every stroke of the combs Rabbi Akiva would say: 'The Rock, His work is perfect; for all His ways are justice; a God of faithfulness and without iniquity, just and right is He.' A heavenly voice was heard to say: Fortunate are you Rabbi Akiva who were just and right and your soul departed with [the words] 'just and right.'"
>
> *"Eleh Ezkerah", Otzar Midrashim* (Eisenstein) 2, p. 442

According to this *midrash*, the same Rabbi Akiva who had accepted God's judgement when suffering befell him during the course of his life, saying "beloved is suffering", did so at the time of his death as well. There is indeed no greater theodicy than this, for if he justifies his own execution, who can possibly reiterate Moses' question "this is the Torah and this is its reward"? The *midrash* further explains the concept of theodicy that is not addressed to God, like Moses' question, but lies in the individual's acceptance of the Judgments he has been given, and is therefore addressed to man. The verse "the Rock, His work is perfect; for all His ways are justice; a God of faithfulness and without iniquity, just and right is He" is taken from the admonitions delivered by Moses in the Torah portion of *Ha'azinu* (*Deuteronomy* 32:4), and the following verse lays full responsibility upon man: "Is corruption His? No; His children's is the blemish; a generation crooked and perverse." Just as Rabbi Akiva was able to say to Rabbi Eliezer: "you have taught us Rabbi (*Ecclesiastes* 7:20): 'for there is not a righteous man upon earth that doeth good and sinneth not'," he was able to apply the same principle to himself and accept his judgement with love. His entire life was about accepting one's judgement and misfortune with love. In accepting his judgement at the hour of his death, he consummated his life's philosophy.

The *midrash* that attests to Rabbi Akiva's theodicy however, is not a central source capable of influencing the views engendered by the entire range of sources that discuss Rabbi Akiva's death. This legend does not appear alongside the talmudic or midrashic legends that tell the story of Rabbi Akiva, but rather in a later work, entirely devoted to the matter of theodicy with regard to the deaths of the Ten Martyrs. So that even if we were to claim that the author had found an appropriate answer to Moses' resounding question — "this is the Torah and this is its reward" — if this indeed resolves the dilemma of the brutal killing itself from a theodical perspective, the question of meaning still remains. Meaning — so important to Rabbi Akiva in his lifetime and at the heart of the earlier *midrashim* that deal with his philosophy and life story — remained a mystery at his death.

The meaning of Rabbi Akiva's death is in fact discussed in a number of places. Some, like the following text, directly relate to his image as the sage of love:

> "The time at which Rabbi Akiva was taken to be executed was the appointed hour for reciting the *Shema*. As they were combing his flesh with combs of iron, he accepted the yoke of heaven, and his students said to him: Rabbi, even now?! He said to them: All my days I grieved at the words 'with all thy soul' (*Deuteronomy* 6:5) — even when it is taken from you. I said: when will I have the opportunity to fulfil this? And now that the opportunity presents itself will I not fulfil it? He drew out [the word] 'one' (*ehad*) until his soul departed on 'one.'"
>
> BT, *Berakhot* 61a[54]

The sage of love gave his final lesson on the philosophy of love at the moment of his execution. His students — who during the years of their studies had learned from him that suffering was beloved — were unable to come to terms with his death. They who had been at his side at the time of his son's death, and even then wondered at his behaviour, find it difficult to maintain their composure, but cannot do otherwise — in light of their rabbi's equanimity. Had they wanted to cry or shout, they could not have done so in the presence of this man, who serenely and devotedly accepted the yoke of heaven while being tortured to death.[55] These circumstances were unlike any they had experienced or learned with Rabbi Akiva before. Even when a person suffers terrible anguish, even when great misfortunes befall him, he is still a living, breathing person, beyond the anguish and the misfortune. The meaning of suffering lies in life itself, and is afforded by the living. We can thus understand, albeit with great difficulty, theodicy and the acceptance of suffering, based on the distinction between the afflicted and the affliction, and based on the hope that one might attain redemption through suffering and from suffering. Here, in the execution of Rabbi Akiva, they experience in an absolute and irreversible fashion, a situation

---

[54] JT, *Berakhot* 9, 14b reads as follows: "Rabbi Akiva was condemned by the wicked Turnus Rufus, and the time to recite the *Shema* came, and he began to recite the *Shema* and laugh. He said to him: Old man, either you are a sorcerer, or you scoff at suffering. He said to him — may that man give up the ghost — I am not a sorcerer, nor do I scoff at suffering, rather all my days I have read this verse and grieved, asking when I would have the opportunity to fulfil all three — 'thou shalt love the Lord thy God with all thy heart, and with all thy soul, and with all thy might'. I had loved Him with all my heart, and I had loved Him with all my possessions, but never with all my soul. And now that I have the opportunity [to love God] with all my soul, and the time to recite the *Shema* has come and my mind is not distracted — that is why I recite and laugh. No sooner had he spoken than his soul departed." See also JT, *Sotah* 5, 20c.

[55] *Cf.* Plato, *Phaedo* 117-118: the description of Socrates' death. His friends burst into tears and he rebukes them. There too it seems as if the circumstances weigh more heavily upon those who remain than upon Socrates himself, who remained calm until the very end.

in which one can no longer distinguish between the man and his fate — which is to cease being a man. Everything they had learned from their teacher up to this point, about theodicy and the meaning of suffering, is no longer applicable, because all they had learned had meaning only for someone who lives in this world. The meaning is manifested in moral behaviour, in observing the commandments and in living up to one's obligations as a human being. Even when unbearable, it is still existence as opposed to non-existence, i.e. the abrogation of existence, that is death.

They watch him as he is executed, with admiration, deep sorrow, anxiety at the imminent separation and their approaching orphanhood. Terribly disturbed by the loss of meaning however, as faithful students who have internalised his philosophy of meaning, they turn to him with a question/cry: "Rabbi, even now?!" Now, as you are being executed and are a hairsbreadth from certain death, have you not reached the point of meaninglessness? Do you even now hold fast to your principles? Do you even now accept God's judgement?

And Rabbi Akiva, clearly, precisely and simply, explains to his students the meaning of his death: love. Ultimate love! The Torah is the Torah of love and its commandment is to love God, and rarely does the opportunity arise to observe this commandment completely. "All my days I grieved at the words 'with all thy soul'" — as the sage of love, Rabbi Akiva well knew that man cannot fully observe love's most important commandment — to love God — and for this he grieved all his life.[56] "And now that the opportunity presents itself will I not fulfil it?" Nothing can compare to doing the right thing — in affording ultimate meaning to something that is in this case the ultimate moment of life — "with all thy soul' (*Deuteronomy* 6:5) — even when it is taken from you!"

As the legionnaires comb his flesh with iron combs to end his life in terrible agony, he accepts the yoke of heaven and teaches — in word and deed — the meaning of his death. This amazing discussion between Rabbi Akiva and his students however, seems to be missing one fundamental element: He chooses not to give the most crucial and obvious answer: life after death. He could have told them that there is no loss of meaning, because the body is merely a vessel, and the soul returns to its source. At the most obvious time however, he does not

---

[56]   It is possible however, to understand from the texts that he was given the opportunity to prepare for this moment at a certain point. BT, *Sanhedrin* 68a reads: "We have learned [in the *beraita*]: When Rabbi Eliezer fell ill, Rabbi Akiva and his friends came to see him . . . He said to them: Why have you come? They said to him: We have come to learn Torah. He said to them: And why have you not come until now? They said to him: We did not have the time. He said to them: I wonder whether they will die natural deaths. Rabbi Akiva said to him: What will mine be? He said to him: Yours will be harder than theirs." The background for this conversation is a visit by Rabbi Akiva and his friends to the bedside of Rabbi Eliezer ben Hyrcanus, whom they had refrained from visiting previously because he had been excommunicated. See also BT, *Bava Metzia* 60b.

resort to belief in the world to come, eschewing the easy solution to the problem of meaning in his death. His emphasis is on what one can still do in this world: to complete the commandment to love God. To his mind, meaning must be sought in life itself and not beyond it. Here too he is consistent, just as he was at the bedside of his teacher, Rabbi Eliezer ben Hyrcanus, as he lay in his death throes. His friends, Rabbi Yehoshua, Rabbi Tarfon and Rabbi Elazar ben Azariah, also present at their teacher's bedside, rose above the smallness of the moment, the pain and suffering, to speak of eternal life and the immortal soul: "and my master is in this world and the next". Rabbi Akiva on the other hand, frankly and determinedly returned Rabbi Elazar to reality, with all its difficulties, as the only place in which man can find meaning — preventing him from escaping for even a single moment to the world of eternity and immortality. "Beloved is suffering" here and now, because of the moral opportunity it provides for true introspection, and for accepting it with love. Even at his own death, he does not want to escape the final terrible moments to the tranquility of the hereafter. He finds his peace in these very moments and the moral challenge they present — a challenge that only life in this world can offer.

It is interesting to compare the discussion between Rabbi Akiva and his students during his execution, and Socrates' discourse with his friends, as the time approached for him to drink the cup of hemlock — in connection with the immortality of the soul.[57] The equanimity with which both men accept their deaths stands in sharp contrast to the agitation of those around them. Rabbi Akiva, who is executed in terrible agony, accepts the yoke of heaven with composure and devotion. His students cannot allow themselves to cry out or weep in the face of their rabbi's composure. Socrates' friends burst into tears, and he rebukes them. There too it seems as if the circumstances weigh more heavily upon those who remain than upon Socrates himself, who remained calm until the very end. The similarity between the two stories ends however, at the composure with which the protagonists accept their deaths. The two discussions regarding the meaning of death and the source of comfort are fundamentally different.

Plato's dialogue also addresses political issues pertaining to government and law that have no parallel in our story. The crux of the discussion however, is Socrates' choice to comfort his friends with the knowledge that his death is not final insofar as his human essence — i.e. his soul — is concerned. Accordingly, the conclusions that he draws pertain to morality:

"But then, O my friends, he said, if the soul is really immortal, what care should be taken of her, not only in respect of the portion of time which is called life, but of eternity! And the danger of neglecting her from this point of view does indeed

---

[57] Plato, *Phaedo, ibid.*

appear to be awful. If death had only been the end of all, the wicked would have had a good bargain in dying, for they would have been happily quit not only of their body, but of their own evil together with their souls. But now, as the soul plainly appears to be immortal, there is no release or salvation from evil except the attainment of the highest virtue and wisdom."

Plato, Phaedon 106-107 (tr. Benjamin Jowett)

In the discussion, he seeks to prove the immortality of the soul, and the body's perishable, ephemeral nature. Socrates (according to Plato) presents theological/ metaphysical arguments, from which he draws moral conclusions, whereas Rabbi Akiva (who in principle does not disagree with Socrates) has no recourse to theology, focusing entirely upon moral arguments. Despite Socrates' moral conclusions however, the main thrust of his parting discourse is his assertion that death is merely a passage to immortality:

"But I do say that, inasmuch as the soul is shown to be immortal . . . let a man be of good cheer about his soul, who hast cast away the pleasures and ornaments of the body . . . and has followed after the pleasures of knowledge in this life; who has adorned the soul in her own proper jewels, which are temperance, and justice, and courage, and nobility, and truth—in these arrayed she is ready to go on her journey to the world below, when her time comes."

Ibid.

He comforts his friends, telling them that they should not grieve at the interment of his body: "I would not have him . . . say at the burial, Thus we lay out Socrates, or, Thus we follow him to the grave or bury him". He does not cling to life, and does not delay drinking the poison until the last possible minute — further emphasising the fact that his death derives its meaning not from life itself, but from the immortality of the soul:

"I do not think that I should gain anything by drinking the poison a little later; I should be sparing and saving a life which is already gone: I could only laugh at myself for this."

Ibid. 621

From the moment that he has come to terms with his death, Socrates no longer values life: what is another hour of life as compared to eternity? It is in these few minutes that we discover the difference between Socrates and Rabbi Akiva. Rabbi Akiva cherishes the most terrible moments of his life, refusing to cease pursuing his moral objective in this world for even a single instant. Socrates believes that man enters this world unwillingly and must strive to live in a good and fitting manner, but there is no point in clinging to life when eternity is so close at hand. When man is about to coalesce with ultimate meaning, he can only laugh at himself for trying to give meaning to another few moments of life.

The differences between these two positions can be summed up in the words of Rabbi Ya'akov Kurshai, teacher of Rabbi Yehudah Hanasi, who offers no solution:

> "One hour spent in repentance and good deeds in this world is better than the whole of life of the world to come; and one hour of satisfaction in the world to come is better than the whole of life in this world."

Mishnah, Avot 4, 22

There is no equivalence between "repentance and good deeds", which are moral objectives; and "satisfaction", which is spiritual fulfilment, because they belong to different worlds. It is therefore up to man to choose between them: Rabbi Akiva decided in favour of one hour spent in repentance and good deeds in this world, and Socrates in favour of an hour of satisfaction in the world to come. In his final words however, Socrates momentarily returns the moral argument to the fore, although in a rather ludicrous way, as if the author (Plato) did not wish to eclipse his earlier message: "I owe a cock to Asclepius; will you remember to pay the debt?" (*Phaedo* 118). It is as if he were saying: "I am going on a journey to eternity with the good deeds I have accrued for my soul in my lifetime. You who continue to live still have a moral obligation". In fact, the cock in question was an offering of thanksgiving to the God of healing for having given him a healthy life. In this context one could say, despite the irreverence in the comparison, that Socrates too returned his soul to his God with an affirmation of his connection to the divine. The focus of Socrates' discussion with his friends however remains essentially different from that of Rabbi Akiva and his students. For Socrates, immortality of the soul is the source of meaning; for Rabbi Akiva there exists only the moral dimension.

In his usual fashion, Rabbi Akiva is not interested in a theoretical discussion of moral behaviour, but in its practice — like the time when he cared for a sick student, washing him, seeing to his needs and saving his life; and only then passing from practice to theory, to teach that one who does not visit the sick it is as if he has shed blood. On other occasions as well, his moral conduct was based upon the principle of combining practice and teaching. So too his final lesson in the philosophy of love, on the complete fulfilment of the commandment to love God, incorporated both theory and practice: "He accepted the yoke of heaven . . . He drew out [the word] 'one' (*ehad*) until his soul departed on 'one'." He actively fulfils the commandment, as he explains its theoretical basis to his students: "All my days I grieved at the words 'with all thy soul' — even when it is taken from you. I said: when will I have the opportunity **to fulfil** this?" He accepts the yoke of heaven, reads the *Shema*, and draws out the word *ehad*, and the completion of the commandment merges with the departure of his soul — thereby actively fulfilling the verse "and thou shalt love the Lord thy God . . . with all thy soul". At that very moment, his life is taken as he fulfils the commandment to accept the yoke of heaven and love God. "He drew out [the word] 'one' (*ehad*) until his soul departed on 'one.'" With all the strength in his body, with all the force of his spirit, with immeasurable love of God, he devoted his final breath to 'one'. "And thou shalt love the Lord thy God with all thine heart, and with all thy soul, and with all thy might" — ultimate love.

Chapter Nine

THE ORCHARD OF LOVE

> "The Rabbis taught: Four entered the (esoteric) Orchard, and they were: Ben Azai, Ben Zoma, *Aher* and Rabbi Akiva. Rabbi Akiva said to them: 'When you reach the stones of pure marble, do not say 'Water water!' because it is written 'he that telleth lies shall not tarry in my sight' (*Psalms* 101:7).' Ben Azai glimpsed and died . . . Ben Zoma glimpsed and was harmed . . . *Aher* slashed among the plants, Rabbi Akiva emerged safely."
>
> BT, *Hagigah* 14b

According to legend, of all the rabbis, only Rabbi Akiva entered the Orchard and emerged from it in safety. Entry into the Orchard should not be seen as a specific event, but a way of life. Rabbi Akiva's death, his comportment at the time of his execution, also constituted entry into the Orchard, and perhaps even its climax.

"For the righteous are called living even in their deaths" (*Otzar Midrashim*, Eisenstein, p. 194)[58] — not "after their deaths", but "in their deaths", when — like Rabbi Akiva — they make their very deaths into life. He emerged safely from his death and the great suffering he endured, transforming the terrible cessation of life into a source of self-perfection and the basis of his connection with eternity.

Rabbi Akiva attributed this unique spiritual achievement — entering and emerging from the esoteric orchard — not to his intellectual achievements, his Torah scholarship or his spiritual accomplishments, but to his moral conduct:

---

[58]   According to *Midrashei Haser Veyater*: A. Berliner, *Peletath Soferim*.

"He [Rabbi Akiva] said: 'Not because I am greater than my fellows, rather the Rabbis taught in the Mishnah: 'your deeds will draw you near and your deeds will distance you'; and of this it is written (*Song of Songs* 1:4): 'the king hath brought me into his chambers: we will be glad and rejoice in thee.''"

Midrash, Shir Hashirim Rabbah 1, 28

Perfection of intellect alone cannot provide the perfection of judgement required by one who enters the Orchard. Consummate intellect enables those who have attained it to enter the Orchard, but it cannot assure that they will emerge safely from it. Perfection of deed complements perfection of knowledge, and Rabbi Akiva, who was perfect in knowledge and perfect in deed, entered and emerged safely. He thus renders the unique spiritual plane to which he alone of all the rabbis ascended, an attainable goal for all Jews. Anyone can have a share in the Orchard and all may approach it through their deeds. While in the eyes of many, knowledge, and especially esoteric knowledge, appears to be the greatest impediment to entering the Orchard, this legend teaches us that entry is within reasonable grasp. The question is not whether it is possible to enter and who may do so, but how to enter in such a manner as to be able to emerge in safety as well.

Love is the driving force behind moral perfection upon which perfection of deed depends, whether action deriving from love of God or actions associated with love of one's fellow man. It is no coincidence that the *midrash* cites a verse from *Song of Songs*, which states that his way is "paved with love": the way to the Orchard, entering it, being there, and emerging from it in safety—all depend upon love, the kind of love that begets worthy deeds. By virtue of the passion in "draw me after thee"—that flows from love of God—all human energy, the full force of "we will run", is harnessed to acting in a worthy fashion:

"Rabbi Akiva ascended and descended in safety, of him the verse says (*Song of Songs* 1:4): 'Draw me after thee, we will run: the king hath brought me into his chambers'.

Tosefta Hagigah 2, 2[59]

The orchard Rabbi Akiva entered and from which he emerged in safety can thus be called the "Orchard of Love", analogous to the orchard in the *Song of Songs* (4:12-13): "A garden shut up is my sister, my bride; a spring shut up, a fountain sealed. Thy shoots are an orchard of pomegranates . . . ". The 'garden shut up' is closed to all but a few remarkable individuals; the 'spring shut up'—evokes the image of the "stones of pure marble" that look like water, but of which one must not say they are water; because "thy shoots"—pools of water that look like water are in reality an orchard of pomegranates . . .

---

[59]   BT, *Hagigah* 14b; JT, *Hagigah* 2, 5.

The Orchard is the plane on which the sage of love's perfection in thought and deed receives expression. Rabbi Akiva's perfect philosophy of love was measured by his deeds, and brought him to attain his unique and exalted place, as one who safely entered and emerged from the Orchard of Love.

Chapter Ten
SUMMARY: THE UNIVERSAL SAGE

Aggadic chronology first introduces Rabbi Akiva ben Joseph to the world and to posterity in a love story. Rachel's love drew out Rabbi Akiva's wisdom and moral perfection, making his Torah and that of his students throughout the generations hers. The sage of love is a woman's creation, since it is a woman's love that begot his wisdom.

Rabbi Akiva "rescued" the *Song of Songs* from oblivion, giving human culture one of its finest and most profound works of love, which has been a source of inspiration for poets and other artists from the very beginning. He brought love into the *sanctum sanctorum*, and created a hierarchy of holiness, with love between man and woman, as depicted in the *Song of Songs*, at its highest level. All other levels of holiness flow from this holy of holies, draw upon it, and are defined in relation to it.

Rabbi Akiva's standing as the sage of love is manifest in a series of halakhic rulings, e.g. in overturning the first sages' decree prohibiting a woman's adornment and use of cosmetics while in a state of menstrual impurity; in establishing clear halakhic guidelines for marriage based on compatibility and harmony between partners; in his lenient approach to divorce; in allowing a woman to remarry based on the testimony of single witness; in accepting *halitzah* (the ceremony releasing a widow and her brother-in-law from their levirate obligations) performed in private, etc. He formulated the principles of marital harmony and declared that perfection can only be achieved through marriage, through the "union" of two: perfection not merely of the union itself, but more broadly defined as a state of harmony characterised by a connection with the spiritually sublime, evoking the presence and involvement of the *Shekhinah* that is sustained by that presence.

Rabbinical literature offers more than just Rabbi Akiva's halakhic and philosophical statements as the sage of love, and the story of his love for Rachel. The sources wished to teach us that he was a man of strong desires, who also possessed the ability to uphold his moral principles. We have seen that one who believes in love as the supreme expression of humanity cannot tolerate its degradation in the form of immediate and partial gratification. Thought and theory were not enough for Rabbi Akiva, who also met with and resisted temptation.

In a discussion concerning the categorical imperative from which all morality derives, Rabbi Akiva asserted that "love thy fellow as thyself" is the greatest principle in the Torah, and the basis of socialisation. The ability to love another requires that one first love oneself. Love of self can develop in two possible ways. One can allow the ego to take control of the man — such love tends to burn itself out; or one can love others, exercising responsibility toward them, performing act of kindness for them — such inter-personal relations eventually develop into love for all human beings created in God's image. "Love thy fellow" strengthens "thyself", and love of oneself provides a solid basis, a mainstay, for love of others. Socialisation based upon "love thy fellow" is in fact a system of love ties between people and themselves that sustain and strengthen one another.

He who first appeared on the stage of history in a love story; who rescued the masterpiece *Song of Songs* — the love poem par excellence — and established its standing in the Holy of Holies; who developed a philosophical and practical system of marital harmony, was stringent in love and lenient in divorce, and resolute in giving love the chance to begin anew; who saw love between man and woman as sacred perfection of body, mind and spirit, and utterly rejected the degradation of love; who withstood temptation and did not give in to desires that demanded immediate and partial gratification; who asserted that "love thy fellow as thyself" is the great principle from which all morality derives; who was known for his love and devotion to his students, was "champion of the poor" and engaged in charity and acts of kindness; who preached love for all who were created in God's image; who accepted all of the misfortunes that befell him with love, and coined the expression "beloved is suffering"; who with every fibre of his being perfectly fulfilled the commandment to love God, loving Him with all his heart, with all his might and with all his soul, even when his life was taken — an expression of ultimate love; such a man, Rabbi Akiva ben Joseph, is worthy of the title sage of love.

THE SAGE OF UNCONSUMMATED LOVE: JUDAH ABRAVANEL'S *DIALOGHI D'AMORE*

Chapter One

INTRODUCTION: PHILO AND SOPHIA

Philo, the sage of love we will discuss in this section, is a literary figure. The great sages of Judaism and humanity are also literary figures, and we relate to the legends about them without committing ourselves to the veracity of the facts they contain, or even addressing the importance of ascertaining their veracity. The great sages of old however, are also prominent historical figures, and the literature that serves as a source of information about them usually enjoys canonical status. Philo, on the other hand, remains the protagonist of a single literary work: Judah Abravanel's *Dialoghi d'amore*.[1]

Abravanel is the only Jewish philosopher to have devoted an entire book to the subject of love, and for whom it is his main literary endeavour. The book comprises three tension-laden dialogues between a pair of lovers: **Philo**, the man who knows more than anyone about love, is not satisfied with platonic love and wishes to consummate his desire and physically unite with his beloved; and **Sophia**, the woman who fears that should she acquiesce to her beloved's desire and her own passions, their pure spiritual love would vanish and be no more. The difference between the intentions of the two protagonists makes this philosophical treatise into a thriller: will the sage of love succeed in consummating his love?!

---

[1] The *Dialoghi d'amore* di Maestro Leon Medico Hebreo, first appeared in Naples in 1535. By 1607, it had been reprinted 26 times, in four languages: twelve editions in Italian, six in French, six in Spanish, and two in Latin. The large number of reprints was due to the fact that the *Dialoghi d'amore* was in considerable demand at the time. The work exerted a great deal of influence, but practically disappeared in the 17th century. For the latest Hebrew edition, see Yehudah Abravanel, *Sihot al HaAhavah* (translation, introduction and notes by Menahem Dorman), 1983.

The names of the two characters are of course symbolic, and derive from the word *philo-sophia*: love of wisdom. Philo thus represents love, and Sophia wisdom. As we see from the story however, things are not quite that simple. Philo wants to consummate his love for Sophia and unite with her in body, while Sophia is interested in a platonic relationship, in studying together — so that their respective names would appear to be appropriate. In fact however, Philo is the source of knowledge and understanding, and Sophia is usually content with her role as the seeker of knowledge who asks questions and awaits their answers. What then is love (*philo*) and what is wisdom (*sophia*)? Is love not the longing to know, the ability to ask, wonder, the curiosity represented by Sophia? And is wisdom not the knowledge, erudition, and reasoning represented by Philo?

Philo, as we have said, wishes to actively consummate his love — in what is called *vita activa*. Sophia represents intellectual contemplation and study — known as *vita contemplativa*. These two terms, as they are generally understood and applied, entail an inherent value judgement in favour of the latter way of life over the former, as the better path to virtue. The positions have been reversed in societies that have held pure study in contempt, considering it to be little more than idleness, and as such immoral.

Some commentators have rejected this simple view of the protagonists of the *Dialoghi*, viewing Philo rather as "form", and Sophia as "matter". In the dialogues, it is in fact Philo who is the source of knowledge, the one who provides the definitions, and Sophia who affords him the opportunity to do so. It may be that Philo does not represent love itself, as his name ostensibly suggests, but rather the longing and searching for it; and similarly, Sophia does not represent wisdom, but the search for wisdom. Their names thus express the desire for love and the desire for wisdom — that converge in their discussions.

As opposed to their respective views regarding the consummation of their love, what they actually represent cannot be described in a dichotomous fashion. Sophia appears as a "midwife", who helps Philo bring knowledge, the wisdom of love, into the world. In this sense, Sophia — wisdom — plays Socrates in Abravanel's dialogue. She represents one who seeks knowledge, the eros and the Parakletos — the forerunner, who inspires her interlocutor or audience to follow the path that she has devised, the direction she has indicated for contemplation and philosophical life. Like Socrates, she offers no assertions, opinions or conclusions, satisfied merely to serve as a guide. She follows the Socratic method inasmuch as she adheres to the patterns familiar to us from the Platonic dialogues: she first arouses her partner's desire to investigate the matter at hand; she then seeks to establish rules for the acquisition of knowledge; and finally, like a midwife, helps him to bring knowledge — the wisdom of love — into the world. To Sophia's mind, the intellectual Socratic process is the perfect act of love. It comprises infatuation, courtship, desire, consummation, and — in the birth of knowledge — even bears fruit. Sophia is not the only Socrates in Abravanel's work however. Philo, the authority on love, is also Socrates, who said of himself: "I profess to understand nothing but matters of love" (Plato, *Symposium*).

Judah Abravanel's philosophy is thus not about the "love of wisdom" but about the "wisdom of love". The philosopher Philo is not a "lover of wisdom", but a "sage of love", and like Rabbi Akiva, whose being stems from the love of Rachel, Philo is also the creation of a woman. It is Sophia who makes Philo the sage of love.

Chapter Two

THE SAGE'S DESIRE

"Knowing you, Sophia, arouses in me love and desire." In his very first statement, Philo shatters a philosophical construct, the product of centuries of intellectual endeavour. I refer to the tremendous efforts invested by Christian philosophers and theologians (also influenced by their Jewish and Muslim counterparts) from the Church Fathers to the end of the Middle Ages, in transforming love, from something concrete that occurs between real men and women, to an abstract concept. Love's proper place, as an abstract concept, was in conceptual discussions, properly applied solely in the realm of the spiritual and the universal. In such contexts it was acceptable to slip in a biblical reference here and there, in which love between man and woman is mentioned, on condition that it never be allowed beyond its allegorical meaning — in keeping with the principle: "a verse never departs from its hermeneutical interpretation . . .".

This kind of extreme insularity however, could only be maintained outwardly. Puritanical control achieved through severe censorship, in fact opened the way for change. Human creativity cannot tolerate for long, a situation in which the last word on everything has already been said. Philosophers, writers, poets and artists cannot help but originate: originality is the *sine qua non* of their work, ready to burst forth the moment the siege is laid and a sense of total repression descends. If you will, here is an explanation (extraneous to historical analysis) of the burst of cultural creativity that "made" the Renaissance. If mediaeval thought "succeeded" in making love purely a concept, it was only a matter of time before a writer, philosopher or poet came along and reopened the discussion of love as an abstract concept versus its realisation and application to men and women.

As noted above, love and desire are intertwined in the very first sentence of the *Dialoghi d'amore*:

Philo: "Knowing you, Sophia, arouses in me love and desire."

Sophia: "To me it seems, Philo, that knowing me arouses in you contradictory feelings, but perhaps it is lust that brings you to say such things."

Philo: "It is your words that are contradictory and lack all coherence."

Sophia: "Not because they contradict one another. Love and desire are contrary voluntary emotions."

Dialoghi d'amore (Hebrew edition, M. Dorman ed.) p. 185

Philo begins by showering his love with terms of endearment — I love you and desire you; but also a good deal more: it is you who arouse in me these feelings of love and desire for you. To the reader's surprise, Sophia does not take up the love challenge, as one might expect. Rather than responding to his words of love, she refuses to see them as an expression of love for her, because he has linked love and desire (although she is willing to concede that he also loves her, asserting that his knowing her has aroused contradictory feelings in him). What she hears is words that arise from "lust", motivated by desire and passion. She believes that love and desire are contradictory feelings: if there is love there is no desire, and if there is desire there is no love. We love that which we have and desire what we have not yet obtained. These are therefore, to her mind, contradictory feelings: a man loves his wife, while he covets and desires another woman. Sophia's words also intimate that as far as she is concerned, Philo still has a long way to go to prove that he is not "like all men" — unfaithful to the object of his love, even when she is his wife. Sophia expresses her fear that once her beloved has achieved his goal and consummated his desire, his love will dissipate. Here too we can see how greatly she values his love for her. She wishes to make it eternal through intellectual inquiry, and fears that if he is allowed to fulfil his desire, he will cease loving her.

In the initial stages of the debate, Philo becomes impatient and weary, since he is unwillingly dragged into a philosophical discussion, when his interest lies in practical love. Expecting an enthusiastic response to his declaration, he is disturbed by the direction in which Sophia leads the conversation: a re-examination of the semantic validity of his words — based, in his opinion, on false premises. He has two choices: to reiterate his words of endearment and profession of love in a romantic fashion, or to present his argument and quickly bring her back to what he considers important. He chooses the second option, but fails to achieve his goal. He thus loses his way completely, and unwittingly follows the path that she has charted:

"Your arguments, Sophia, prove the keenness of your mind more than the truth of your views . . . I have come to you, Sophia, in search of a cure for my suffering, and you ask me for a solution to your doubts. Perhaps you do so in order to distract me from a matter you consider undesirable, or perhaps you care as little for my poor opinion as you do for my ardent longing."

Ibid. p. 186

Once again, Philo protests to his beloved, who has surprised him by failing to respond to his overtures. If previously, he arbitrarily claimed that her arguments were false, without offering any support for his assertion, he now accuses her, albeit not explicitly, of not really loving him. He had expected her to provide a "cure for his suffering", by granting him her favours, and discovers that she considers this undesirable. His argument is not meant to be contentious, but stems from his view of desire as the embodiment of love. Desire is the "lover's suffering", the result of his ardent longing, and not "lust" per se. This argument leads to a hidden dispute — conducted alongside the open debate — with regard to the essence of desire. Philo behaves modestly, as befits a true sage, and cautions Sophia not to expect too much of his intellectual capacity. He even claims, albeit cautiously and in an implied fashion (grasped immediately by the sensitive Sophia) that her rejection of his aspirations attests to a lack of love on her part. Sophia proceeds gently, trying to draw him with her words, to entice him into a relationship of intellectual love, while ignoring his self-effacing remarks regarding his mental faculties. Without speaking explicitly of love, she tells him that she is attracted to him, implying physical attraction as well, but referring mostly to what she considers to be his best feature — his mind:

> "I do not deny that pure and delightful mind are more attractive to me than desirous love, but I do not believe that I do you injustice in admiring in you that which is nobler. And if you love me, as you say, you would do better to assuage my mind than arouse my desire. Therefore put all of that aside and resolve my doubts."
>
> *Ibid.*

Sophia makes it absolutely clear that her preference for platonic love does not derive from the predilections of her body, but from the reasoning of her mind, since her desire may indeed be aroused. Her position expresses a thoroughly dualistic approach to the inclinations of the body and the intellectual desire for knowledge. She clearly, albeit implicitly, accuses her beloved of giving in to his physical urges and preferring the "base" to the "noble".

Sophia's declaration that she finds matters of the mind more attractive than love that stems from desire; her reference to Philo's mind as the focus of her love and interest in him; her intellectual restlessness and her request that he assuage that disquiet — move the conversation away from romance and the chance to consummate his desire, inescapably drawing him into intellectual discourse. Philo instructs her in the concepts of love and desire, but always thinks of his own love and desire: their consummation rather than their conceptualisation. Every time he tries to lead the conversation in that direction however, digressing to the subject of his practical intentions, Sophia guides the conversation to the intellectual plane. It is she who asks the questions, presses, and determines the direction of their conversation, while he, who is not interested in a theoretical discussion but in fulfilling his desires, responds for the sake of love:

"Although I have arguments against this claim, I must do as you wish, because such is always the law of lovers who are weary and defeated by their triumphant loves . . . "

Ibid.

Philo makes a big concession. Although he continues debating the nature of their relationship, he accedes to Sophia's wishes that it be founded upon intellectual discussion. It is obvious that he has no choice in the matter, and merely hopes to persuade Sophia that their relationship should be based upon the consummation of both desire and love. They thus continue to investigate the matter of love and desire, and Philo admits that giving in to desire can be detrimental in cases of extreme libidinousness. The best solution is to follow the middle road, to cultivate a sense of balance. It is thus possible to satisfy both love and desire. Both are voluntary emotions: the one pressing to attain the desired object and the other to take pleasure in it. Sophia need not be concerned therefore that love will cease once desire is fulfilled.

The discussion of love and desire and the tension between the two, demonstrates the sophistication of the criticism levelled by the author, Judah Abravanel, at Christian puritanism. We have already noted that the author, in the first sentence of the book, through his character Philo, associates love and desire with one another. In this sense, he declares his intentions and goals at the very outset. Should anyone wish to prevent publication, there would be no need for the inquisitors to read the entire book and inquire into Rabbi Judah's philosophy. The reason for their possible objection awaited them in the opening words. The author must have said to himself: "I will write a book in which I will challenge puritanical Christianity in a sophisticated manner (as we shall see below), but I must not underestimate 'the enemy': he is educated and by no means stupid. There is therefore no point in hiding the subject and couching it in esoteric terms that might conceal the true meaning and the author's real intentions, were I writing a philosophical treatise on abstract matters of faith. In matters of love however, the human sensibilities common to us all will alert the censors to any hidden discussion. It is therefore impossible and in any case undesirable to conceal the subject: love and desire — dichotomy and illegitimacy of desire, as an expression of original sin; or harmony and acceptance of desire, as a positive phenomenon, without guilt. The danger is obvious: the puritans will prevent the book's publication for merely raising the issue. Nevertheless, even puritans are human, and as such possess a number of excellent human qualities: it is unlikely that they will put down a book on love after having read only a single sentence . . . If they read on they will discover that it does not advocate licentiousness . . . that it presents the questions in a clear fashion, and usually leaves it up to the reader to provide the answers . . . A wise puritanical censor [in the age of reformation] will in this case allow publication of the book."

The sophistication of the author's criticism of Christian puritanism is reflected in the fact that he does not criticise Christianity directly, even once, in the entire book. In every case, he criticises non-Christian philosophers or schools of thought, such as those of ancient Greece, that profess the same or similar views to those of Christians. He can therefore not be accused of criticising Christianity, since his criticism is levelled at others. He is not satisfied however, merely with the cautionary measure of indirect criticism. The dialectic form allows him to criticise puritanism through Philo, and rebuff that criticism through Sophia. In this way, for example, Philo may reject the celibacy advocated by some of the Stoics and Academics (students of Plato at the school founded in 385 BCE in a place called *Akademia*). Contrary to Philo, Sophia immediately embraces the idea, since it essentially advocates a life devoted to study and contemplation, and the renunciation of worldly pursuits. Philo sees this renunciation as a mistake that prevents one from attaining virtue: only a balanced choice, avoiding extremes of all kinds and following the middle road, can ensure a moral life. The Aristotelian golden mean of which Maimonides was so fond, and which in sexual matters, was adopted even earlier by Saadia Gaon in his *Book of Beliefs and Opinions*, makes it possible to associate love and desire with one another. Rejecting celibacy does not imply advocating sexual licence, which he rejects no less forcefully. Such an Aristotelian approach had already gained favour in the Christian Church and among a number of its most important thinkers. Many within the Church establishment thus saw in this approach, a practical solution to the problem of sexual relations within the framework of marriage, and an appropriate model for the public at large. Criticism of celibacy per se was therefore not a problem, because it led to a realistic and moderate solution.

Philo however (referring to the character himself, without further digressions concerning the author), employs the principle of the middle road to refute Sophia's dualistic approach to love and desire, and her attempt to present intellectual-spiritual love as the only worthy path. Not only is there nothing wrong with consummating desire and engaging in physical love in an appropriate fashion, but it is sinful to despise it and afford it less than its due. Hiding behind spirituality and study does not protect man from sin. It is in fact those who distinguish between "noble" spiritual love, and "base" physical love, that will in the end bring man to the commit the sin of abstinence on the one hand, or that of licentiousness on the other.

Sophia does not reject his argument, and appears as if she might even accept it. She allows Philo to further elaborate on the subject of love between men and women, but leads him toward a discussion of love between marriage partners. The two lovers themselves are not married, and Sophia's question can perhaps be understood as a hint or wishful thought, that she and her beloved might be joined in matrimony. We must remember however that their marrying would make the discussion regarding the relationship between love and desire moot, and the question of whether fulfilling desire will make love disappear can only be addressed before that love has been physically consummated. Marriage however might keep them together — certainly according Christian views and Jewish practice at the time — even if the harmony has gone out of their relationship, and they no longer love each other.

Philo senses a great opportunity and eagerly answers his beloved's question. As expected, he tries to assuage Sophia's fear that their love would disappear were she to yield to their desires, and assures her that the very opposite is true: physical pleasure not only helps perpetuate love, but even enhances it. The response to physical pleasure is emotional and intellectual, and the sense of satisfaction it brings enhances the love that exists between the partners. Marriage enables them to derive pleasure from one another consistently and over time, and not only is the physical consummation of their love pleasurable, but it also contributes to the longevity of their love and their marriage. From Philo's point of view, this is practically a proposal of marriage. Sophia however, once again fails to respond in a germane fashion, and drags her beloved to further intellectual/theoretical discussion.

Having little choice, Philo, the sage of love, skilfully uses their theoretical inquiry to lead his beloved toward his goal — the realisation of his desires — in her own way, and in keeping with her wishes. He discusses various manifestation of love: love between men and women; love of wisdom; love between the various elements of the universe; divine love; and the deep connection between all of these loves. Philo expresses a unifying view of love: love is one, and it is only its manifestations in the cosmos that are variegated. In this sense, he gives further literary expression to love as it is portrayed in the stories of the Bible. He also reflects Maimonides' view that love is a single concept of varying degrees, with the highest form of love including rather than negating its lower forms.

The author, Judah Abravanel, is only partially faithful to this approach, and contradicts himself from time to time, in his somewhat clumsy description of the various "types" of love. His is less a method at odds with the harmonious and unifying approach, than a lack of method stemming from the eclectic nature of his philosophy. Abravanel strives toward harmony, balance and virtue, but he also tries to satisfy everyone, and therefore cannot avoid contradictions. The desire to satisfy everyone is interesting, because it appears not only at the philosophical level, but also at the literary level, i.e. in relations between the two protagonists. Philo, whose views, it can be assumed, are more representative of those of the author than Sophia's are, often yields to her: not only bowing to her wishes regarding the nature of their relationship, but also accepting some of her theoretical assertions. This is accomplished by having Philo withdraw at the last moment, sometimes employing an artificial and forced literary style, leaving readers in suspense regarding possible developments in their relationship.

The *Dialoghi d'amore* give us the opportunity to study the phenomenon of love and attraction between the sexes from a philosophical point of view. While trying to discover the character of Philo however, let us pay attention to the expressions of his desire on the practical as well as the philosophical level.

In the book's opening sentence, as noted above, Philo declares his love and desire for Sophia. Although he is the first to make a distinction between the two ("knowing you, Sophia, arouses in me **love and desire**"), by the very fact that he presents them as separate concepts. He does so because he feels he should express his physical intentions, and because he fears that a general declaration of love might be understood in a purely abstract fashion, thereby preventing him from fulfilling his desires. He is therefore compelled to present love and desire to Sophia as separate concepts, but immediately rejects her dualistic approach, going on to describe the two as being inter-related and mutually inclusive. It is not a simple equation however, since the two terms are not equal — the concept of love is more extensive, and offers a more widely accepted definition of the relationship between them. Love includes desire, and desire is a form of love, since love has three possible manifestations: the noble, the expedient, and the pleasant.[2] In the noble and the expedient, love should be eternal. Pleasure on the other hand, appeals to the physical senses, and once these have been satisfied, desire is calmed for a time, until it is aroused again.

Philo thus asks Sophia to satisfy his physical desire in the name of his love for her, and the satisfaction of desire is both natural and justified inasmuch as it is part of love. The non-satisfaction of his desire causes him physical and emotional anguish, which he seeks to assuage by its satisfaction. His main effort in their initial discussion is therefore devoted to rejecting the dualism with which Sophia characterises love and desire, and presenting the unity of the two:

> Philo: "It is not easy to find a definition for love and desire that will encompass all of their manifestations . . . For the purposes of our discussion, let it suffice to define desire as a voluntary emotion, that something considered good that we lack will come into being or become ours; and love as the voluntary emotion that seeks to take pleasure in something considered good, by uniting with it."
>
> *Ibid.* p. 193

Before discussing the two important definitions presented here, let us address the keyword "emotion" (*pathos*) — a fundamental concept in Aristotelian and mediaeval Neo-Aristotelian thought. And this is what Aristotle writes on the concept of emotion:

---

[2]   Aristotle, *Nicomachean Ethics*, 2.3.7.

"A state of the soul is either an emotion, a capacity, or a disposition; virtue therefore must be one of these three things. By the emotions, I mean desire, anger, fear, confidence, envy, joy, friendship, hatred, longing, jealousy, pity; and generally those states of consciousness which are accompanied by pleasure or pain."

Aristotle, *Nicomachean Ethics* (ed. H. Rackham) 2.5

Emotion is thus an external influence that acts upon our thoughts or wills. It is the result of impressions exercised upon us by the people and things we encounter. In the present case, Philo's emotions are the result of his impressions of Sophia. This gives rise to the following definitions:

— Desire is the will to obtain that which we consider to be good and we lack.
— Love is the will to take pleasure in that which we consider to be good, by joining with it — whether the good is not yet in our possession and we yearn for it; or whether we have already obtained it and we seek to unite with it in our love.

Philo's desire is clearly reflected in both definitions — both of which lead to physical union. Philo however, brilliantly attributes the pleasure in the realisation of physical union mainly to the definition of love, rather than to that of desire. Desire is unfulfilled voluntary emotion, and the fulfilment to which it aspires occurs within the realm of love. Rejecting desire as a base manifestation of love or of some other phenomenon will thus not help Sophia's argument, since Philo's claim for union in the name of love would still stand. Moreover, his compliance with Sophia's request that he assuage her mind, limit their love to philosophical inquiry, and avoid arousing her desire is, as far as he is concerned, a temporary concession on the way to attaining his goal — physical union with his beloved. As they proceed along the intellectual paths of Sophia's choosing, he believes that she incurs a debt to him, that will — at the time of its repayment — enable him to apply all of the theories of love he is painstakingly teaching her. The abstract discussion is at times exhausting, but does not deter Philo from pursuing his goal, or assuage his desire. On the contrary, the desire aroused at their first meeting, combined with the love that followed, increases as they deepen their acquaintance through intellectual inquiry. Her questions on the subject of love and desire, their essence, meaning and causes — as well as his own answers — arouse and intensify his desire for the object of his love, who brings him to contemplate matters of love. The sage of love's desire, like that of all people, derives from the action of emotion upon his will to obtain that which he considers good, as explained above: his desire arises from the impression and external influence exerted upon him by knowing or meeting with his beloved. Unlike other people however, the sage of love's desire is profound and powerful, because it intensifies as he contemplates and deepens his understanding of the wisdom of love.

The better he explains the joy in intellectual enlightenment and divine love, the more he raises love and true pleasure to their spiritual plane, the more difficult Sophia makes it for him to associate them with his physical desire:

> "That is to say, the more spiritual the pleasure, the less satiable [the desire] and the less odious. However, according to the way of the world, the pleasure that you seek from me is satisfaction of the sense of touch, which more than any other sense, brings in its wake a sense of satiety and repulsion, and that is why I deny it to you."
>
> *Dialoghi d'amore, op. cit.* p. 220

Contrary to the effect that the intellectual discussion of matters of love has on Philo, i.e. arousing and intensifying his physical desire, Sophia is strengthened in her convictions and her resolve to withhold from her beloved that which he seeks to obtain. Her words drive Philo to deliver a learned discourse on the senses. One must distinguish between sight, hearing and smell, that man can live without; and taste and touch upon which man depends if he is to eat that he may survive, and have sexual relations that he may perpetuate the human race. The first three were not limited in their capacity since they do not bring man to loss of control and intemperance. The senses of taste and touch may lead to the destruction of one who overindulges them, and it was therefore necessary that they be given natural limits. The natural limit is the satiety one feels after having obtained the object of desire, and as such is a good thing, which allows indulgence, yet prevents the loss of control and overindulgence. Regarding Sophia's fear that Philo will come to despise the object of his desire, and his love for her will dissipate once he has reached satiety, he says:

> "And although the lover's desire will be satiated coupling with the one whom he desires, and desire or passion abate immediately, the love in his heart is not diminished. On the contrary, it strengthens the expectation of their future union, and the lovers change places — or more precisely, the two become one with the removal of all distinction between them, as far as possible. And love thus perseveres, with greater unity and perfection, and the lover's desire to take pleasure in his beloved in their lovemaking will not cease — and that is the true definition of love."
>
> *Ibid.*

Philo strives to provide an answer to Sophia's main objection to indulging their physical desire. Not only will love not fade when they are satiated with lovemaking, but it will be strengthened in the expectation that the pleasure they have just experienced will recur at their next coupling. Indeed, desire disappears for a while, but attaining the object of one's desire and the pleasure in doing so, intensify love and strengthen it, rather than weaken or eliminate it, as Sophia fears. Furthermore, love would not be complete without the experience of lovemaking, since it reinforces the element of anticipation of their next union. Faithful to his assertion that desire is part of love and is instrumental to it, Philo offers a definition of love: "the lover's desire to take pleasure in his beloved in their lovemaking". There is far more to this definition than the desire for sexual gratification, since the lover longs to take pleasure in his beloved, and the fact that they are lovers is what gives the definition its true meaning. Philo is in effect rephrasing his previous definition of love: "love is the voluntary emotion that seeks to take pleasure in something considered good, by uniting with it" — which refers to the situation before the lovers have united with one another, while this definition refers to the situation after desire has been fulfilled and wanes for a time, lacking independent existence. At this point, it merges with love, in anticipation of the lovers' next union — achieved through lovemaking, which is the realisation of love, the "changing of places" that makes lover beloved and vice versa.

This would appear to be the final word on the doubts raised by Sophia, who can no longer return to her main arguments against desire. Instead, she uses what she has just learned from Philo:

> "If so, you admit that all your desire is bound to the most physical of the senses, that is the sense of touch, and I wonder that you associate the ultimate purpose of love with something so base, if love is indeed as spiritual as you have said."
>
> *Ibid.* p. 221

Sophia compels Philo to respond on two levels: to promise that fulfilling his desire will not cause his love to disappear; and to justify his focus and interest in fulfilling seemingly base, physical desires, when the spiritual possibilities presented by love are infinite, as he has claimed. He seems to have successfully clarified and proven the first claim — desire is not a contrary emotion to love, and the fulfilment of the former will not eliminate the latter. It still remains however, for him to explain why one should engage in the base, when all one's efforts can in fact be devoted to the spiritual and the lofty:

> "I said only that lovemaking does not eliminate true love, but reaffirms and strengthens it through the act of physical love, desired inasmuch as it is a symbol and a sign of the love the two lovers have for one another. Moreover, when the souls unite in spiritual love, the bodies also seek to take pleasure in this union, to the extent possible, so that there will be no difference [between the lovers] and their union will be complete in every way. Furthermore, through physical union, spiritual love is also intensified and becomes more complete, when it is accompanied by fitting actions."
>
> *Ibid.*

The sage of love's desire thus flows from his love and is a tangible expression of it. Desire is, in this sense, a "product" of spiritual love, and what is more, intensifies and deepens spiritual love, so that the lofty actually requires the base. The test lies in their chronological sequence. In Philo's case, as in his opening remark, love preceded desire ("knowing you, Sophia, arouses in me love and desire"). Here too he argues that his love for her was not born of his desire, but on the contrary, his desire is the child of the love that bore it.

True between a man and a woman entails an exchange of places, born of mutual desire and realised in its fulfilment. The lover thus strives to enter his beloved's personality, in order to exchange personalities with her. The driving force is desire, fulfilled on a spiritual as well as a physical plane. It is only in this way that lover and beloved can change places with one another, based on equality in their love.

These words of Philo's make an impression on Sophia, but she is not yet willing to give in. She claims once again that experience has shown that many lovers, once they have satisfied their physical passions, forsake desire and lose their love, which sometimes even turns to hatred, as in the case of Amnon with Tamar.[3] It is important to note that she does not speak from personal experience, and Philo in fact uses this against her, claiming that she has no experience in matters of love. Furthermore, her choice of example — the incestuous relations between Amnon and Tamar — reflects a position whereby there is something taboo in all sexual love.

Abravanel's treatment of the subject (*ibid.* 221-222) can be viewed as a hidden debate over the Christian doctrine that all physical contact between lovers, even when they are married, bears vestiges of man's original sin. The claim of lack of experience in matters of love can also be seen as being directed at the Church, whose representatives — the celibate priests who preach to others — themselves lack experience in love.

According to Philo, the story of Amnon and Tamar is not an example of love, but of purely physical desire, a flawed condition in which one merely covets another. Indeed desire or lust is negative when it is purely physical. The love and desire of which Philo speaks to Sophia however, are interconnected and interdependent, since spiritual love preceded and gave rise to desire. Unlike the love of Amnon and Tamar that is not love at all, Philo's love for Sophia is flawless and true, due to its spiritual source; and spiritual love gives rise to physical desire, which is the longing to achieve complete unity. Love comes before desire, proof of its completeness. Sexual gratification is not only a welcome addition to spiritual love, to lofty intellectual understanding, but also strengthens and heightens spiritual delight.

As he completes his arguments regarding the unity of love and desire, it is clear to Philo that he has not yet succeeded in convincing his beloved and leading her along the path he would like them to follow together. He now

---

[3]   On Amnon and Tamar, see 2 *Samuel* 13.

attributes this to her unfamiliarity with love and its place in the world. While he does not despair of leading her down his path, he continues to follow the road of academic inquiry she has paved for him, and their intellectual love grows stronger.

Philo presents weighty arguments and succeeds in proving his claims regarding the essence of love and desire, the necessary connection between them, and the essentiality of desire to the attainment of true and complete love. Sophia's arguments against desire are not unfounded, but they are based upon imbalanced situations that lead to negative results — extreme, uncritical indulgence and the gratification of desires that do not arise from love. Philo, as we have seen, has appropriate responses to such negative phenomena, enabling him to sustain his theory regarding love and desire, and to hope that Sophia will give him a chance to realise it and subject it to the test of reality.

The texts concerning Philo's desire, in the end, teach us very little about Philo himself. If we are to understand him, we have no alternative but to turn to the philosophy of love in which he instructs Sophia, and us.

Chapter Three
LOVE AS A UNIVERSAL PHENOMENON

Sophia misinterprets Philo's words at the end of the first dialogue. To him, they are a summary of his clams in favour of the connection between love and desire, between the spiritual and the physical, and the need that spiritual love has for physical love and vice versa. To her however, they are an invitation to further discussion regarding the source of love, its causes and origins. She wants to know about the birth of love, and Philo explains that love must first be understood as a general phenomenon before its source can be discussed. Sophia wonders a little at this — wisely and correctly asking whether it would not be better to first address something's origins, and only then proceed to inquire into its manifestations and general nature? Philo tries to dismiss her question with a rather weak argument: the general nature of love is well known, whereas its source is not, and it is better to proceed from the known to the unknown. Sophia accepts this, and is pleased with the result, despite the argument's logical weakness. For her, the important thing is that they spend time together, engaged in intellectual discourse. The order of the subjects they discuss is unimportant to her. It is a tactical move on Philo's part, in the belief that skipping the question of love's origins and going directly to a discussion of its general nature may shorten the way to achieving his goal.

The second dialogue focuses mainly on the generality of love as a universal phenomenon, a cosmic principle pertaining to heaven and earth, the animate and the inanimate. At least on this issue — the universal nature of love — there is complete agreement between the debating lovers. The intimacy created by this accord, gives Philo — and even some readers — a sense of hope.

The generality of love, as we have noted, is reflected in its all-pervasiveness. Philo begins with a description of love among the animals, and goes on to discuss its presence in the universe as a whole.

The dialogue opens with a comparison between the reasons for love among the animals and those that prevail among human beings.

Reasons for Love
Reasons that animals and humans have in common:
Desire: the delight and pleasure in procreation — male and female
Continuity of the species: parents and children
Giving: acts of kindness — giver and receiver, nurse and nursed
Similarity: affinity among the like — human and human, dog and dog, etc.
Society: the habit of living in the company of others
Reasons that exist only among humans:
Compatibility of nature and disposition
Morality and intelligence

The purpose of this comparison is to rebuff the dualism of spiritual versus physical love. Love in its general form exists in a basic, fundamental way, among both animals and humans. Among humans however, it possesses a number of additional characteristics that, according to Philo, are insufficient in and of themselves to sustain human love without the physical, instinctive basis common to man and animal. Philo's assertion regarding the generality of love among all living creatures — human and animal alike — strengthens his claim regarding the unity of love. There are of course those who reject this assertion, seeing the spiritual characteristics that are unique to human beings as the only way to love that is truly worthy of them, and that sets them apart from the animals.

Philo draws a parallel between the planets and spheres — the movement of which symbolises the generality of the cosmos — and the sensory organs, the cognitive organs located in the head and the internal organs involved in the creation of semen (according to prevailing scientific views in the 15th century). He explains that just as the human organs play specific roles in procreation and the continuity of the human race, so the stars play specific roles in the constant creation of nature, the continuity of the cosmos. The comparison serves to illustrate the generality of the human phenomenon, linking it to the universal and the abstract.

Although cosmic love is usually considered to be an abstract, spiritual phenomenon, it is given substance here, highlighting once again the connection between intellectual-spiritual love, its physical manifestation, and the universe:

Stars	Generative Organs	Cognitive Organs
Sun	Heart	Right eye
Moon	Brain	Left eye
Jupiter	Liver	Right ear
Saturn	Spleen	Left ear
Mars	Gallbladder/kidneys	Right nostril
Venus	Testicles	Left nostril
Mercury	Staff	Tongue/mouth

The celestial processes expressed in the movements of the spheres and the stars, are organs responsible for the cosmic insemination of the world, as described in the table above. The world is not inanimate or static, but a sentient, feeling entity — or more precisely, a series of entities possessing such characteristics, that engage in relations that are both physical and spiritual. These relations are reflected in the constant motion, love, cosmic insemination and its consequences. According to this approach, man is a world unto himself, and the world is a living being — an animal (according to the Aristotelian approach), or a man (according to certain mystical approaches). The expression "small world" also appears in the writings of the Rabbis, and this ancient concept can be found among the works of the mystics and the pre-Socratic philosophers.[4]

Sophia is struck by the images of cosmic love. She is particularly moved by the image of the love of heaven and earth — in which heaven is male and earth female. She remarks that the concept "man" (*adam* in Hebrew) comprises both male and female, according to the interpretation that "*Adam*" is the common name of man and woman, who are complete only when they are together. The love of heaven for earth is the love of male for female, but also the love of a mother for the fruit of her womb, since the earth was born of the heavens and is nourished by them.

At the end of the dialogue, Philo offers a recapitulation of the principle of generality of love as the driving force of the cosmos, uniting man and the universe:

"The Supreme God creates and guides the world with love and binds it into a single unity, for inasmuch as there is one God in absolute simple unity, that which is drawn

---

4   See *Midrash Tanhuma, Pekudei* 3: ". . . and to the creation of man who is a small world. How so? When God created his world, he made it like a creature woman born. Just as a woman-born creature commences from the umbilicus and stretches here and there to the four sides, so God began to create his world from the foundation stone (*even hashtiyah*), whence the world was founded."

from him must also be one in complete unity; because from one comes one, and from pure unity — complete unity. The spiritual world too unites with the physical world through love, and even the Intelligences, or divine angels, would never unite with the heavenly spheres, shaping their forms and becoming souls that give them life, if they did not love them; and the intellectual souls would not unite with human bodies to make them sentient, were they not compelled by love; and the soul of the world would not unite with this sphere of birth and demise were it not for love. The lower elements thus unite with the higher, the physical world with the spiritual world, the finite with the infinite, and the entire universe with its creator in the love that they have for Him and their desire to unite with him and delight in his divinity."

Ibid. p. 310

Love is the force of unity in the world, emanating from the creator. The essence of love is unity of matter and spirit, and it is the unifying force on all levels and in all worlds:
— Unifying God-creator and world-created.
— Unifying the spiritual beings.
— Unifying the angels and their spiritual source.
— Unifying intellectual soul and physical body in human beings.

The generality of love does not mean only that it is ever-present and all-pervasive, but also that it enables the unified existence of the cosmos and affords meaning to all that exists. Love is universal in that it repudiates plurality in the created world, bringing it to unity and overall unification with the one creator.

There are few such clear and unequivocal statements on the harmony/unity of the physical and spiritual worlds and spiritual and physical love, in the *Dialoghi d'amore*. The author carefully offsets and conceals his Jewish approach, which rejects the dichotomy of two "kinds" of love: one of the spirit and the other of the flesh. The dialogue itself often provides the necessary counterweight, when Sophia accepts or refuses to accept Philo's position, and views desire as distinct from or even perilous to love. The author sometimes maintains a balanced approach by presenting a number of views — some in keeping with Christian puritanism and the dichotomy of the "lofty" and the "base", and some rejecting it. In general, Abravanel takes care not to state his own opinion explicitly. He rejects those approaches that preach abstinence, but does so with redoubled caution: nowhere in the *Dialoghi* does he refer directly to Christian views on celibacy, referring rather to the Stoics and pre-Socratics mentioned earlier; and even then not in an aggressive fashion, claiming only failure to live up to moral standards. The above passage and its unmistakable message regarding the unity of the spiritual and the physical, is therefore all the more remarkable. The message is reinforced by the fact that Sophia makes no comments or corrections, but simply agrees with Philo:

"If so, love is the animating spirit that pervades the entire world, and the bond that unites the cosmos."

Ibid p. 310

It is evident from the fascinating and amusing discussion at the end of the second dialogue that the author intended to leave readers under the impression of the unity of spiritual and physical love. They do not return to the subject of love and desire, but devote a long passage — more than a page long — to the question of which of them loves the other. It is clearly the type of verbal repartee that could only take place between lovers.

Sophia concludes their exchange as follows:

"It would be unbecoming of me, Philo, were I to openly admit that I love you, and cruel, if I were to deny it. Believe therefore that which appears the more correct to you in your wisdom, although you fear the contrary. And since the hour calls upon us to retire, we would do well to yield to it and go our separate ways, and it shall not be long before we meet again. For the present, rest at ease and remember your promise. Farewell!"

Ibid. pp. 311-312

In the final words of the dialogue, Philo wins a great victory: Sophia insinuates, but also admits explicitly, that she loves him. It would appear to be the natural outcome of the greater intimacy created by their agreement on the subject of this dialogue — the universality of love. This agreement distanced them somewhat from the contentious issue of the first dialogue — the relationship between love and desire. The shortcut employed by Philo may have helped him, and Sophia seems almost convinced of the necessity of desire, and of its connection to love. Perhaps she will accept his suit, and Philo, the sage of love will succeed in consummating his love. It may also be however, that Sophia is more willing to reveal her love because she has succeeded in basing their platonic relationship upon love of wisdom and intellectual inquiry. In any event, her words here are practically a promise for the future, and as such may arouse great hopes in Philo, and of course in the readers as well.

Chapter Four

THE PARADOX OF ABSTRACT PERCEPTION

Philo and Sophia's conversations take place in the city streets, probably in a shaded central square, or in one of the public gardens. Their meetings are not planned in advance. Sophia apparently arrives at the place she knows her beloved passes on his way to or from his affairs, and it is she who notices him first. She is therefore also the first to speak, hoping to persuade him to continue their discussion of love:

> Sophia: "Philo, O Philo, do you not hear, or do you not wish to reply?"
> Philo: "Who is calling me?"
> Sophia: "Do not pass me by in such haste. Listen for a moment."
> Philo: "Are you here, Sophia? I did not see you. I was so deep in thought that I passed by without noticing you."
>
> *Ibid* p. 313

Why is Philo so deep in thought that he does not notice his beloved standing in their usual place, passing by her without recognising her as soon as she calls to him? Sophia wishes to find out, since it is clear that she is a little offended by his lack of attention. The reason undoubtedly, she says to herself, lies in the matter for which he left his house and in which he is utterly engrossed. It immediately becomes clear however, that this is not the reason for his detachment from his surroundings. Philo tells her that he is on his way to deal with a trifling matter, meaning that having met her, he wishes to stay with her and all else is of little consequence. Sophia however, does not take this answer as a compliment, and her astonishment/offence grows:

> "A trifling matter? It is inconceivable that a trifle would keep your open eyes from seeing and your open ears from hearing!"
>
> *Ibid.*

And she has a disturbing thought: how could a trifling matter keep him from noticing her, standing there and waiting? Philo replies that his senses may not be so keen because he is distracted by an internal rather than an external matter:

> "My soul, that is weary of worldly affairs and the need to engage in trifling matters, seeks refuge within itself."
>
> *Ibid.*

Philo expects Sophia to understand of her own accord that she is the reason for his introversion; that she has penetrated to the depths of his soul, where he is completely engrossed in thoughts of his beloved, to the point that his senses are weakened and he becomes detached from his surroundings. He believes that she herself is aware of this, and when she denies it, he cannot accept her denial. Sophia continues to probe him, trying to extract further details regarding the reason behind his having been so lost in thought, and finally receives a clear answer:

> "Since you entreat me to speak that which you already know, I admit that my spirit was seized with wonder as I gazed upon your beauty, the image of which engraved

upon my soul is always the object of its desire. And that is what distracted me from my external senses.

Ibid. p. 314

These words do not flatter Sophia or set her mind at rest, but bring back her sense of affront at his having passed by without noticing her. She expresses her jealousy of the Sophia of his imagination, wishing that she herself, the real Sophia, could command all of his attention:

Sophia: "Ha ha, you make me laugh! How can something be so ingrained in your mind that when it actually appears before you it cannot penetrate even open eyes?"

Philo: "Just as you say, Sophia, had your shining beauty not penetrated my eyes, bored as deeply as it has into my feelings and imagination; and were it to penetrate to my heart, would it not choose my heart as its abode, engraving upon it your image for ever? Even the rays of the sun do not penetrate the celestial bodies or the elements beneath them to the earth more speedily than the image of your beauty penetrated to my heart of hearts and the depths of my spirit."

Ibid.

These beautiful words of love are not enough to set Sophia's mind at rest, and her modesty does not allow her to admire herself overly or take pleasure in the intense effect she has had upon Philo. She is willing to accept the fact that her image is engraved upon his soul, but not to the extent that he would ignore her physical presence:

Sophia: "If your words were correct, I would marvel all the more that despite my presence in your spirit and my sway over it, the gates of your eyes and ears are barely open to me."

Ibid.

She now casts aspersions on his romantic account of the workings of his soul and imagination. Were his words correct, he should have shown greater sensitivity to her actual appearance before his eyes, and responded immediately when she called to him. He claims that he is completely absorbed with her, how could this preoccupation possibly befuddle his senses?

Philo senses his beloved's umbrage, and seeks to reassure her. What ensues is a discussion of the function of the senses in relation to internal cognition, awareness of the spirit or the subconscious.

Cognition is the consequence of sensory and mental perception. Philo distinguishes between these two types of perception: the senses responsible for perception of the physical world — the five senses and particularly sight; and the mind, that perceives the abstract, spiritual world, and leads to intellectual cognition. The mind also serves as arbiter and purifier of the senses. The cognitive process — from sight, the most important of the senses according to Philo, to intellectual contemplation — creates an awareness that rises above sensory perception, and at times even obfuscates it.

It would thus appear that Sophia, who fears yielding to their desires, is not the main obstacle to consummating their love. Philo has created an abstract image of his beloved, which he contemplates in his every waking moment, to the point that he does not notice the flesh and blood Sophia as she stands before him, or recognise her when she calls to him. Philo's consciousness and self-awareness are thus an obstacle to the consummation of his love. Or perhaps Sophia has succeeded beyond her own intentions, and Philo is already consummating his love in the enlightenment that accompanies the deep philosophical contemplation of the wisdom of love. Perhaps Philo — who has successfully proven the unity of the spiritual and the physical through the power of love — has consummated his love in his intellectual world, so that he no longer has any need for consummation in the physical world.

Paradoxically, the process whereby Philo develops as a sage of love prevents him from consummating his love, and he becomes **the sage of unconsummated love**. Some will say of course, that here is no greater consummation than wisdom, attained through intellectual perception. Others will cite the verse "neither make thyself overwise; why shouldest thou destroy thyself?" (*Ecclesiastes* 7:16)

Chapter Five
LOVE AND BEAUTY

The subject of beauty, fundamental to Renaissance culture, appears a number of times in the third dialogue, pursuant to the earlier discussion of sensory and intellectual perception. The mind purifies beauty's effect, but retains its impression. It is fascinating to discover how the author adopts beauty — a central and exciting new theme in Italian culture of his day — making it an intrinsic part of his faith and an important component in his theology.

The source of beauty is divine, and God is beauty itself. The world was created by Sublime Beauty and Supreme Wisdom. The entire universe is the product of the desire and coupling of Sublime Beauty — the Father, with Supreme Wisdom — the Mother. The coupling of human male and female emulates the celestial coupling. In this we see kabbalistic influences on the work of Judah Abravanel.

The main issue here is the importance of the subject of beauty to a discussion on the essence of love. The puritans saw desire and lust as purely physical and external, as opposed to deep, spiritual and internal. They characterised the mutual attraction between men and women — often born of sight, aroused by the other's physical beauty — as something superficial and external. Renaissance culture reawakened ancient approaches, different and positive, to the role of beauty and aesthetics in inter-personal relationships, and the world in general. Far from being considered purely external, beauty was seen to play an important role in arousing as well as sustaining love.

Furthermore, beauty is not merely a means of arousing love and desire, but something deep and internal. In its first appearance on earth, beauty came from God, Sublime Beauty: an external revelation of that which had been separate and concealed. In its other appearances, it expresses the artist's creative ability, flowing from the most profound and sublime wellsprings of man. Externality is not something to be rejected or ashamed of, as long as it is not accepted as such, but is associated with its lofty and internal sources. Beauty indeed stems from the depths of creativity, but is renewed each time it is looked upon, recreated "in the eye of the beholder".

The potential in a theology of beauty to present a comprehensive unifying approach to love is great. The author however, fails to exploit this potential to the fullest. Careful study of his work reveals that, despite his enthusiasm for this innovative approach, he had not fully internalised it, and his eclectic writing is full of contradictions. Words that Judah Abravanel places in Philo's mouth later in the dialogue show that he does not entirely reject the baseness of physical love, and in effect fails in his attempt to present physical love as complete unity, as an integral part of spiritual love. Although he does not accept the extreme dualism proposed by Sophia, he does not escape it completely either. It may be the incompleteness of the arguments assigned to Philo by Abravanel that prevent the protagonist from attaining his goal: the consummation of his love. Time after time, when he presents an argument he believes will convince his beloved to yield to him, she succeeds in eluding him, and returns the story to its starting point.

> Sophia: "Do you not see that what I seek from you is the philosophy of love, while you seek from me the act of love? And you cannot deny that knowledge of the theory must precede its practical application, and since you have already afforded me some ideas concerning love, such as its essence and its generality, it would seem that my understanding in this matter would be lacking without knowledge of its source and its consequences. You must therefore finish without delay that which you have begun, and satisfy the remainder of my desire. For if you truly love me (as you claim), you must love my soul more than my body. . . "

> *Ibid.* p. 336

Philo is lavish in his praise of the spiritual, and adopts a certain dualism in order to elicit his beloved's agreement, and also because he has failed to construct a holistic contradiction-free model. Sophia herself now uses the model that he has constructed, as she continues to lead him along the path of their intellectual/ platonic relationship and away from his goal. Philo is obliged to accept her assertion that he must love her soul more than her body, since he has never laid the foundation to contend with this claim, having justified the physical world inasmuch as it ministers to the world of the spirit and derives from it. He is unable, or perhaps uninterested in claiming unity of matter and spirit, and must therefore accede to her demand.

Sophia will not concede in the matter of a clear distinction between spiritual, and even emotional love, and physical love. At this point, they would appear to be on an inevitable collision course, but the author does not allow it to happen: Sophia does not completely negate physical love, and Philo's position in neither absolute nor immutable. For Sophia, this represents significant progress. With gentle hints, she persuades Philo to continue their philosophical discussion, and sustains his hope that his desire to consummate his love will in the end be satisfied. Sophia understands, and ostensibly accepts Philo's desire, but claims that before she herself engages in the act of love, she must first be educated in its theory, and then perhaps . . . but only "perhaps", because all that she yet desires, as she claims, would appear to lie in the realm of the intellect. Philo's love, if it is true, must first take far greater interest in her soul than her body.

Chapter Six
WHEN AND WHERE WAS LOVE BORN?

As the sage of love, Philo addresses countless questions, the object of which is to shed light on love and understand its complexities. The third dialogue is, for the most part, dedicated to the five questions that Sophia asked Philo, and which he recapitulated as follows:

— **Love and cause**: Has love always existed, independent of any preceding factors; or was love born, i.e. its existence a result, and if so, who brought it into the world?

— **Love and time**: Is love eternal — for even if it was born of a cause, that cause lies beyond time? And if its duration can be measured, was it born at the time the world and everything in it was created, or at another, later time?

— **The source of love**: Is its source physical, celestial or divine/spiritual?

— **The parents of love**: Does it have a father and a mother, two that joined together to conceive it? Were its parents divine or human?

— **The purpose of love**: What necessity gave rise to love and what is its ultimate purpose in the world?

Sophia does not doubt the existence of love per se. All of her five questions posit its existence, and all of the discussions in the *Dialoghi* in fact take place between lovers who argue their respective positions in the name of love. Before focusing their attention on such specific questions however, they must first address the issue of love's existence:

> Philo: "If we wish to define matters concerning the birth of love, we must first posit love's existence and come to know its essence."
> Sophia: "Of course love exists, and each of us can attest to its existence, for there is no one who does not feel it inside himself or see it in another."

> *Ibid.* pp. 339-340

Sophia ignores those who would deny love's existence, and determines the discussion's context in keeping with her own feelings and emotional world — "for there is no one who does not feel it inside himself". Although her statement is a general one, Philo immediately associates it with their relationship and attributes it to his beloved's personal feelings, to which he cannot remain indifferent:

> Philo: "It is no small matter in my eyes that you confess to feeling the existence of love within yourself. I feared that perhaps (for lack of experience) you might ask me for   proof of its existence."
> Sophia: "In this, I have spared you travail."

> *Ibid.*

Philo receives considerable encouragement to elaborate upon the wisdom of love on the basis of Sophia's questions. First, he returns to the beginning of their discussion, and reiterates his definition of love (see first dialogue above), as comprising both love and desire.

Love, replies Philo, arises from the cause that created it, and is not primordial or eternal. The lover precedes love, and in loving creates it. Man can exist without love, but love cannot exist without man, or more precisely without two people: lover and beloved. The beloved is the active and generative cause of love in the soul of the lover. The beloved is thus the father of love, and the lover its mother, who gives birth to it after having been impregnated by the beloved.

The connection between love and time is fairly complex, and Philo answers with difficulty. On the one hand, the first love revealed to man was the divine love expressed in the creation of the world, but for a number of reasons, creation has not remained fixed in the human mind as the beginning of love. The complexity of the question of creation and time leads to the conclusion that love is eternal, if only because its divine source is eternal. God is therefore also the progenitor of love, or in the words of Philo, its "progenitors", in plural — father and mother of love. He thus follows in the footsteps of the *Zohar*, which describes the divine coupling in the world of the *Sefirot* as the sublime expression of unity and the source of the emanation (*Atzilut*) born of this love.

Philo thus goes on to describe the cause of the yearning of the elements of the cosmos for one another, and answers Sophia's questions. From this point, Sophia leads her partner to a discussion of divine love, and ever further from his goal. Philo does not give in, and deep philosophical inquiry into divine love brings him back to his original goal:

> "Hence, the radiance of divine love lavished upon man is what brings him first to the height of pleasure and joy, and then to his own burning love, which leads him to the blessing of unity with Sublime Beauty and joy. And that you might well understand this thing, observe the reflection of this love in man and woman who love each other with all their hearts, for if the man truly burns in his love for the woman, he will not, in his love, achieve pleasurable union with her (which is the purpose of his love) without the glowing of her eyes, the sweetness of her speech and the pleasantness of her ways, in which she shows him the measure of her acceptance of his love, affording him the strength and courage to achieve that unification of lover with his beloved that is the purpose and completeness of ardent love."
>
> *Ibid.* p. 477

Philo tries to highlight the principle that divine love is not a spiritual and abstract concept, unrelated to love between man and woman. Divine love is first and foremost God's love for man, which in turn, arouses man's love of God. Following Maimonides, Abravanel asserts that the essence of divine love cannot be understood without observing love between man and woman, which is the epitome of divine love.

Of course, this too fails to convince Sophia to set aside — even for one moment — her intellectual desire and the great pleasure she derives from it, for the sake of physical desire. She persists in her questions, and the third dialogue too, concludes with a number of topics for further discussion, and a promise from Philo that he will continue to instruct her in the theory of love.

Chapter Seven
UNCONSUMMATED LOVE

The dialogues on love are endless, and the tension between Philo and Sophia can be sustained as long as they love and converse with one another. Philo does not succeed in achieving his goal (although there is no clear avowal to this effect, and there is always the hope that he might have had greater success during the course of their subsequent, unrecorded conversations), yet he cannot be said to have failed: the philosopher cannot attain perfect wisdom, and fulfils his destiny in his very desire and quest for it. The essence of human life is the search for truth, and the essence of love the desire to unite. Sophia draws nearer to Philo, and finally reveals her love to him:

> "Just as this beauty draws the lover to unite spiritually and intellectually with it, and in this way returns its love, so I do not deny that I love you and long to unite with your mind."
>
> *Ibid.* p. 480

This is of course quintessential platonic love. The book can be seen as a kabbalistic critique of the platonic approach — an assertion worthy of further study, including examination of the kabbalistic concepts involved. Sophia represents belief in platonic love, while Philo claims that her approach suffers from narrow-mindedness and one-sidedness: that of a person in search of wisdom. Philo represents the other sides of the matter: love and the desire for beauty, and the longing of form to unite with matter. Sophia fails to understand this longing; she fears it, and cannot put aside the dualism of "lofty" and "base".

> "As for the other union, the physical, that lovers are wont to desire, I do not believe in it, and I do not want us to lust after one another at all, for just as spiritual love is full of good and beauty and all its consequences joyous and beneficial; so I believe that physical love contains aught but evil and ugliness, and its consequences are generally painful and harmful. And that I might judge this matter properly, tell me, as you have promised, the consequences of human love."
>
> *Ibid.* p. 481

Sophia remains steadfast in her conviction, rejecting every physical aspect of love "that lovers are wont to desire". She feels secure in spiritual love, which she believes will ensure joyous and beneficial consequences, and associates physical love with painful and harmful consequences — at least "generally". Nevertheless, she is not so overly arrogant or confident that she is without doubt. She is prepared to put her position to the test once again, and asks Philo to join her in further inquiry, to determine love's consequences. The third dialogue and the book itself end with Philo's response to the challenge with which Sophia, his beloved, presents him, but not before he reminds her once again of her debt to him. Philo thus becomes the sage of unconsummated love.

We could have analysed Sophia's questions and the structured process that she develops as the platform for Philo's wisdom of love, and consequently claim that she is no less the sage of love than he. We must remember however, that such an analysis would not have constituted a worthier, feminist approach, since Sophia, like Philo, is the literary creation of Judah Abravanel. The book's characters as well as its gender conceptions were all created from his point of view, and Sophia does not offer a woman's perspective, but a man's perspective of a woman.

Philo and Sophia's dialogues on love show that wisdom of love is not enough. Reasoning and eloquence do not stand up to the practical test. Love's fulfilment still requires mutual intent, a meeting of choice and will in a pair of lovers.

The necessary connection between love and desire, and the necessity of desire's consummation if true and complete love is to be achieved, in the end place Philo, the sage of love, in a trap that renders his love unconsummated.

SECTION IV

WRITTEN FOR MEN BY MEN: FEMINIST REVOLUTION AND INNOVATION IN THE CANONICAL SOURCES

Chapter One

INTRODUCTION: IDENTIFYING REVOLUTIONARY AND INNOVATIVE APPROACHES IN CULTURAL SOURCES

Jewish canonical literature was written by men. In that, it is no different from all classical cultural works, created over thousands of years, within cultural and social contexts that discriminated against women and excluded them from public circles. The exclusion of women from the field of literature was absolute — not because women did not write but also because women did not read. In other words, women in general had no connection to literature; its writers and readers were all men. The books of the Bible, the Mishnah, the Talmuds, the Midrash, Gaonic literature, medieval Jewish philosophy, Kabbalah literature and the *Zohar*, were all written by men for men.

This fact, which is the product of particular social and cultural circumstances, must be recognised by those who seek to reveal the "feminine voice" in the traditional sources, and by those who would discover the truth regarding the slow development of the status of women over the generations. Accepting the fact that women were excluded from the world of literary creation and consumption, and even the attempt to understand the socio-cultural environment that brought about this fact, are not enough. The important question is whether the men who produced literature took this reality for granted, or strove to change it? Was their position on the status of women in keeping with the gender reality of their time, or did it differ? Did the male writers dare to offer new interpretations? Did they have a message to convey to their contemporaries, or did they merely reflect contemporary culture?

As noted, these important questions pertain to human culture in general. This research only addresses Jewish canonical sources. One example however, of the universal relevance of the discussion, can be found in Sophocles' *Antigone*. This play, written in the fifth century BCE by a man and for men (who also performed the women's roles), raises the problem of the status of women at the time, in all its intensity. As such, it conveys a message to the contemporary culture, and does not merely make due with reflecting it. Antigone was ahead of her time, as a woman who had the ability to choose freely, and who accepted the moral imperative on an equal level, without hiding behind a man or in the shadow of a man's authority, even if that man was the king.[1] She pays with her life for having been ahead of her time. The real tragedy in this play however, does not lie in her death but rather in the ruin of the king, whose order she disobeyed of her own free will, in order to uphold the moral imperative. In effect, Antigone afforded the king another chance to obey the moral code. In rejecting this code, he brought destruction upon himself, undermining society as a whole. The feminine voice in the play, that of Antigone, is a heroic one, and Sophocles — the man who wrote for men — can therefore be said to have given expression to feminist innovation in his play.

The attempt to describe and document feminist innovation and revolution in Jewish sources may be misleading inasmuch as it presents an idyllic picture that inadequately expresses a discriminatory socio-cultural reality, and the prevailing views among the men who wrote these works. It is important to emphasise that the terms "innovation" and "revolution" merely refer to positions that diverge from the prevailing social and cultural norm. The idyllic picture that may arise from the fact that this article focuses on innovation within the traditional sources, is not presented intentionally in order to describe a non-existent reality. Nevertheless, we must guard against the widespread tendency toward anachronistic judgement of views expressed in traditional texts. Any judgement of the positions taken by these writers and thinkers must be done within the context of the socio-cultural reality in which they lived. We must not impose upon them the values and concepts of our own culture. The force of feminist innovation and revolution in the canonical sources is measured in relation to the cultural surroundings and values of the society in which these works were created.

Chapter Two

A MONOGAMOUS MESSAGE TO A POLYGAMOUS CULTURE

Polygamy, practised to this day in various parts of the world, was the accepted social norm throughout all of the periods in which Jewish canonical literature was created. The Bible itself tells us of polygamy in biblical times, but again, this was the prevailing practice throughout the world, practically up to the modern

---

[1]   I thank my daughter, Inbal, for this distinction.

era.[2] Having many wives was an expression of wealth and social status — meaning that women who were their husbands' only wives were not necessarily better off.[3] The culture of marriage between a single man and a number of women — and among the aristocracy, princes and kings, a single man and many women — was deeply ingrained in the common identity, among men and women alike. Polygamy declined however, in those areas that came under Christian influence, despite the fact that vast majority of Christian converts — both willing and unwilling — hailed from the lower classes, and thus could not afford more than one wife anyway. This was especially true of Europe. Later, European-Christian imperialism attempted — not always successfully — to impose monogamy upon the cultures it conquered in the west and the east.[4] European-Christian influence often persisted long after the liberation of Muslim and far-eastern countries from European rule. In some Muslim countries, polygamy has only recently been outlawed, as a result of democratisation and policies aimed at limiting population growth, while some Muslim countries still allow men to marry a number of women. In eastern cultures, polygamy continued into the 20th century, and only the erosion of traditional culture, particularly under communist regimes, reduced its prevalence.

If this was the case in polygamous societies 1,000-2,000 years after the biblical era, how much more so at the time of the Bible: 2,500 and more years ago. During these periods, monogamous concepts were foreign to the prevailing culture and identity, as if from another world, and their appearance in the Pentateuch is a veritable revolution — the beginning of a revolution adopted by most of the world thousands of years later — which made little headway when it first began, even in later biblical times.

In the Bible, we find ample evidence of polygamy. At the very beginning of the book of *Genesis*, the Bible tells us about the first bigamist: "And Lamech took unto him two wives: the name of the one was Adah, and the name of the other Zillah" (*Genesis* 4:19). The commentators and midrashists[5] saw in Lamech's

---

[2] "Post-modernists" claim that men have never ceased being polygamous, but rather that changing family structure and sexual mores have enabled them to renounce legal polygamy. A discussion of such assertions however, is beyond the scope of this section. We must keep in mind that the monogamous family structure has always been the target of ideological attacks. In the *Republic,* Plato proposes that the family be eliminated for the members of the upper classes, and such notions are reiterated in various utopian works from the late Middle Ages to the 1960s.

[3] Bigamy and polygamy often served as a means of rescuing and helping women in distress or those who had fallen captive and been raped. The Rabbis encouraged such marriages. See BT, *Yevamot* 63a, and JT, *Kidushin* 4, 4, as well as Friedman *Ribui Nashim Beyisrael,* pp. 3-4.

[4] See Amnon Linder, *The Jews in Roman imperial legislation,* pp. 138-139, 285-287; and Friedman *op. cit.,* p. 13.

[5] Midrash, *Bereshit Rabbah* 23, 2.

action, the beginning of a flaw in human behaviour. The practice spread and was adopted by many, and was one of the expressions of the decadence of the generation of the flood. The commentators suggest that many men at the time would marry one wife for procreation, and another solely for the sake of sexual pleasure. The latter would drink a certain liquid that would induce sterility, in order to prevent her from becoming pregnant:

> "Rabbi Azariah said in the name of Rabbi Yehudah bar Simon: Such was the custom of the generation of the flood: a man would take two wives — one for procreation and the other for sexual relations. The one who was for procreation would sit like a widow in her lifetime (var. in the life of her husband), and the one who was for sexual relations would be given a sterilising draught that she might not conceive, and she would sit near him, adorned like a harlot."
>
> Midrash, *Bereshit Rabbah* 23, 2

Lamech was apparently unsuccessful however, in inducing sterility in one of his wives, because the Torah emphasises that both bore children:

> "And Adah bare Jabal: he was the father of all such as dwell in tents, and of such as have cattle. And his brother's name was Jubal: he was the father of all such as handle the harp and organ. And Zillah **she also** bare Tubal-cain, an instructer of every artificer in brass and iron: and the sister of Tubal-cain was Naamah."
>
> *Genesis* 5:20-22

Contrary to expectations or common practice, "Zillah **she also** bare". The very fact that the two women are even mentioned is unusual, since the Bible usually lists only fathers and sons in its accounts of the generations, and women are not mentioned at all — as if having no status in the births of their children.

Later, the Bible tells of Abraham who, prompted by his wife Sarah, takes her handmaiden Hagar, and begets Ishmael with her. According to the plain meaning of the text, Abraham also had a third wife: "Then again Abraham took a wife, and her name was Keturah" (*Genesis* 25:1), whom he married following the death of Sarah. The Midrash[6] tells us that Keturah was in fact Hagar, whom Abraham had reinstated — possibly supported by the account in *Chronicles*: "Now the sons of Keturah, Abraham's **concubine**: she bare Zimran and Jokshan . . . " (1 *Chronicles* 1:32). According to this verse, Keturah was not Abraham's wife, but his concubine, possibly none other than Hagar. This is a matter of dispute however, and a number of important commentators reject this interpretation, asserting that Keturah was not Hagar.[7] The Bible then

---

[6]   *Bereshit Rabbah* 61; *Tanhuma, Hayei Sarah,* 9; *Pirkei deRabbi Eliezer* 29.

[7]   This is the opinion of Rabbi Avraham Ibn Ezra and Nahmanides. See also Radak on *Chronicles, loc. cit.,* who infers from Gen 25:6 — "But unto the sons of the concubines, which Abraham had, Abraham gave gifts . . . " — that Abraham had a number of concubines.

tells us of Esau's three wives. The first two were Canaanite women (*Genesis* 26:34), "which were a grief of mind unto Isaac and to Rebekah"; and the third, whom he married in order to satisfy his parents, was his cousin Mahlath, the daughter of Ishmael (*Genesis* 28:8). His brother Jacob intends to marry Rachel, his sweetheart (*ibid.* 29:18-28), but is tricked by her father: "And it came to pass, that in the morning, behold, it was Leah". Jacob does not give up on Rachel, and marries her as well. His two wives later present him with two concubines — Zilpah and Bilhah (ibid. 30:1-5) — and together, the four women give birth to the tribes of Israel.

Despite the biblical injunction against a king of Israel[8] marrying many wives, the phenomenon of polygamy is particularly evident among the kings. David marries Abigail, wife of Nabal the Carmelite, and Ahinoam the Jezreelite, as well as other women, wives and concubines, and of course Bathsheba.[9]

The prime example of polygamous culture in the time of the Bible was King Solomon, who submitted to no restriction on the number of women or their nationality, and took hundreds of wives and concubines, including many foreign women:

> "But king Solomon loved many strange women, together with the daughter of Pharaoh, women of the Moabites, Edomites, Zidonians, and Hittites; Of the nations concerning which the Lord said unto the children of Israel, Ye shall not go in to them, neither shall they come in unto you: for surely they will turn away your heart after their gods: Solomon clave unto these in love. And he had seven hundred wives, princesses, and three hundred concubines: and his wives turned away his heart."
>
> 1 *Kings* 11:1-3

His wisdom did not prevail in this case, and the Rabbis[10] as well as the Bible criticise him for it, noting that his foreign wives turned his heart after other gods.

Rehoboam, King of Judah after Solomon, had 18 wives and 60 concubines (2 *Chronicles* 11:21). Abijah, who ruled after Rehoboam, had 14 wives (*ibid.* 13:21). Further passages attest to polygamy among wealthy men and judges, including Elkanah, the father of Samuel, who had two wives (1 *Samuel* 1), and Gideon, whose many wives gave him 70 sons (*Judges* 8:30).

---

[8]   *Deuteronomy* 17:17: "Neither shall he multiply wives to himself, that his heart turn not away . . . ". This is a general prohibition against *multiplying* wives, without in fact requiring monogamy. A discussion naturally ensues regarding the precise definition of "multiplication". See BT, *Sanhedrin* 21a and corresponding sources.

[9]   Royal polygamy and the many biblical descriptions of the sexual sins in the house of David, but this subject has already been discussed at length by many commentators and scholars. See for example Bial, *Eros Vehayehudim*, pp. 24-32. See also 1 *Samuel* 25:39-44; 2 *Samuel* 5:13, 11:27; and the commentaries on these passages.

[10] BT, *Sanhedrin* 21b. See also JT, *Sanhedrin* 2, 6, where Solomon is heavily criticised, and Rabbi Shimon bar Yohai accuses him of harlotry.

All of these accounts illustrate the well-known fact that the various cultures of the biblical period were polygamous. Any discussion of messages dating from this period regarding relations between the sexes and the status of women, must therefore take this into consideration.

Biblical accounts of polygamy, as an immanent part of the culture of the day, include criticism, sometimes intimated and at other times explicit, of the phenomenon itself. We have already mentioned the figure of Lamech, the first bigamist, who does not appear in a positive light. The fact that he had taken two wives is not sanctioned, although not explicitly condemned. The phenomenon that began with Lamech proliferated, as suggested perhaps by the following verses:

> "And it came to pass, when man began to multiply on the face of the earth, and daughters were born unto them, That the sons of God saw the daughters of men that they were fair; and they took them wives of all which they chose. And the Lord said, My spirit shall not always strive with man, for that he is also flesh: yet his days shall be an hundred and twenty years."
>
> *Genesis* 6:1-3

These verses are considered to be rather enigmatic, but one might take them to mean that "the sons of God", i.e. the sons of the rich and powerful[11] were not satisfied with taking a single wife, as did most of their ancestors. The first man had one wife, and this was the practice, until the time of Lamech, as noted above. When the population increased however ("when men began to multiply"), those who could afford to do so, socially and economically, "took them wives of all which they chose", without any moral qualms. The Bible sharply criticises the phenomenon, which, according to the plain meaning of the text, might be considered one of the causes of the terrible punishment that was the flood.[12]

---

[11] Onkelos (Aramaic translator of the Pentateuch) translates "*benei ravrevaya*" — the sons of the great, the leaders; in *Bereshit Rabbah* 26, 5, "*benei dayanaya*" — the sons of the judges; and *ibid.* "any breach that does not originate with the great, is not a breach", i.e. the process of social corruption in this matter began from a "breach" initiated by the sons of the leaders. Similarly, Rashi explains "*benei ravrevaya*" as "the sons of the princes and the judges".

[12] The language used by the Bible to describe the increase in population is interesting. As in *Genesis* 1, where it is written "Let us make **adam** in our image, after our likeness: and let **them** have dominion . . . ", the word *adam* appears first in the singular, but is later treated as plural: "when **adam** began to multiply . . . and daughters were born unto **them**". This further supports the version appearing in chapter 5: "Male and female created he them; and blessed them, and called their name *Adam*", i.e. the name *Adam* ("man") is common to both male and female, indicating a state of wholeness when they are together. See below in this section, and in Section I above.

The taking of many wives by the rich and powerful may thus be seen as an immoral act, an expression of corruption numbered among the causes of the flood. It is therefore clear that in the process of saving creation, through Noah and the ark built by God's command, the message of monogamy is emphasised. The Bible tells us that Noah went into the ark with **his wife**, his sons, and **their wives**. The idea of pairs however does not end with man, but is extended to the animals as well, who — clean and unclean — are brought to the ark in pairs of male and female. The language of the verses describing this is unusual:

> "Of every clean beast thou shalt take to thee seven and seven, man and wife; and of the beasts that are not clean two and two, man and wife."
>
> *Genesis* 7:2

The commentators discuss use of the expression "man and wife" in reference to animals. There is clearly an overemphasis of couples and pairs in the flood story, suggesting that the text seeks to establish the idea of monogamy as a moral standard for all mankind.

It would thus appear that the Bible does not merely criticise polygamy, but expresses a clear preference for monogamy. Despite repeated accounts of polygamous relationships — reflecting socio-cultural reality — it has been quite evident to readers throughout the ages that the Bible prefers relationships comprising one man and one woman. This biblical message concerning relationships is highlighted by the prevailing polygamous culture of the time. This unique biblical view appears at the very moment man first sets foot on the earth:

> "And God said, Let us make *adam* in our image, after our likeness: and let them (in plural! and according to the next verse, it is clear why — there are two, man and woman) have dominion over the fish of the sea, and over the fowl of the air . . . So God created *adam* in His own image, in the image of God created He him; male and female created He them. And God blessed them, and God said unto them, Be fruitful, and multiply, and replenish the earth, and subdue it."
>
> *Genesis* 1:26-28

According to the simple meaning of the passage, the creation of *adam* "in our image, after our likeness" included both male and female. Following creation, the word "*adam*" came to refer only to the male, although at the time of creation the concept comprised both sexes, and appears as a designation for both male and female together:

> "This is the book of the generations of Adam. In the day that God created man, in the likeness of God made He him; Male and female created He them; and blessed them, and called their name Adam, in the day when they were created".
>
> *Genesis* 5:1-2

"God's image" is manifested in their creation as male and female, together constituting the image of God in the world. "Adam" is the joint name of the first couple, in whose creation God imprinted the model of monogamy for all generations to come.

The story of man's creation appears three times in *Genesis*. In the account of the six days of creation, there are three verses pertaining to man's creation on the sixth day, in which we are told that man was created male and female in God's image. In chapter 5, the Torah repeats the story in two verses, again noting that man was created male and female in God's image. In between these two passages however, there is a third passage, which appears to differ significantly from the other two. The plain meaning of the story told in *Genesis* 2 is that at first man was created male alone, and only afterward was woman fashioned from his rib. The text refers neither to creation in God's image, nor to the equal creation of male and female:

> "And the Lord God formed *Adam* of the dust of the ground, and breathed into his nostrils the breath of life; and *Adam* became a living soul . . . And the Lord God said, It is not good that *Adam* should be alone; I will make him an help meet for him . . . And the Lord God caused a deep sleep to fall upon *Adam*, and he slept: and He took one of his ribs, and closed up the flesh instead thereof. And the rib, which the Lord God had taken from *Adam*, made He a woman, and brought her unto Adam. And Adam said, This is now bone of my bones, and flesh of my flesh: she shall be called Woman, because she was taken out of Man. Therefore shall a man leave his father and his mother, and shall cleave unto his wife: and they shall be one flesh."
>
> *Genesis.* 2:7, 18, 21-24

The plain meaning of these verses is not consistent with the egalitarian version of *Adam's* male and female creation, as told in chapter 1 and chapter 5. It leaves little room however, for polygamy. On the contrary, it carries a strong message in support of monogamous relationships. One woman was created from a rib taken from one man, and for her sake he will leave his father and his mother and cleave unto her and they will be one flesh. Leaving his father and his mother who gave him life and raised him to adulthood, cleaving to his wife and the unity of flesh, are raised here to the level of the purpose of mankind's existence. Paradoxically, man on his own, as an individual, is not united and harmonious within himself, but rather alone and isolated. Unity is manifested through cleaving to a single partner, who is bone of his bones, flesh of his flesh, taken from him, and without whom he is not whole, not "one", except in cleaving to her. There is no room here for other women. This is the beginning and the foundation of the message of monogamy conveyed by the Bible to the polygamous society and culture of its time.

The commentators went even further, and interpreted the story of man's creation in *Genesis* 2 in such a fashion as to be consistent with the egalitarian version of man's male and female creation. The Adam-androgyne myth was well suited to this purpose, and it appears time and again throughout rabbinic literature.[13] Man was created both male and female — attached at the back, according to some midrashim, or at the side according to the *Zohar*.[14] Man was alone in the sense that male and female in a single body cannot achieve sexual union. God helped them by making woman "meet" for man, i.e. in a separate body. The myth that man was created androgynous, male and female in a single body, undoubtedly conveys a clear monogamous message, entirely rejecting polygamy. The subject at hand is not creation however, but rather the monogamous message conveyed by the Bible to polygamous cultures, and that message is not weakened even by the simple meaning of the version of creation presented in *Genesis* 2. On the contrary, it is reinforced, and afforded independent validity, as if to say that monogamy neither derives necessarily from equality, nor depends upon it.

Abraham did in fact have a concubine, or a concubine and another wife, as noted above. The biblical narrative however does not discuss his relationships with Hagar or Keturah. On the other hand, the reader is left with a very strong impression of his relationship with Sarah. This relationship takes a broad, central and important place in the story of Abraham's life. Of the eleven verses describing Abram's journey to Egypt, nine relate to Abram and Sarai's pretending to be brother and sister, and the consequences of their ploy (*Genesis* 12:10-20) — one they later repeated in the kingdom of Abimelech (*ibid*. 20:1-18). Taking Hagar as a concubine upsets the structure of Abram's relationship with his wife. Being unable to bear him children, it was however, Sarai who suggested that Abram take her handmaid Hagar as a concubine:

> "And Sarai said unto Abram, Behold now the Lord hath restrained me from bearing: I pray thee, go in unto my maid; it may be that I may obtain children by her. And Abram hearkened to the voice of Sarai."
>
> *Genesis* 16:2

From Sarai's point of view, Hagar was to serve as a kind of "surrogate mother", to give birth to a son whom she would then raise. Abram is passive, expressing neither joy nor enthusiasm, but merely obeying his wife. When Hagar conceives, and begins to exhibit independent behaviour, to the point that "her mistress was despised in her eyes", Sarai complains to Abram, and he responds: "Behold, thy maid is in thy hand; do to her as it pleaseth thee . . . " — in other words, I have no interest in her or in a lasting relationship with her. What passed between us,

---

[13] Midrash, *Bereshit Rabbah* 8; *Vayikra Rabbah* 14; *Tanhuma, Tazria* 1; BT, *Eruvin* 18a; BT, *Berkhot* 61a.
[14] *Zohar* 3, 44b.

was by your initiative, and therefore pertains only to the relationship between us. You are my only wife, even if I have known Hagar and she has conceived a child by me.

Abram and Sarai's different approaches might be attributed to the fact that Abram still believed God's promise that he would grant him progeny, as it is written: "And he believed in the Lord; and he counted it to him for righteousness" (*ibid.* 15:6), whereas Sarai had given up hope of conceiving at such an advanced age. Their different attitudes are clearly reflected in their respective reactions to the message brought by the angels: "And he said, I will certainly return unto thee according to the time of life; and, lo, Sarah thy wife shall have a son . . . " (*ibid.* 18:10). While Abraham accepts the prediction, the Bible stresses Sarah's scepticism: "Therefore Sarah laughed within herself, saying, After I am waxed old shall I have pleasure, my lord being old also?" (*ibid. ibid.* 12).

Sarah's first complaint regarding Hagar did not result in a crisis in her relationship with Abraham, since he remained passive, leaving the matter entirely in his wife's hands. The first crisis occurs after the birth of Isaac, in response to Sarah's criticism of Hagar's son:

> "And Sarah saw the son of Hagar the Egyptian, which she had born unto Abraham, mocking. Wherefore she said unto Abraham, Cast out this bondwoman and her son: for the son of this bondwoman shall not be heir with my son, even with Isaac. **And the thing was very grievous in Abraham's sight** because of his son. And God said unto Abraham, Let it not be grievous in thy sight because of the lad, and because of **thy bondwoman**; in all that Sarah hath said unto thee, hearken unto her voice; for in Isaac shall thy seed be called."
>
> *Genesis* 21:9-12

One cannot help but notice the marked change in Abraham's attitude. On the previous occasion, he reacted to the fate of his pregnant handmaiden with equanimity, allowing Sarah to do with her as she saw fit. Now all of a sudden, "the thing was very grievous in Abraham's sight". Regarding the issue of whether Hagar had upset Abraham's relationship with Sarah, assuming a place in his life, it is important to note that his concern is entirely directed toward his son and not to the boy's mother, and it is God who responds: "Let it not be grievous in thy sight because of the lad, and because of thy bondwoman", as if to remind Abraham that there is another person involved, also worthy of concern, and that He would in fact look after them both: "And also of the son of the bondwoman will I make a nation, because he is thy seed".

The final narrative worthy of attention in the context of the relationship between Abraham and Sarah is that of Sarah's death, and Abraham's efforts to bury her — described in no less than 20 verses (in the Torah portion of "*Hayei Sarah*"). Beyond the profound sadness that envelops Abraham — "and Abraham came **to mourn for Sarah, and to weep for her**" (*ibid.* 23:2) — her death also marks his own demise, since he cannot live without her, and her grave will also become his. He will do one final thing following her death: he will send a slave to find a wife for his son Isaac.[15] Once this task is completed, and Sarah's tent is once again inhabited, Abraham will join his wife in their final resting place: "And his sons . . . buried him . . . in the field . . . which Abraham purchased of the sons of Heth: there was Abraham buried, and Sarah his wife" (*ibid.* 25:9-10). The message of monogamy is further strengthened by the name Makhpelah (from the Hebrew root kf"l, meaning twofold), which means the tomb of the couples, as the Talmud explains:

> "Why [is it called] Makhpelah? Rabbi Yitzhak said: It is the place of the four couples: Adam and Eve; Abraham and Sarah; Isaac and Rebekah; Jacob and Leah."
>
> BT, *Eruvin* 23a

Abraham's entire adult life, from maturity to old age, is characterised by full partnership with, and absolute loyalty to his one and only partner: Sarah. Nevertheless, Hagar's presence cannot be ignored. The paradigm for future generations is therefore not Abraham, and certainly not Jacob, who had two wives and two concubines, but rather Isaac.

Isaac is portrayed in the Torah as the paragon of stability and virtue. He, who was bound by his father to the altar as an unblemished sacrifice, never breaks his connection with the Land. Unlike his father Abraham, Isaac never leaves the Land, even in times of famine and hardship. Nor does he break his connection with one woman, Rebekah, even during difficult and trying times, remaining, in this as well, a symbol of marital fidelity.

Their relationship is not merely the result of an arrangement negotiated by Eliezer on behalf of Abraham, but is founded upon love kindled at their very first meeting. According to many commentators, it was, at least for Rebekah, "love at first sight". When she saw Isaac, and did not yet know who he was:

> "And Rebekah lifted up her eye, and when she saw Isaac, she lighted off the camel. For she had said unto the servant, What man is this that walketh in the field to meet us? And the servant had said, It is my master: therefore she took a veil, and covered herself".
>
> *Genesis* 24:64-65

The Bible shares a romantic and moving moment. Rebekah and Abraham's servant Eliezer, travel a long way to Canaan. The Bible however, jumps directly to Isaac and Rebekah's first meeting—a chance encounter between the two

---

[15] Other *midrashim* claim that he wed Keturah after Isaac's marriage, some say at the behest of his sons. See Midrash, *Bereshit Rabbah* 60, and corresponding sources.

intendeds. Isaac impresses Rebekah greatly from the first moment she lays eyes on him — so much so, that she falls off her camel, an image that is both touching and amusing to readers. Rebekah however, is not amused, but probably embarrassed. Let us consider her situation for a moment. She rides a long way to meet her future husband, a man she does not know, and she does so not because she is forced to, but of her own free will:

> "And they said, We will call the damsel, and enquire at her mouth. And they called Rebekah, and said unto her, Wilt thou go with this man? and she said, I will go."
>
> *Ibid.* 57-58

During the course of her long journey, she must have given a great deal of thought to the new life awaiting her as a married woman, and wondered considerably about her husband to be: What does he look like? What kind of person is he?

And at the very end of the trip, Rebekah happens to see a man, who so impresses and moves her, that she has that embarrassing fall from the camel. What went through her mind at that moment? Did she pray that he might be her intended? Or perhaps, on the contrary — that it might not be her future husband seeing her in such an embarrassing situation? The Bible does not tell us our mother Rebekah's thoughts, only that she immediately wished to know who that impressive man coming toward her was, openly and unashamedly asking the servant who had been charged with the task of bringing her to his master — her future husband: "What man is this that walketh in the field to meet us?" When she discovered who he was, she responds by covering herself. Is this an indication of her embarrassment, her shyness, or perhaps the reaction of a woman who has fallen in love at first sight?

For Isaac as well, this is not mere "taking", but a relationship based from the outset on love. The Bible does not give us the usual terse description of so-and-so who took so-and-so for a wife, but emphasises a process that occurred between the two, the height of which can be seen in a love that fills all of the previous voids:

> "And Isaac brought her into his mother Sarah's tent, and took Rebekah, and she became his wife; and he loved her: and Isaac was comforted after his mother's death."
>
> *Genesis* 24:67

This marriage, based from the very beginning on love, displaced every previous feeling of absence or loss, establishing a strong foundation for a perfect relationship.

As with Abraham, and more so, Isaac's relationship with Rebekah lies at the heart of his life story. Isaac's marriage to one woman is not merely a fact, speaking for itself to whatever extent possible, but a central and highlighted message in the biblical narrative of his life. The two do not always see eye to eye, but they complement each other. In all of the events described following their marriage, the presence of both is always felt: when they are staying with Abimelech at the time of the famine; in their negative (and identical) feelings about Esau's wives; in their (different) attitudes to their sons, Esau and Jacob. It is in fact the latter, an example of disagreement between them, which makes the story of their relationship more real and credible. Love is not a state of complete compatibility and agreement, and it is not conditional upon a lack of disagreement.

The Bible wishes to emphasise Isaac's loyalty to Rebekah in that even when she was unable to bear him a child, he does not take another wife, as was the custom, but chooses rather to focus on prayer:

> "And Isaac intreated the Lord for his wife, because she was barren."
>
> *Genesis* 25:21

Why did he need to pray? He could have done the simplest and most common thing when a first wife is found to be barren: take a second! Or at least a concubine or a handmaiden. That is what all of the men around him did when they found themselves married to a barren woman. That is what his father did, and what is more, it was at his mother's instigation. Does the Torah teach us that Abraham of his own initiative prayed to God, entreating him for sons? God says to Abram: "thy reward will be exceeding great", to which he replies that reward is meaningless to him: "what wilt thou give me, seeing I go childless", there is no one to inherit from me. This is not an explicit request to God that he be granted progeny, but perhaps a mild complaint over something with which he has already come to terms. Nevertheless, God promises him: "so shall thy seed be", and Abraham's response is: "And he believed in the Lord; and he counted it to him for righteousness" (see *ibid.* 15:1-6).

Isaac's unusual behaviour was not, as far as we know, emulated by his son. He did not pray when his beloved wife Rachel bore him no children, being satisfied with the offspring of her sister and co-wife Leah. Moreover, he treats her rather callously:

> "And when Rachel saw that she bare Jacob no children, Rachel envied her sister; and said unto Jacob, Give me children, or else I die. And Jacob's anger was kindled against Rachel: and he said, Am I in God's stead, who hath withheld from thee the fruit of the womb?"
>
> *Genesis* 30:1-2

Isaac was indeed unusual in his great love for Rebekah, special in his loyalty to her. He entreated God "for/before his wife" ("*lenokhah ishto*"), who was always before him, **the only possible female presence in his life**. Even for the sake of procreation and continuity, a matter of paramount importance, he never considered giving up this loyalty.

The patriarchs play important symbolic historical roles in the eyes of future generations, and Isaac and Rebekah well express this symbolism in its purest form, largely due to their stable, loving relationship. The paradigm presented by Isaac and Rebekah stresses to us once again that while polygamy was an expression of normative, prevailing culture at the time, worthy love between the sexes is that which is attained in marriage between one man and one woman.

The ideal relationship between lovers, and violations of such a relationship, are an endless source of imagery in the Wisdom Books and the Prophets. The prophets employed love and the monogamous relationship to describe spiritual experiences and convey religious messages, and as an expression of the bond between God and the People of Israel. Great intensity is ascribed to first love, young love, love of the betrothed, love between bride and groom. The memory of this formidable bond helps sustain husband and wife (God and his People) through periods of crisis, and it is to this bond they strive to return when the relationship is once again on sound footing:

> "Thou shalt no more be termed Forsaken, neither shall thy land any more be termed Desolate; but thou shalt be called, My delight is in her, and thy land, Espoused; for the Lord delighteth in thee, and thy land shall be espoused. For as a young man espouseth a virgin, so shall thy sons espouse thee; and as the bridegroom rejoiceth over the bride, so shall thy God rejoice over thee."
>
> *Isaiah 62:2-4*

In these verses, the couple metaphor is twofold: God is the bridegroom, and the People of Israel the bride. The Land of Israel is female and her sons return to her with the vigour of nascent love between a young man and a virgin. The main theme in both relationships described by the prophet is novelty and freshness: as a "young man" (= virgin) espouses a "virgin" — rekindling the initial passion between the People and the Land of Israel; and as a "bridegroom" rejoices in his "bride" — awakening the incipient love between God and His People.

Jeremiah, in the following well-known verses, also compares God to a bridegroom returning the love of His bride Israel:

> "Thus saith the Lord; I remember thee, the kindness of thy youth, the love of thine espousals, when thou wentest after me in the wilderness, in a land that was not sown."
>
> *Jeremiah 2:1-2*

"The kindness of thy youth" expresses freshness and purity. "The love of thine espousals" provides the ardour of devotion, the strength required to ignore the hardships of the desert. Memory of that first and absolute love ensures the success of the relationship — or in its allegorical sense, ensures redemption. It expresses not only the kindness of God, recalling his bride's devotion, but also God's loyalty to his beloved, whom love has exalted to a level at which she too can bestow kindness upon her beloved — even if he is God. During the difficult journey through the desert, in a land not sown, you could have left me, but you showed me kindness, "the kindness of thy youth", sustained by "the love of thine espousals".

This relationship is monogamous in essence, but is violated by one of the partners: the woman who betrays her divine husband and commits adultery with other lover-gods. Any assertion that God may have deserted his People is immediately dismissed:

> "But Zion said, The Lord hath forsaken me, and my Lord hath forgotten me. Can a woman forget her suckling child, that she should not have compassion on the son of her womb? yea, they may forget, yet I will not forget thee."
>
> *Isaiah* 49:14-15

Images of Israel as a treacherous woman and a harlot abound in the prophecies of Jeremiah ("... that which backsliding Israel hath done ... there hath played the harlot ... yet her treacherous sister Judah feared not, but went and played the harlot also" — Jer 3:6-7), Isaiah ("How is the faithful city become an harlot!"), and most prominently, Hosea, in which the metaphor of harlotry and betrayal is a central theme. Nevertheless, it is Hosea who provides us with one of the most fascinating expressions of return from adultery and harlotry to a loving and faithful relationship which, like the examples above, looks to the relationship's glorious beginning, the period of betrothal:

> "And it shall be at that day, saith the Lord, that thou shalt call me 'my man' (*ishi*); and shalt call me no more 'my master' (*baali*). For I will take away the names of Baalim out of her mouth, and they shall no more be remembered by their name ... And I will betroth thee unto me for ever; yea, I will betroth thee unto me in righteousness, and in judgement, and in lovingkindness, and in mercies. I will even betroth thee unto me in faithfulness: and thou shalt know the Lord."
>
> *Hosea* 18-19; 21-22

One cannot help but presume that the proposed change from perceiving one's partner as "master" (*baal*) to perceiving him as "man" (*ish*) is far more than a play on words and remonstration against the *Baalim* — the gods with which Israel had committed "adultery". It would not be too much of an anachronism to say that the language of man-woman (*ish-ishah*) expresses a greater state of equality between the partners and the uniqueness of each partner to the other, than the term master-possessor, which gives sanction to the husband's possessing other women and the wife's seeking other masters. From the prophet's point of view, there can be no room for polygamous relations, and love between the sexes is manifested in monogamous, one-woman-one-man relations: " And I will betroth thee unto me for ever"!

The use of images and metaphors of love between the sexes to convey spiritual and religious messages, demonstrates the importance, centrality and deep significance ascribed to such relationships. Love between men and women is portrayed in the ancient sources as the most significant phenomenon in human life, to the point that it serves as a primary source of imagery in describing transcendence from the human to the divine.

We use "the divine" in its usual sense, to express the yearning of man or a people for God. It is also however an expression of the bond, aspiration and yearning man feels toward wisdom and ideas and the search for them, as reflected in *Proverbs* 4:5-8, and many other places. These same sources however, constantly reiterate the message of monogamy, while voicing criticism of male tendencies toward polygamy:

> "Drink waters out of thine own cistern, and running waters out of thine own well. Let thy fountains be dispersed abroad, and rivers of waters in the streets . . . Let thy fountain be blessed: and rejoice with the wife of thy youth. Let her be as the loving hind and pleasant roe; let her breast satisfy thee at all times; and be thou ravished always with her love. And why wilt thou, my son, be ravished with a strange woman, and embrace the bosom of a stranger?"
>
> *Proverbs* 5:15-20

Wisdom is compared to water, and its attainment requires perseverance and fidelity. It is difficult at first, evoking images of "when thou wentest after me in the wilderness, in a land that was not sown" and "who led thee through the great and terrible wilderness, wherein were fiery serpents, and scorpions, and drought, where there was no water" (*Deuteronomy* 8:15). This allegory too relates to the difficulty presented by the lack of water and the effort entailed in obtaining it. It must be collected in a cistern or drawn from a well, but if you are loyal to your own cistern or well, you will profit therefrom. You yourself become a fountain of knowledge, whence it is dispersed abroad to all who wish to drink of it.[16]

While the image of the unfaithful wife abounds in the Prophets, *Proverbs* ascribes such perfidy to the man, whom it exhorts ("rejoice with the wife of thy

---

[16] This metaphor brings to mind the well-known interpretation of the verse "But his delight is in the law of the Lord; and in his law doth he meditate night and day" (Ps 1:2): First it is "the law of the Lord", but after he has meditated in it night and day, it becomes "his law". Rashi: "First it is called 'the law of the Lord', and once he has toiled over it, it is called 'his law'". See BT, *Kidushin* 32b; Rashi *loc. cit.*; and *Yalkut Shimoni, Beshalah* 228.

youth") to be faithful to his one and only love, and whom it admonishes for embracing a stranger. The relationship portrayed here rejects any possibility of polygamy, and strengthens the biblical message of monogamy.

These verses from *Proverbs*, like others in the Bible, some of which have been cited here, attach great importance and centrality to monogamous relationships. This centrality is not reflected however, in the precepts of the Torah, which include neither a negative injunction against polygamy nor a positive commandment to practise monogamy. The Torah merely presents a rather broad system of sexual injunctions (*Leviticus* 18 and 20) that slightly narrows the possibilities, limiting the number of women available for marriage to a specific individual. This would have been significant in a society with a tribal-family structure, since marriage within the extended family would have been easier than marriage between members of different extended families or tribes, which would have involved more complex monetary arrangements and difficulties concerning inheritance. Gradually and indirectly, the system of sexual prohibitions had a certain influence on the reduction of polygamy.

The Torah also provided the option of divorce for cases in which marital harmony has come to an end (*Deuteronomy* 24:1). Allowing divorce is a fundamental statement in favour of monogamy, with far-reaching ramifications regarding the importance of relations between the sexes. In a polygamous culture, a man is not expected to live in harmony with all or even one of his wives. The polygamous ethic is not based on love and mutuality, and at most address the man's ability to provide for and protect his wives against the aggression of others. The Torah in fact does not forbid polygamy, but in allowing divorce, it introduced the issue of marital harmony into the heart of polygamous culture. It is done by negation, but one cannot ignore the force of this realistic position and its potential influence on attitudes toward relations between men and women within the framework of marriage. Allowing divorce is in effect a statement in support of monogamy: If the relationship doesn't work out, taking another wife in addition to the first one is not a recommended course of action. As difficult as such a course of action may be in a patriarchal society, it is better to divorce the first wife and only then to marry another, rather than to have more than one wife at a time.

Polygamy is also portrayed as a recipe for strife and hatred:

"If a man have two wives, one beloved, and another hated, and they have born him children, both the beloved and the hated; and if the firstborn son be hers that was hated . . . he may not make the son of the beloved firstborn before the son of the hated, which is indeed the firstborn. But he shall acknowledge the son of the hated for the firstborn . . . "

Deuteronomy 21:15-17

According to the Torah, the practically inevitable consequence of a man's having two wives is that one will be beloved and the other hated. The difficult relationships within such a family are a given, even if they come to a head only later when there are disputes between the sons of the two wives over their father's inheritance. The Torah does not forbid marriage to more than one woman, but it certainly sees the problems posed by such relationships.

The passage in the book of *Deuteronomy* that deals with the appointment of a king is one of the most fascinating and controversial in the Torah. The commentators argue whether the appointment of a king is mandatory or merely permitted. All agree however the sovereign described in Deuteronomy — unlike his counterparts in other nations — is bound by certain restrictions:

> "When thou art come unto the land which the Lord thy God giveth thee, and shalt possess it, and shalt dwell therein, and shalt say, I will set a king over me, like as all the nations that are about me; Thou shalt in any wise set him king over thee, whom the Lord thy God shall choose: one from among thy brethren shalt thou set king over thee: thou mayest not set a stranger over thee, which is not thy brother. But he shall not multiply horses to himself, nor cause the people to return to Egypt, to the end that he should multiply horses: forasmuch as the Lord hath said unto you, Ye shall henceforth return no more that way. Neither shall he multiply wives to himself, that his heart turn not away: neither shall he greatly multiply to himself silver and gold."
>
> *Ibid.* 17:14-17

One of the above prohibitions is relevant to the subject at hand: kings are charged not to have many wives. This prohibition reflects an attempt to change the polygamous behaviour of the king, who serves as a role model for society as a whole. This can be seen as an attempt to effect socio-cultural change, from polygamy to monogamy — or at least to a less polygamous society. The biblical injunction does not seek to prevent a king from taking more than one wife, but imposes a certain limitation upon one who had never been limited before. On the contrary, the very fact that he was king had enabled him, more than any other man, to have as many wives and concubines as he saw fit. Kings would have many wives in their palaces as an expression of control, power, political alliances, and a source of images and legends about them, and the Torah wished to hold this practice in check. Such limitations imposed on the king, who was seen as a general role model, would have had a significant effect. The prohibition against a king of Israel's taking many wives also raises the question: How many wives may a king marry without violating the injunction against "multiplying"?

The Rabbis discussed this issue without stressing the innovation in limiting a king's right to take as many wives as he wished. Regarding the question of whether this prohibition stems from the Torah's desire to restrict polygamy to some extent, or from the fear that his wives would cause his "heart to turn away" from God, there is some disagreement in the Mishnah:

"'Neither shall he multiply wives to himself' — but only eighteen. Rabbi Yehudah said: He may multiply [wives], as long as they do not turn his heart away. Rabbi Shimon said: Even if one will turn his heart away, he may not marry her. Why then is it written (*Deuteronomy* 17) 'Neither shall he multiply wives to himself'? Even [if they are] as Abigail."

Mishnah, Sanhedrin 2, 4

The sages of the Mishnah were fully aware of the biblical sources that chastise Solomon in this matter (1 *Kings* 11:1-3), but fail to criticise other kings, who may not have had harems like that of Solomon, but who certainly had numerous wives. The numerical limit imposed by the Mishnah was inspired by King David, who had six wives, and the prophet permitted him to take a further 12 concubines. It is unclear whether the prophet was stating that David actually had 18 wives, or that this number was the limit imposed upon him by the Torah, i.e. whether King David's behaviour is the source of the law, or merely provides evidence of it. Either way, David serves as a source for the laws pertaining to kings, including the halakhic quantification of the prohibition against a king's "multiplying" wives. The Bathsheba affair does not mar the image of David as a righteous king and founder of Israel's royal dynasty. Indeed the Rabbis strove to absolve David of wrongdoing, despite biblical indications to the contrary: "Rabbi Shmuel bar Nahmani said in the name of Rabbi Yonatan: 'He who says David sinned is mistaken'" (*Shabbat* 56a). There is therefore no reason not to learn this halakhah from King David.

Contrary to the general opinion (the first) cited in the above mishnah, whereby a king may marry a maximum of 18 women, Rabbi Yehudah believed that a king might marry as many women as he wished — even more than 18 — on condition that they do not turn his heart away from God's commandments. Rabbi Yehudah's opinion is not accepted, and established halakhah in this matter is that a king may not take more than 18 wives. Other opinions in the Talmud, suggesting figures of 24 and even 48, are rejected.[17] This restriction may seem utterly meaningless to someone who takes monogamy for granted, but as we have noted, the positions in this matter should be judged in their cultural and historical context, and as compared to the behaviour of other kings.

"Neither shall he multiply wives to himself" is thus not a sweeping ban. It does express a basic moral position however. A king of Israel is required to limit the number of wives he takes, as compared to the norm among other kings and the prevailing cultural environment. Thus, in respecting this injunction, the king serves as a paragon for the entire people.

Another figure worthy of emulation is that of the high priest. Although the Torah does not explicitly forbid the high priest to have many wives, it states that

---

[17] See BT, *Bava Metziya* 115a; BT, *Sanhedrin* 21a; *Sifre, Deuteronomy*, 159; Maimonides, *Hilkhot Melakhim* 3, 2.

he may not marry any woman who is not a virgin, thus restricting his choice of women and hence his ability to "multiply wives":

> "And he that is the high priest among his brethren, upon whose head the anointing oil was poured, and that is consecrated to put on the garments . . . And he shall take a wife in her virginity. A widow, or a divorced woman, or profane, or an harlot, these shall he not take: but he shall take a virgin of his own people to wife. Neither shall he profane his seed among his people, for I the Lord do sanctify him."
>
> *Leviticus* 21:10; 13-15

There is in fact, no biblical injunction against a high priest marrying many women — as long as they are all virgins. The Talmud however, infers such a prohibition from the Torah: "'An atonement for himself, and for his house' (*Leviticus* 16:6) — not for two houses", and "'but he shall take a virgin of his own people to wife' (*Leviticus* 21:14) — one and not two" (BT, *Yevamot* 59a). There is thus an individual of very high standing in the Jewish people — not the highest, but the second highest — who is specifically barred from marrying more than one woman, thereby becoming the first monogamist by force of Halakhah.

We have seen that the kings failed to observe the minimal restrictions imposed upon them by the Torah. Were the high priests strictly monogamous, in keeping with the absolute prohibition against high-priestly polygamy? We have no evidence of any violation of the monogamous norm among any of the high priests. A passage worthy of closer scrutiny is:

> "Joash was seven years old when he began his reign, and he reigned forty years in Jerusalem. His mother's name also was Zibiah of Beersheba. And Joash did that which was right in the sight of the Lord all the days of Jehoiada the priest. And Jehoiada took for him two wives; and he begat sons and daughters. And it came to pass after this, that Joash was minded to repair the house of the Lord."
>
> *2 Chronicles* 24:1-5

This chapter tells the history of King Joash, who ruled 40 years in Jerusalem, and of the High Priest Jehoiada. It reviews the reign of King Jehoram's wife, Athaliah, who killed all of the descendants of the royal house of Judah — all of the males who might lay claim to the throne. Jehoiada the Priest conspired against Athaliah, anointed Joash — the child hidden by Jehoshabeath — thereby rising to prominence. Jehoiada's influence was great, and there is no doubt that he was the strong man in the kingdom and the only high priest reported to have been buried in the tombs of the kings. Among the verses pertaining to the history of Joash, we find the following: "And Jehoiada took for him two wives; and he begat sons and daughters". Some have taken the verse, detached from its context, simply to mean that the high priest was a bigamist, in contravention of the Talmudic law that forbids (by inferred biblical injunction) a high priest to marry more than one woman.[18] As noted however, the subject of this passage is not Jehoiada, and the meaning of the above verse is that Jehoiadah the priest took for Joash two wives simultaneously or in close succession, in order to enable him to beget sons and re-establish the House of David, of which Joash was the sole survivor, following Athaliah's massacre. Josephus writes: ". . . and when he (Joash) was of age, he married two wives, who were given to him by the high priest, by whom were born to him both sons and daughters".[19]

Discussion of the verse's possible, anomial meaning, confirms the importance ascribed to the high priest's obligation to practise monogamy. The injunction against the highest religious authority's marrying more than one woman, and the requirement that the king limit the number of wives he takes to the greatest extent possible, that he might serve as a role model for the nation and its leaders — together constitute an expression of the canonical Jewish position on polygamy.

We must stress once again that polygamy was the norm at the time, and that any opposition to the norm represents a new and revolutionary approach, or in the words of Goody: **"It is not polygamy that needs to be explained, but it's absence, i.e. monogamy; the former is common, the latter rare".**[20]

Monogamy thus joins all of the other revolutions the Torah sought to foment: the Sabbath, social justice, and above all — monotheism. None of these goals can be attained all at once. They are rather, ongoing processes, offering fresh revolutionary challenges on a daily basis, in every generation, for society as a whole and for each individual member.

The rejection of polytheism parallels the departure from polygamy, and the idea of the unity of God is applied to the unification of man and woman in a single entity. While the biblical message of monotheism is accompanied by a broad system of negative and positive precepts, as well as various decrees, amendments and legal minutiae pertaining to idolatry, the message of monogamy is conveyed as an idea, a moral position, but lacking practical expression in the form of laws and precepts — beyond that which we have described above. The Torah's approach in this matter would appear to avoid unrealistic legislation. That is how the Torah's allowing a soldier to take a foreign wife is viewed, and that is perhaps how one should view the fact that the ideology of monogamy

---

[18] See Maimonides, *Hilkhot Issurei Biyah* 17, 13, which states: "he may never marry two women at the same time"; and Ravad's gloss, in which he cites the verse "and Jehoiada took for him two wives" as proof against Maimonides ruling — here is a high priest, Jehoiada, who in fact did take two wives. A printer's gloss on Ravad's comment however, reads as follows: "The Sages have already explained that the verse refers to Jehoiada's having wed two women to Joash". See also *Tosafot Yeshanim* on Yoma 13b, pass. beg. "*Velo ba'ad shnei batim*", which needlessly suggests an implausible solution.

[19] *Antiq.* 9, 7.

[20] J. Goody, 2000, p. 176.

receives no clear and obvious legal expression in the Bible or the Talmud. Despite an aversion to polygamy, and recognition of the fact that man and woman can only find true fulfillment within a monogamous relationship — no attempt was made to legislate against the cultural norm, in an attempt to create a new and different constitutional standard, knowing full well that it could never withstand the test of reality in society steeped in polygamous culture.

The absence of legislative support notwithstanding, we must not underestimate the force of the Bible's monogamous message, and the inescapable comparison with its monotheistic message. The concepts of unity and unification are essentially the same, strengthening, supporting and largely dependent upon one another.

Belief in a single God, i.e. juxtaposing the individual with her/his God within the context of the belief in unity, parallels the juxtaposition of one woman and one man; and their complete physical union within the harmony of mind and emotion parallels the idea of the unity of God.

This is, in itself, a very powerful comparison. Some however, have gone beyond merely drawing a parallel between monogamy and monotheism, asserting that the two concepts are in fact one and the same. Adherents of the latter approach maintain that monogamy in fact derives from the principle of divine unity. A clear expression of this approach can be found in the Kabbalah.

Kabbalistic sources do not merely assert the fact of divine unity, but — in keeping with their characteristic use of language from the realm of imagination, emotion and spirit, — illustrate this unity with sexual imagery. Love, desire and divine union in the world of the *sefirot*, are the source of all existence, the blueprint of creation, a path for man and a connection between all worlds. The concept of the ten *sefirot* of divinity is central to all Kabbalistic thought. The *sefirot* appear in the *Zohar* in the form of a variety of images and attributes of the divine. One of the most well-known of these attributes and images is that of the Supreme Man (*Adam Elyon*) — an anthropomorphic image used to describe, discuss it, or make various assertions concerning the world of the divine. This figure is the source of all abundance in the cosmos, an abundance that flows from the *sefirah* of *Keter* (Crown), or from the *sefirot* of *Hokhmah* (Wisdom), *Binah* (Understanding), *Hesed* (Love/Mercy), *Gevurah* (Power), *Tiferet* (Beauty), *Netzah* (Eternity), *Hod* (Majesty), and *Yesod* (Foundation). The figure of the Supreme Man, which comprises all of the above *Sefirot*, is male, and its female partner is the *sefirah* of *Malkhut* (Kingdom). The *Zohar* calls the divine male and female: God and the *Shekhinah*, or the *Melekh* and *Matronita*.

The use of sexual symbolism to represent connection and union, recurs in various forms, not only between the *sefirot* that describe the divine world and are in turn described as the Supreme Man — male — and *Malkhut* or the *Shekhinah*, connected with or facing the world of creation, but also within the world of the divine, at its highest and most secret levels. The two highest *sefirot*, *Hokhmah* and *Binah*, are the father and mother of the lower *sefirot*, created by their sexual union, and seeking sustenance from them.[21] The relationship between them is described in terms of male and female from which the world of *Atzilut* (Emanation) derives, creating harmony throughout the divine — which is based upon male and female images and the relations between them. The lower *sefirot* existed within their father and mother, *Hokhmah* and *Binah*, and were created through their sexual union. At first, they were inside *Binah*, like a foetus in its mother's womb, then they emanated from *Binah*, which gave birth to them. Kabbalah compares the idea of emanation to the mystery of birth. Following the birth of the lower *sefirot*, the father and mother, the supreme couple — i.e. *Hokhmah* and *Binah* — continue to serve as a source of sustenance, and as role models for their progeny. The enduring, unceasing and infinite love of *Hokhmah* and *Binah*, serves as an example and an inspiration. Their everlasting relationship is a paragon of love at its highest, toward which all aspire. The love of *Hokhmah* and *Binah* arouses the love of the lower *sefirot* for one another, and creates a harmonious relationship among them as well. It is from this relationship between the lower spheres, often described as the relationship between God and the *Shekhinah*, that souls are born.[22]

All souls are created as the product of the desire and sexual union of God and the *Shekhinah*, and comprise both the male attributes of *Tiferet*, and the female attributes of *Malkhut*, and are thus bi-sexual:

> "Come and see: All of the souls of the world, which are the fruit of God's labour, are one in the secret of one. And when they descend to the world they all separate in the form of male and female, and are male and female joined as one. And come and see: The female passion toward the male creates life, and the male passion toward the female creates life, and the pleasure of the male passion toward the female and his joining with her brings forth life . . . And when the souls go forth, they go forth male and female as one, and when they descend, they separate one to the one side and the other to the other side, and God unites them later, and [the task of] uniting them is given to no other but to God alone, who knows how to unite and join them suitably."
>
> *Zohar* 1, 85b

All souls, which are the fruit of God's labour — i.e. products of the divine sexual union, as they reside in the world of divinity, in the *Shekhinah* — are "one in the secret of one". The secret is that of unity comprising both male and female indistinguishable from one another, and the assertion that the soul is "one" signifies a unity of male and female. The female essence within the soul

---

21   *Zohar* 1, 246b.
22   *Zohar* 1, 209a; 2, 223b. For further discussion of the joining of souls, see Section I above.

is created by female passion toward the male, "creating life" — bestowing the female spiritual essence. The male essence within the soul is created by the male passion toward the female — bestowing the male spiritual essence. All of this occurs "in the secret of one": the secret of divine unity, which is also a unity comprising both male and female. When the soul descends to the world of creation however, the world of plurality and separation, it separates "in the form of male and female", and God unites them later.

Kabbalah is full of messages about love relationships: Not only does love exist in the world of the *sefirot*, sustaining the divine and thus serving as a paragon for man to seek and adhere to the harmony of union between the sexes, but if the relationship between a man and a woman is successful, it is because they were created within the *Shekhinah* as a single soul, and when that soul descended to earth, it was divided in two, until reunified in their relationship. The idea of bisexuality of souls at the time of their creation in the *Shekhinah* thus has deep and far-reaching significance for the relationship between a man and a woman — who cannot attain wholeness except in their union.

Kabbalah's approach to love relationships in terms of the nature of souls is uncompromising and stems from a hermetic spiritual paradigm. According to this paradigm, bachelorhood is completely untenable, even in the most exceptional circumstances. The deficiency of bachelorhood is absolute, and only love within the context of a male-female relationship — two half-souls uniting in their love — can bring man to fulfil his purpose in the world of creation and return the soul to its divine source.

Kabbalistic interpretation, in all its discussions pertaining to relations between the sexes, refers exclusively to monogamous marriage: one man and one woman, with no mention whatsoever of polygamy.[23] The principle whereby every soul is created both male and female, separated upon descent into the world, and re-united later, makes simultaneous marriage to more than one woman completely unthinkable.

Both early and later canonical sources present monogamy as the meritorious path, whereas polygamy is presented as an undesirable phenomenon. The creation story sets the tone, stressing the principle of the couple relationship. Polygamy is seen as one of the expressions of the corruption that characterised the generation of the Flood. Our forefather Isaac, symbol of loyalty, stability and purity is also the paradigm of monogamous fidelity.

The prophets who used the couple relationship as an allegorical device by which to convey spiritual and religious messages, viewed polygamy as a source of negativity, and monogamy as the ideal state. Some have thus compared monogamy to monotheism, equating the rejection of polytheism with the rejection of polygamy, and acceptance of monotheism with acceptance of

---

[23]   Tishbi, *Mishnat Hazohar*, vol. 2, p. 613.

monogamy. This is the basis of the theological assertion that monogamy is a divine principle, upon which beliefs regarding the origin and nature of the human soul are founded. In the course of philosophical and ideological development, monogamous ideas were planted in a normatively polygamous society millennia ago, causing the progressive exclusion of the phenomenon of polygamy from the norm.

Chapter Three

ONAH: THE OBLIGATION
TO HAVE SEX FOR PLEASURE

There are two separate precepts that require married couples to have sex: "be fruitful and multiply" (procreation), and "*onah*" ("conjugal rights"). The former requires that a man contribute to "populating the world", the continuity of his seed, that is having children, and in this matter Halakhah has determined that one who has begotten a son and a daughter has fulfilled his obligation.[24] Of course, this precept requires that one have sex with his wife during the fertile part of her cycle, at least until he has children. Sex for the sake of procreation however, is merely a means to an end.

The Torah established another precept however, unrelated to the continuity of the seed and populating the world, but to sex itself, and the marriage relationship. The *onah* obligation (*Exodus* 21:10) requires that the husband regularly have sex with his wife — not as a means to have children, but as an end in itself, for the sake of their mutual pleasure.[25]

The frequency of this obligation is determined by the husband's physical strength, and the extent to which his work (providing for the family) allows him to be at home. One whose work enables him to spend more time with his wife is also required to have sex more frequently. As noted, this obligation has absolutely no connection to procreation, and thus applies to one who has already fulfilled the requirements of "be fruitful and multiply" and cannot have more children, on days when the woman is not fertile, and even during pregnancy. A woman has the right to demand that her husband not change his occupation to one in which he will be away from home for extended periods, or that he not go away at a certain time — since her conjugal rights would thus be affected.

---

[24] See Mishnah, *Yevamot* 6, 6: "One must not refrain from procreation unless he has children. Beit Shamai say two males, and Beit Hillel say one male and one female, as it is written (Gen 5): 'male and female created He them.'" See also corresponding sources.

[25] BT, *Nedarim* 15b. For a detailed account of the relevant *halakhot*, see Maimonides *Hilkhot Ishut* 14.

The significance of *onah,* as the husband's duty to satisfy his wife, is also reflected in the specific requirement that a husband have sex with his wife before departing on a journey:

> "Rabbi Yehoshua ben Levi said: A man must have marital relations with his wife when he departs on a journey . . . This teaches us that a woman desires her husband when he departs on a journey."
>
> BT, *Yevamot* 62b

The husband's duty is presented here as a direct consequence of the fact "that a woman desires her husband when he departs on a journey", i.e. his obligation to respond to his wife's desire. This is an important statement regarding the nature of relations between man and wife. The woman is not bound to serve her husband and satisfy his needs. It is rather the husband who must serve her and satisfy her needs.

The background behind this *halakhah* is a discussion elsewhere in the Talmud regarding women's desires and the manner in which they are expressed:

> "'And thy desire shall be to thy husband' (*Genesis* 3:16) — This teaches us that a woman desires her husband when he departs on a journey. 'And he shall rule over thee' — This teaches us that a woman demands in her heart, and a man gives voice to his demands. This is a positive quality in women, for they demonstrate affection toward their husbands."
>
> BT, *Eruvin* 100b

The expression "and he shall rule over thee" is interpreted in an unusual fashion here. The sages of the Talmud charge the man with the responsibility of responding to his wife's desires, taking her nature into consideration. Unlike men, who are more wont to give full verbal expression to their desires ("a man gives voice to his demands"), a woman "demands in her heart", rather than explicitly voicing her desires. The Talmud sees this as "a positive quality in women", attesting to their greater modesty. A woman's desires however, are no less ardent, and the man is therefore charged with the responsibility of responding to them. Women have their own ways of expressing desire: "they demonstrate affection toward their husbands", and expect them to understand what they mean. Women's sexual communication differs from that of men: the ways in which a woman strives to arouse her husband are delicate, and not explicit or direct like those of men. The Rabbis did not however, wish to silence women and keep them from expressing their desires. On the contrary, they encouraged women to give clear expression to their needs and desires:

> "Rabbi Shmuel bar Nahmani said in the name of Rabbi Yohanan: A woman who demands marital relations of her husband will have sons the like of which did not

exist even in the generation of Moses. Of Moses' generation it is written 'Take you wise men, and understanding, and known among your tribes' (*Deuteronomy* 1:13), and it is written 'So I took the chief of your tribes, wise men and known' (*ibid.* 15), and 'understanding men' could not be found. Of Leah however, it is written 'and Leah went out to meet him, and said, Thou must come in unto me; for surely I have hired thee' (*Genesis* 30:16), and it is written 'And of the children of Issachar, which were men that had understanding of the times, to know what Israel ought to do' (1 *Chronicles* 12:33)."

BT, Eruvin, ibid.

Leah, wife of Jacob, demanded that her husband have sex with her, after she had hired him from her sister and co-wife Rachel, for the night, with her son's mandrakes. Leah is presented here as a role-model for women, who are called upon to act as she did, for she did not restrain her desire, but demanded that her husband satisfy her. Not only did she insist upon exercising her basic right, by virtue of her husband's *onah* obligation, but the Rabbis even reinforce such behaviour, claiming that such intercourse, initiated by the woman, will produce splendid children "the like of which did not exist even in the generation of Moses"! Moses sought men possessing three important leadership qualities — wisdom, understanding and renown — but could find only men with two of these qualities. No understanding men could be found. Intercourse between Leah and Jacob on that night, initiated by Leah, produced Issachar, whose descendants are described in the Bible as "men that had understanding of the times" — indeed "the like of which did not exist even in the generation of Moses".

It is interesting to note that in the traditional sources, "understanding" is considered a female quality. It is written in the Talmud: "God granted women greater understanding than men" (BT, *Sotah* 38b). It is apparently for this reason that the Rabbis believed that when sex is initiated by the woman, there is a greater chance that sons born of such a union will inherit their mother's understanding.

According to talmudic law, the obligation of *onah*, sex for the sake of pleasure, requires "proximity" of the flesh — direct physical contact between the man and the woman:

"Rabbi Yosef taught: '*She'erah*' (*Exodus* 21:10) means proximity of the flesh, that he may not do as the Persians, who have marital relations in their garments. Rabbi Huna offers further support, for Rabbi Huna said: He who says I will not have marital relations unless I am clothed and she is clothed, must divorce his wife and give her the benefits stipulated in her marriage contract."

BT, Ketubot 48a

Rabbi Yosef, an *amora* (later talmudic sage), reported an earlier (tannaitic) tradition, whereby in addition to a man's obligation to have sex with has wife, i.e. *onah*, the Torah also stipulated the manner in which he must do so. The Torah requires "proximity of the flesh"—inferred from the word "*she'erah*" (*Exodus* 21:10). Based on this teaching, Rabbi Huna ruled that a man who refuses to have marital relations when both partners are naked, but insists rather that they be clothed, should be compelled to divorce his wife and pay her the amount promised to her in the marriage contract. The husband is obligated to concern himself with his wife's pleasure, and may not perform the *mitzvah* of *onah* as one compelled, or as one who is merely fulfilling a duty. The assumption that he does so for "reasons of modesty" does not stand in his favour, and he is considered to have violated his obligation toward his partner. This halakhah reinforces the understanding that *onah* was established as a distinct obligation for the sake of sexual pleasure, since the obligation to procreate does not require the partners to be naked. *Onah* on the other hand, requires physical contact between the partners, in the sense of "and [he] shall cleave unto his wife: and they shall be one flesh".

Further support for the Rabbis' position whereby *onah* is a fundamental part of love and harmony between marriage partners, can be deduced from the laws concerning a "rebellious wife"—a woman who refuses to have sex with her husband. If the reason she has refused is because she despises him, he is compelled to divorce her, "for she is not as a captive, to lie with one whom she despises".[26] Behind this law is the principle of a woman's right to a satisfying sex life, including the right to refuse to have sex with a man she does not love. The "rebellious wife", whose behaviour is by definition negative, appears here to be a woman who stands up for her rights, and Halakhah recognises her stance, requiring that she be released from a marriage to a man she does not want. The Rabbis blame the husband for her refusal, and utterly reject the possibility of sexual relations without her consent, as we see in the following passage, as well:

> "Rami bar Hama said in the name of Rabbi Assi: A man may not coerce his wife to have marital relations, as it is written 'and he that hasteneth with his feet sinneth' (Prov 19:20). And Rabbi Yehoshua ben Levi said: He who coerces his wife to have marital relations will have indecent sons ... We have also learned: 'Also that the soul be without knowledge, it is not good' (*ibid.*)—That is one who coerces his wife to have marital relations. 'And he that hasteneth with his feet sinneth'—That is one who has intercourse twice. But how could that be, for Rava said: He who wishes to have male children should have intercourse twice! The latter is with consent, and the former without consent."

> BT, *Eruvin* 100b

---

[26]   Maimonides *ibid.*, 14, 8. She is entitled to a *get* (writ of divorce), but incurs financial loss. See *Ketubot* 63b, and *Kesef Mishneh* on Miamonides *loc. cit.*.

The Talmud rules that a husband may not coerce his wife to have marital relations (referred to in the Talmud as "fulfilling the commandment"). That is not the way in which to fulfil one's obligation to procreate. In order to reinforce the prohibition, the Talmud cites the words of Rabbi Yehoshua ben Levi, who asserts that non-consensual relations will produce indecent sons who will not be a source of pride to their father. It is interesting to compare this threat to sinners, with the Talmud's promise to a woman who demands sex (also referred to as "fulfilling the commandment") of her husband, that she will have sons "the like of which did not exist even in Moses' generation". The two situations represent the opposite poles of correct and incorrect behaviour between man and wife: sexual coercion on the part of the husband is the negative pole, and the result is indecent sons; sexual relations initiated and explicitly demanded by the woman are the positive pole, and the result is children the like of which did not exist even in Moses' generation.

The Talmud also makes a clear distinction between one who has intercourse a second time without his wife's consent and is considered a sinner, and one who does so with his wife's consent — undoubtedly with the common hope of having male offspring. In various talmudic and midrashic sources, the sex of a child is said to depend upon which parent achieves sexual satisfaction first:

> "Rabbi Isaac said in the name of Rabbi Ami: If the woman climaxes first, she will give birth to a son. If the man climaxes first, she will give birth to a daughter".
>
> BT, *Nidah* 25b and 3a [27]

Since the birth of a son is considered preferable, men are thus encouraged to concern themselves with their wives' sexual satisfaction. The commentators explain that when the second act is consensual, the chances that the woman will climax first are greater, since her desire will have been aroused by the first act. Nevertheless, as we learn from the case of Jacob and Leah, when both partners climax together, there is a greater chance of having twins: a boy and a girl.

Onah — sex for the sake of pleasure — is founded upon shared intention, mutual consent. This obligation is referred to in the Talmud as "the joy of *onah*" (*Pesahim* 72b), since mutual consent and shared pleasure will bring the partners sublime joy. The stabilising element in love, as stated in a number of places in the *Zohar*, is joy. A man must ensure that there is a joyous atmosphere in his relationship with his wife in general, avoiding sadness and strife, but particularly during their sexual union. The *Zohar* sharply criticises one who has sex in an atmosphere of sadness and strife, to the extent that it compares such conduct to illicit sexual relations.[28] This can also be seen as a condemnation of one who

---

[27]   See also BT, *Berakhot* 60a; *Yalkut Shimoni*, *Tazria* 547; and corresponding sources.
[28]   *Tikunei Hazohar*, introd., 4a; *tikun* 69, 109b-110a; and *tikun* 56, 89b.

has sex reluctantly, for fear of committing a supposedly "unspiritual" act. Sex is first and foremost a religious duty, and as such is treated as a joyous occasion. The *Zohar* completely rejects the notion that expressions of human physicality should be treated as "base" needs. The joy expresses release and religious exaltation, raising the physical act to a high plane, by means of the strongest human emotions, and not merely by intellectual reasoning. True union between man and woman cannot be attained without joy:

> "A man must therefore gladden his wife at that time, invite her, in a single desire with him, and they must share the same intention; and when the two are together then all is one in soul and in body. In soul, to cleave one to the other in a single desire. And in body, as we have learned, a man who is not married is like half a body, and when male and female are joined, they become one body. They are thus one soul and one body, and are called one person. Then God descends upon the one and imbues that one with a holy spirit, and they are called God's children, as it is written. And thus 'Ye shall be holy: for I the Lord your God am holy.'"
>
> *Zohar* 3, 81b

Sex in itself can arouse joy naturally, but here a man is told not to take this for granted, but to make a deliberate effort to bring joy to his wife. Joy is the basis — the substructure upon which complete harmony in sexual union is built. It will help a man to bring his wife to desire it as he does, and to co-ordinate their intentions. Joy contributes to comprehensive and sweeping unity. It fosters unity of will and intention, and renders the moment of sexual union one of unity of body and soul, complete and utter harmony. In this, joy is the actualising force of love between the partners.

Refusal by one of the partners to have sex is cause for divorce, since regular sex for the sake of pleasure establishes harmony in married life. Lack of physical attraction is sufficient cause for divorce.

Sexual desire is presented in many traditional sources as a sublime quality, associated with the highest human expression of "knowing" and "remembering":

> "'And Adam knew his wife again', desire was added to his desire. Previously he had no desire unless he saw her."
>
> Midrash, *Bereshit Rabbah* 23, 5

Adam's attaining knowledge is reflected in the fact that his desire for his partner had risen to higher plane. Previously, Eve would arouse his desire only when she was present, when he actually laid eyes on her. Now he "knew her" — desire became a matter of consciousness, and he desired her even in her absence, even when he could not see her. The language of the *midrash* is reminiscent of the reflections of the Greek philosophers on the concept of "*orexis*" — desire associated with memory and knowledge.

Desire is so important that there is a special angel charged with responsibility over it (*Bereshit Rabbah* 53, 6); and above all, it brings harmony and peace between the partners:

"That is desire, which establishes peace between man and his wife."

Midrash, *Vayikra Rabbah* 18, 1

Desire is essential to a complete relationship between man and wife. In cases of disagreements, arguments and even fights, matters are not always resolved verbally, and the physical bond plays a crucial role in establishing peace between them, making for a healthy and complete relationship.

Relationships will always have ups and downs, and sex plays a vital role in improving relations, particularly during the downs. Investing in the physical relationship, having sex for the sake of pleasure, is a very worthy matter according to Halakhah, and it is one of the ways in which to ensure success in married life.

This approach, whereby desire is seen as a positive human quality, is reflected in many other traditional sources, which assert that the creator did not instil any negative impulses in man. Man possesses the freedom to choose to act in a positive or negative manner, and he may use natural impulses such as desire or jealousy, for good — deepening the bond with his wife; or for bad — engaging in illicit sex, and causing suffering to his wife.

The obligation of *onah* — whereby a man is required to have sex with his wife for the sake of pleasure, and is charged with the responsibility of ensuring her pleasure — is a central expression of feminist innovation and revolution in the canonical sources. The status of women in talmudic times or even a thousand years later did not require the development of a halakhic, practical and behavioural approach of this kind. The obligation of *onah* was not a natural outgrowth of prevailing culture, but rather a determination aimed at changing social reality and hierarchy between the sexes. It stems from a deep moral conviction that women were not meant merely to serve men. This conviction ran contrary to the norm, which saw women as bound to serve their husbands, and marital relations were referred to in Hebrew as "*tashmish hamitah*" — "bed-service" (an expression that could in fact be understood in two ways: she serves him, but he also serves her).

The moral principle that women were not meant merely to serve their husbands has independent merit of course, but in the context of relationships, it is also rooted in understanding of the concept of love. Love has the power to sweep aside disparity and differences of class, to ignore hierarchy, and to create a state of equality for those who are touched by it. The canonical sources we have seen here, view the marriage relationship as one founded upon love. Love would appear to rise above the common rules, having the power to change cultural reality at a given time and place. Love, in this sense, rises above law and accepted norm, raising up those who would otherwise have been considered inferior. It has the ability, as in the case of *onah*, to change the norm and create a new law.

The obligation of *onah*, mandating sex for the sake of pleasure and stressing the woman's pleasure, is a revolutionary law, which not only does not stem from the normative culture, but actually collides with it. Consequently, traditional sources tend to ignore it, or to incorporate it into the obligation to procreate. In this sense, there is a discrepancy between the general creative and literary discourse on the subject of *onah*, and its actual fulfilment by loving couples, over millennia. Normative culture did not allow *onah* to take an independent place in literature, but apart from the fact that it is plainly a matter of some delicacy, its rightful place is indeed within the intimacy of marriage, and it has no place in the centre-stage of public discourse.

It is no coincidence that the right to sexual pleasure has been a fundamental part of feminist ideology in the modern era, and there are those who see it as one of the most important expressions of the feminist revolution. This fact can help give us an appropriate sense of proportion when we learn about the application of a similar principle that developed in talmudic law and subsequent halakhic literature, hundreds and thousands of years before the feminist revolution.

Chapter Four
THE LOVE RELATIONSHIP AS PERFECTION:
THE END OF MALE EXCLUSIVITY

The Midrash constantly reiterates the belief that perfect man, the "crowning glory of creation", comprises both genders — male and female. The height of this perfection lies not only in the emotional aspects of the marriage relationship, but in sexual intercourse between spouses; a physical manifestation perceived as spiritual perfection both on a human plane and in the higher worlds.

The Rabbis ascribed great importance to "populating the world" — assuring continuity of the species, expressed in the commandment to "be fruitful and multiply" — but there is nothing new in that. What is unique about the Rabbis' approach is the importance it ascribes to the relationship itself, unrelated to procreation:

"Although a man may have a number of sons, he must not be without a wife."

BT, *Yevamot* 61b

Being "without a wife" would make him incomplete. This wholeness is not related to procreation, but rather to the harmony one can attain only as a couple. The unique element in the Rabbis' approach is not their objection to distinguishing between spiritual and physical love, or their rejection of the concepts of "original sin" and celibacy. These positions stem from a unique belief that sees perfection in the relationship between man and woman, and lays the foundation for the ideal of harmonious love.

In this discussion of harmony and reciprocity, it is important to remind ourselves once again, that all of the texts, without exception, were written from a male perspective. "*Adam*" (man) in rabbinic terms is a male, and it is he who "must not be without a wife". It is the man for whom being single will deny him everything good in this world. The man is an incomplete, divided "*adam*", if he lives without a woman. Although we can assume that women also benefit and gain wholeness through marriage, the traditional sources emphasise the fact that it is she who complements him. It is therefore surprising that this focus on the male does not preclude the development of positions advocating reciprocal harmony in love between man and woman. This can be explained in light of the Rabbis' approach to the biblical messages in this matter.

It is possible, and even desirable to infuse the old sources with new and valid meanings, and to highlight rabbinic statements upon which we can base relationships between the sexes in our own cultural and social environment. In order to avoid currently popular anachronistic approaches to the traditional sources, discovering feminism and supposedly egalitarian views in rabbinic literature, I feel it is important to stress the true content of the sources and their precise cultural context. It is conceivable that refusing to ignore the original meaning of the texts may make the messages they convey even more meaningful and revolutionary. In this sense we can see the Rabbis as doing more than just conveying their contemporary culture. They are the bearers of change to those who follow their teachings and to Jewish society as a whole.

The Midrash lists every possible deficiency of a man who lives alone:

"Rabbi Yaakov taught: He who has no wife dwells without good, without help, without joy, without blessing, without atonement. Without good — 'It is not good that the man should be alone' (*Genesis* 1:18). Without help — 'I will make him an help meet for him' (*ibid.*). Without joy — 'And thou shalt rejoice, thou, and thine household' (*Deuteronomy* 14:26). Without blessing — 'That he may cause the blessing to rest in thine house' (Ezek 44:30). Without atonement — 'And shall make an atonement for himself, and for his house' (*Leviticus* 16:11). Rabbi Simon said in the name of Rabbi Yehoshua ben Levi: Without peace as well, as it is written: 'Peace be both to thee, and peace be to thine house' (1 *Samuel* 25:6). Rabbi Yehoshua of Siknin said in the name of Rabbi Levi: Without life as well, as it is written: 'Live joyfully with the wife whom thou lovest' (Ecc 9:9)."

Midrash, *Bereshit Rabbah* 17, 2

The list presented by the *midrash* includes central elements that give life meaning: good, help (= support), joy, atonement, blessing, peace, and of course life itself. All of these things are enjoyed by married men and are lacking in the lives of those who "have no wife". Some of these things can be direct consequences of a harmonious relationship; for example, mutual support or companionship, which is the opposite of "man being alone", the joy that certainly results from a love relationship and enriches the relationship itself. Other components, according to the Rabbis, would seem to depend upon divine blessing: good, atonement, blessing and peace — and these are not bestowed upon one who lives alone. One who is not married is deemed unworthy of these blessings! This approach is the complete opposite of the Christian concept of "original sin", which perceives something inherently negative in married life, possibly requiring constant atonement. It is inconceivable that a Christian would be denied atonement because of his celibacy.[29] According to the Rabbis, marriage is a fundamental obligation and is the purpose of life; God does not give atonement for other sins to one who does not fulfil this commandment, but rather chooses to live alone.

Rabbi Simon in the name of Rabbi Yehoshua ben Levi adds a further component to the bachelor's list of deficiencies: "Without peace as well". The concept of peace can be seen as the sum total of all of the previous elements without which man is incomplete. Rabbi Yehoshua ben Levi however, well-known for his statements concerning the importance and centrality of peace in general, makes no distinction between human perfection and peace. He sees personal peace — that which exists within the family unit — as the basis for peace between people and throughout the world. The bachelor, who lacks peace, is vulnerable to his passions, and may therefore channel his energies into fighting and war. Married life is thus the basis for peace throughout society.

Based on all of the above, the conclusion of Rabbi Yehoshua of Siknin that the life of a man without a woman is not life, is unavoidable. Life beyond the framework of a monogamous relationship is pointless, and man is incomplete except as part of a couple — man and woman — who together create a single, perfect whole:

> "Rabbi Hiya bar Gamda said: Nor is he a complete man, as it is written: "And he blessed them, and called their name *Adam*" — the two together are called *Adam*."
>
> Midrash, *Bereshit Rabbah, ibid.*

Rabbi Hiya bar Gamda bases his words on the verse in *Genesis* that notes that the name "*Adam*" is the shared name of man and woman, and that only their union in marriage can ensure perfection. Despite the semantic convention of calling

---

[29]   Bailey 1959, pp. 19-29, 92; Nooman 1965, pp. 29-135.

only man *"adam"*, Rabbi Hiya reminds us that only "the two together"—when they are together -"are called *Adam"*, and man alone is not complete.

The talmudic source cited above goes on to describe life together as a precondition for intellectual-spiritual development, and the meaning of life itself, similar to the midrash:

> "Every man that is without a wife dwells without joy, without blessing, without good . . . . In Palestine they say: Without Torah, without wisdom."
>
> BT, *Yevamot* 62b

The Babylonians, according to this text, valued marriage highly, attributing great virtues to it, and the lack of these virtues to one who is guilty of the sin of bachelorhood. As further support for their assertion, they cite the words of the Rabbis of *Eretz Yisrael*, who believed that knowledge of the Torah and intellectual development also depend upon marriage. A man requires his wife's support in order to acquire Torah knowledge and attain intellectual development.

The idea that man, woman and God join together to form a single whole can be summed up in the words of Rabbi Akiva to Rabbi Ishmael in the Midrash:

> "Neither man without woman nor woman without man nor both of them without the *Shekhinah*."
>
> Midrash, *Bereshit Rabbah* 22, 2

Among traditional sources, this midrashic source is interesting and unusual in that it emphasises reciprocity. Most of the sources we have cited refer only to the man—the deficiencies of his bachelorhood, the great good he can expect if he marries, and his lack of prospects if he fails to marry. Rabbi Akiva notes the need of both—"neither man without woman", immediately followed by "nor woman without man". Neither can be complete without the other. The meaning of the togetherness they share, if it is a deep and real bond, will transform the two-way relationship into a three-way relationship: "nor both of them without the *Shekhinah*". There are those who assert that the absence of the *Shekhinah* will cancel "both of them", i.e. annul their relationship, while the presence of the *Sekhinah* will uphold it. Others understand that the presence of the *Shekhinah* depends on both of them: If they are together in every sense, the *Shekhinah* will necessarily be together with them. "And a threefold chord is not quickly broken" (*Ecclesiastes* 4:12). Such descriptions of reciprocity in relationships between men and women take on even greater prominence in light of the fact that we have stressed a number of times here that we are dealing with texts "written by men and for men".

The dominant approach in the Talmud, whereby human perfection is manifested in the union of the sexes, creates a certain linguistic difficulty, since the Hebrew word "*adam*" is used to express both "man" and the unity created by the joining of man and woman:

> "Rabbi Elazar said: A man (*adam*) who has no wife is not a man, as it is written: 'Male and female created He them . . . and called their name Adam' (*Genesis* 5:2)."
>
> BT, *Yevamot* 63a

"*Adam*" is the common name shared by man and woman, who in their unified creation constituted one whole, as we have seen in the rabbinic versions of the myth of androgynous creation. They were created as a single whole, and it is to this whole that they must strive to return throughout their lives. This idea appears above in a similar statement ascribed in *Midrash Rabbah* to Rabbi Hiya bar Gamda. Rabbi Elazar goes a step further than Bar Gamda however, asserting that a man who has no wife is not only "unwhole", but does not even merit the name "*adam*". Man is worthy of being called "*adam*" only when he has a wife — as God called them *Adam* only after He had created them male and female.

The systematic, deep-seated and complex approach developed by the Rabbis, based on the belief that the love relationship between men and women is perfection, was not a natural outgrowth of the culture in which they lived and worked or of the social norms of their time. This clearly male-dominated society, which failed to outlaw polygamy, would have had little interest in the far-reaching assertions regarding man's total dependence upon woman, in every aspect of life, including intellectual development. Recognising their own deficiency and incompleteness without a female partner in their lives, making the achievement of perfection conditional upon marriage, was in fact a tremendous concession in terms of their belief in male superiority and independence, and in effect eliminated the very concept of male exclusivity. This systematic process laid the foundations for the revolution in the status of women, and the possibility of creating truer love relationships between men and women.

Chapter Five
SUMMARY: INNOVATION AND THE NORM

Feminist innovation and revolution in the canonical sources appear in a number of contexts:

— Intention to change the social norm with regard to the status of women in the family: A message of monogamy to a polygamous culture. This message appears as a central motif throughout the Bible, and is given practical emphasis in the words of the Talmud and the personal history of many of the talmudic sages.

— Defining an ideal paradigm for love relationships between men and women: A harmonious approach based on reciprocity and emotional, intellectual and physical attachment. The dichotomous approach has demonised woman as instruments of evil, who by their very presence arouse desire in men. The harmonious approach requires a physical relationship and pleasure from sex within the framework of marriage, and moreover, recognises a woman's right to enjoy sex, and imposes the duty upon the man, in a special precept, to have sex with her for the sake of pleasure. This approach thus constitutes a gateway to change in the status of women and in men's attitudes toward women in general.

— Presenting man as a divided, incomplete creature, whose intellectual, moral, spiritual and physical wholeness and perfection depends upon his female partner and the harmony in their reciprocal relationship. In terms of male society, it is as if the men had ceded control over part of their territory, making room for women.

— Including the gender phenomenon, male and female, in an equal fashion in the concept of "God's image", and later, in divinity itself, affords supreme legitimacy to harmony and reciprocity between the sexes, and serves as a solid ideological and theological basis for change in the status of women.

Without delving into the specific motives behind such innovation in the writings of male authors throughout the generations, I believe that at the heart of their work lies a moral conviction that refused to accept the social and cultural norm, compelling them to lay the foundation for change.

CONTRAST AND HARMONY IN MARRIED LIFE: ON SPIRITUALITY AND ABSTINENCE

Chapter One

INTRODUCTION: THE DUALISTIC APPROACH

The belief that spiritual growth entails withdrawal from physical and material life is ingrained in human consciousness. As one attains lofty spirituality, most believe, one will forswear matters of the body — beyond satisfying one's basic needs. At the highest levels of spiritual accomplishment such needs will be restricted to the minimum necessary to sustain the body that it might sustain the spirit within it. Sex is one of the needs that can be denied while preserving physical existence.

One who has achieved supreme understanding — becoming truly righteous, pious or saintly — is often viewed as no longer being a part of society. To the general public, and sometimes to their own minds as well, such people are a breed apart, to whom the rules of socialisation do not apply. They are free to study, contemplate and pray, to seek wisdom or God.

Married life is perceived as antithetical to the spiritual and intellectual development of such people, or at least as an awkward companion: in and of themselves — as individuals who limit their physical concerns to satisfying only those needs required for subsistence — and as a result of the socialisation they are denied, due to their separateness. At best, one who experiences spiritual growth and leads a normal married life is seen as someone who "does both things". According to prevailing notions, married life and spirituality cannot coexist on the same plane.

On the basis of this perceived reality, we shall discuss the relationship between marriage and intellectual/spiritual development in traditional Jewish sources; investigate various positions regarding the possibility of partial or complete abstinence; and examine the legitimacy, need or absolute necessity of abstinence for those on a high spiritual level.

Chapter Two

MARRIAGE AND INTELLECTUAL GROWTH:
HELP OR HINDRANCE?

The Rabbis considered harmonious marriage — including the physical relationship crucial to marital harmony to be a prerequisite for human spiritual fulfilment. Is this the case however, on all spiritual levels? Are there no circumstances under which abstinence, if only limited, is required?

There is no one answer to these questions in Rabbinical literature — at least not in the clear and systematic fashion found in some of the later mediaeval writings. To some extent, this issue underlies the discussion of what takes precedence: Torah study or marriage?

> "The Rabbis taught: [What takes precedence:] Torah study or marriage? One should first study Torah and then take a wife, and if one cannot be without a wife, he should first marry and then study Torah ... One should therefore first marry and then study Torah. Rabbi Yohanan says: How can one engage in Torah with a millstone around his neck? There is no dispute: the one is for us, and the other for them."
>
> BT, *Kidushin* 29b

In juxtaposing Torah and marriage in a situation of some conflict, the *tosefta*[1] raises the question of temporary abstinence. There is no dispute over the fact that a man is obligated to marry. The question is merely whether he should postpone marriage in order to study Torah first. The tannaitic source left open the question of a young man's Torah study and intellectual development versus his marriage. The answer to this question depends upon the nature and predilections of the individual. Deep intellectual involvement in Torah study demands dedication, and this might be affected by the need to devote time to a wife and growing family. Nevertheless, just as the Rabbis recommend that one build a home, ensure his livelihood, and only then marry, Torah proficiency is also important as the foundation of the family's spiritual life. If however, one cannot withstand the pressures of desire, and is distracted by his sexual needs — "if one cannot be without a wife" — then he should first marry, and only then set aside time for Torah study. Thus, according to the *tosefta*, it depends upon one's nature, predilection and behaviour. This opens the way to further discussion of the source. The Talmud concludes that the Rabbis do not disagree in principle, but reflect different customs: "the one is for us, and the other for them" — this is our custom and that is theirs. In other words, the assertions of the various *amoraim* — Rabbi Judah in the name of Shmuel, and Rabbi Yohanan — pertain

---

[1]   *Tosefta, Bekhorot* 6, 3, and commentators.

to differences between the community in *Eretz Yisrael* and that in Babylonia. Early talmudic commentators however,[2] differ on the essence of the difference between *Eretz Yisrael* and Babylonia: was the Palestinian custom to marry and then study Torah whereas the Babylonians saw this as an obstacle to intellectual growth — or vice versa?

From the various sources and later commentaries on this debate, we can conclude that it was the sages of *Eretz Yisrael* who advocated early marriage and spiritual and intellectual development within the framework of marriage.[3] Explicit talmudic sources relate to the Torah study of married scholars as superior:

> "'The fear of the Lord is pure, enduring for ever' (*Psalms* 19:10) — Rabbi Hanina said: This is one who studies Torah in purity. Who is that? One who marries and then studies Torah."
>
> BT, *Yoma* 72b

The subjects under discussion in the tractate of *Yoma* are what constitutes a sage worthy of the name, one who is as virtuous inside as outside and, aspects of Torah that might be detrimental and an elixir of death, or beneficial and an elixir of life. The scholar must beware of Torah, and it is in this context that Rabbi Hanina proposes the principle of studying Torah in purity. And what is this purity? That he marry and then, untroubled by desire, study Torah. Elsewhere, the Talmud compares the Torah "offered" to God by scholars to the incense and meal-offerings performed in the Temple — actions which required a state of purity:

> "Scholars who engage in Torah everywhere — it is as if they are offering incense to my name. And a 'pure meal-offering' — that is one who studies Torah in purity: who first marries and then studies Torah."
>
> BT, *Menahot* 110a

The purity of Torah scholars and the virtue of Torah study thus require that scholars marry in order to preserve their virtue and purity. These talmudic sources played an important role in the debate with Christianity on the question of original sin. The Jews were seen by the Church Fathers as depraved because they engaged in procreation, whereas Christian monastics were accused by the Jews of impurity specifically because of their celibacy.

The conclusion that it was the sages of *Eretz Yisrael* who advocated early marriage and spiritual/intellectual development within the framework of marriage is consistent with another talmudic source, cited in the previous chapter, that credits the sages of Palestine with the view that marriage is a prerequisite for spiritual development:

---

[2]   Rashi and Rabeinu Tam, *ibid.*, par. beg. "*Ha lan ha lehu*".
[3]   See *Hidushei Maharsha* and *Tosafot Ri Hazaken*, *ibid.*; the words of Rabbi Akiva in BT, *Sanhedrin* 76a; and Midrash, *Vayikra Rabbah* 21.

"Every man that is without a wife dwells without joy, without blessing, without good [. . .]. In Palestine they say: Without Torah, without wisdom."

BT, *Yevamot* 62b

The sages of Babylonia held marriage in high regard and attributed great virtues to it, and the lack of these virtues to the sin of bachelorhood. The sages of *Eretz Yisrael* ("in Palestine they say") added Torah study and intellectual development — the ability to attain wisdom — to the list of virtues contingent upon marriage, upon the support with which a woman provides her husband.

We must remember however, that we are discussing commentary and opinion, not a description of reality. Actual circumstances may have been very different from halakhic requirements, or perhaps the sages sought to change reality by recommending a certain type of behaviour.

Such early marriage often involved a temporary separation for the sake of travel to "a place of Torah", or to the academy of one of the famous rabbis. Absence from the home for the sake of Torah study for determined periods of time usually enjoyed the support and agreement of the wife, who favoured her husband's intellectual development and success. Modern scholarship has determined that early marriage — followed by lengthy periods of separation — was in fact more prevalent in Babylonia than in Palestine. Daniel Boyarin for example, offers an extremely original and interesting analysis of the dilemma of Torah study versus married life,[4] in which he asserts that Babylonian culture created "a class of married monks, men who had the pleasure and benefit of marriage for parts of their lives but who would absent themselves from home for extended periods of study." While original, Boyarin's thesis appears to exaggerate the "unresolved tension" between the demands of marriage and dedication to Torah study. Every intellectual pursuit, and Torah study in particular, entails a desire to dedicate oneself wholly to study, to "immerse" oneself in the world of learning, undisturbed by mundane concerns. One who has had such an experience may wish to postpone marriage or detach her/himself temporarily from family — to some extent or other. In this sense, we are not discussing a phenomenon unique to the talmudic period, but one that is extremely well-known in our times as well, and in many different cultures. Boyarin himself is very cautious. He is aware of the fact that his sources lend themselves to very different interpretations, and treats his assertion as a "possible interpretation" rather than a research conclusion. His choice of the word "monk" is unfortunate however. Torah scholars who parted from their wives did not do so in order to be purer or holier, or because they viewed sexual relations as base physicality. On the contrary, the concept

---

[4]   D. Boyarin, *Carnal Israel*, University of California Press, 1993, pp. 134-167.

of purity is associated specifically with married life — free from the dangers of sinful thoughts or desires that can arise from abstinence. It was not a matter of fleeing or avoiding marriage, but of undisturbed dedication to something else: Torah study. The word "monk" is therefore not appropriate.[5]

An analysis more in keeping with traditional sources[6] would find that the difference in practice between the two communities was not significant, and people married or married off their children as soon as they could afford to do so financially. Once married, some parted from their wives for short or extended periods of time, as people do today. They did so in order to dedicate themselves to Torah study, or to other matters — less extensively documented in the talmudic literature — that resulted in prolonged absences, such as earning a livelihood or amassing wealth.

The Rabbis present us with a fascinating debate regarding man's self-fulfilment and intellectual development. To what extent do such achievements help create a firm foundation for family life and to what extent is marriage an impediment to intellectual growth? The discussion affords equal weight to both sides of the dilemma and is therefore, as we will show, of practical and universal relevance.

Chapter Three

CATEGORICAL REJECTION:
ABSTINENCE IS PUNISHABLE BY DEATH!

Although a number of talmudic anecdotes would appear to support the scholarly view that it was common practice in Babylonia for men to leave their wives for the sake of Torah study, such cases were not widespread,[7] but rather exceptions to the rule. Sages such as Rabbi Ada bar Ahavah, who wished to justify absences of this kind under certain conditions, were in the minority, as we shall see below. Most of the Rabbis completely rejected this practice, and sharply condemned it:

---

[5]   Regarding attempts to understand social reality from written sources, see Adiel Schremer's article: "*Ben Shemonah Esreh Lehupah? Gil Hanisu'in shel Yehudei Eretz Yusrael Bitkufat Habayit Hasheni, Hamishnah Vehatalmud*". Schremer, who makes no reference to Boyarin, provides a thorough and cautious historical analysis, asserting, *inter alia*, that Rabbinical texts are insufficient as sources of historical information.

[6]   Without citing any specific source, sufficient support for this claim can be found in the many references in the Mishnah, Tosefta and Talmuds, regarding "a woman whose husband went abroad".

[7]   See Maharsha, *ibid.*, par. beg. "*Ha lan*" (second half).

"Rava said: There were scholars who relied on the words of Rabbi Ada bar Ahavah, and led their lives[8] [accordingly] (absenting themselves from their homes for the sake of study), as in the case of Rabbi Rahumi, who studied before Rava in Mahoza. It was his custom to return home every Yom Kippur eve. One day, he was deep in study [and forgot to go home]. His wife was expecting him, [thinking]: 'now he will come, now he will come'. [When] he did not come, she became discouraged and shed a tear. He was sitting on a roof [at the time]. The roof gave way beneath him and his soul departed."

BT, *Ketubot* 62b

Scholars who were absent from their homes for extended periods of time without their wives' consent, sometimes tried to justify behaviour that ran contrary to the halakhic norm by citing various customs. Rabbi Ada bar Ahavah believed that Torah scholars were permitted to leave their wives for a number of years. The Talmud however, sharply rejects this position and presents those who do so as deserving of death. Rava said that scholars who relied on the opinion of Rabbi Ada bar Ahavah "led their lives accordingly", i.e. although this was the halakhic opinion of Rabbi bar Ahavah, it is not accepted Halakhah, and they acted of their own accord ("led their lives"), for they should not have relied on this opinion. Of course, the expression "led their lives" also foreshadows the outcome: they relied on Rabbi Ada bar Ahavah, and risked their lives. We thus discover that not only did their Torah study not justify their absence, it did not even protect them from danger, as witnessed by the terrible punishment suffered by Rabbi Rahumi, who died because he had made his wife unhappy. Although he did not mean to cause her sorrow, he was punished for having left her to study Torah, living away from home.[9]

The strong message against leaving home is not limited to a single story or a few statements in the Talmud. It is repeated on numerous occasions. The case of Rabbi Rahumi involved a severe violation of his marital relationship, involving year-long absences from home. The following however, is the story of a Torah scholar who was absent from home only during the week — respecting his wife's conjugal rights (*onah*) on the Sabbath eve:

"When is the *onah* (marital duty) of Torah scholars? Rabbi Judah said in the name of Shmuel: every Sabbath eve. 'That bringeth forth his fruit in season' (*Psalms* 1:3) — Rabbi Judah — and some say Rabbi Judah and some say Rabbi Nahman — says: that is one who has marital relations every Sabbath eve. Judah, son of Rabbi Hiya, son-in-law of

---

[8]   The expression "*avdei uvda benafshaihu*" simply means that they acted of their own accord. It can however, also be understood to mean that they acted against or endangered their lives.

[9]   "It was his custom to return home every Yom Kippur eve" would seem to imply that he was away the entire year. This is not necessarily the case however. See Y. Frankel, *Darkhei Ha'agadah Vehamidrash* 1, p. 101.

Rabbi Yanai would go to the house of study, and return to his home every Sabbath eve. And when he came, a pillar of fire would appear before him. One day, he was deep in study [and forgot to go home]. Since he did not see that sign, Rabbi Yanai said to them: turn his couch over (a sign of mourning), for were Judah alive, he would not have failed to perform his marital duty. It was 'as an error which proceedeth the ruler' (*Ecclesiastes* 10:5), and his soul departed."

Ibid.

This is not the story of an abstinent scholar who left his wife for an extended period of time — like Rabbi Rahumi in the previous story. The rabbis determined the appropriate frequency of marital relations for Torah scholars to be once a week — on the Sabbath eve — and Judah, son of Rabbi Hiya, adhered to this principle, returning from the house of study every Sabbath eve at twilight.

In this story, the Talmud seeks to condemn those Torah scholars and men in general who neglect their wives' conjugal rights, and the message, that there can be no justification for abstinence, is absolutely clear. Rabbi Judah was, after all, a Torah scholar, who on a single occasion became so absorbed in what he was studying that he "forgot himself" — a natural occurrence for one who studies Torah so profoundly. Rabbi Yanai however, was absolutely convinced of his death, for had he been alive, he would not have neglected the obligation of *onah*. Neglecting this obligation of physical union with his partner, made him dead while he was yet alive! And the fact that he did so out of devotion to his intellectual, spiritual calling — Torah study — does not protect him or the vitality he lost by his abstinence.

This message appears repeatedly — from the early *midrashim* that stress the tremendous deficiencies of bachelorhood, that one who does not have a wife is incomplete and his life is not worth living, to the Talmud's sharp denunciations of sexual abstinence. Such abstinence, even when it is only temporary and for the important purpose of studying Torah, can sometimes lead to death. Apart from showing sensitivity to a wife's feelings, the Rabbis wished to make a clear statement: there is no aspect of life — as spiritual or lofty as it may be — that can replace or come at the expense of married life. Nothing can compensate for the deficiencies of bachelorhood or sexual abstinence.

Chapter Four

THE DILEMMA OF ABSTINENCE FOR INDIVIDUALS ON A HIGH SPIRITUAL PLANE

Many are the talmudic and midrashic (earlier and later) sources that condemn bachelorhood. In this context, it is worth mentioning the well-known talmudic story of Ben Azai, one of the greatest of the *tanaim*, who was unusual in that he was a bachelor. Ben Azai himself denounces, in unusually sharp terms, those who eschew marriage:

> "We have learned [in the *beraita*]: Rabbi Eliezer says: One who does not engage in procreation it is as if he sheds blood, as it is written 'whoso sheddeth the blood of man in man shall his blood be shed' (*Genesis* 9:6), followed by 'and you, be ye fruitful, and multiply' (*ibid. ibid.* 7).
>
> Rabbi Yakov (var. Akiva)[10] says: It is as if he diminishes the image [of God], as it is written 'so God created man in his own image' (*ibid.*), followed by 'and you, be ye fruitful, and multiply'.
>
> Ben Azai says: It is as if he sheds blood and diminishes the image, as it is written 'and you, be ye fruitful and multiply' (Rashi: it is written after both and so it is as if he has done both things).
>
> They said to Ben Azai: Some speak well and do well, others do well but do not speak well, and you speak well but do not do well?!
>
> Ben Azai said to them: What can I do, for my soul desires Torah? The world can be perpetuated by others."
>
> BT, *Yevamot* 63b

Rabbi Eliezer and Rabbi Akiva (or Yakov) express sharp condemnation of bachelorhood: one accuses the bachelor "spilling blood", i.e. committing murder (!), and the other of "diminishing God's image" in the world — an expression that can be taken to imply heresy. According to Rabbi Eliezer, the bachelor's sin is toward his unborn children — since he has failed to marry, it is as if he has taken their lives. According to Rabbi Akiva, his sin is against God: the bachelor in his wickedness, diminishes the divine presence in the world — achieved by the positive actions of every person created in his image — by preventing potential sanctifiers of God's name from being born.

Both approaches harshly condemn bachelorhood. Not satisfied however, Ben Azai goes further in condemning one who fails to marry, by uniting the other two approaches: the bachelor is accused of both murder and heresy! Ben Azai's words astonish his colleagues, who see their bachelor friend's extreme approach as hypocrisy. It is worth noting that the talmudic text does not end with a condemnation of bachelorhood in general or of Ben Azai in particular, but with Ben Azai's words of self justification: "What can I do, for my soul desires Torah? The world can be perpetuated by others." This conclusion opens the way for an anomaly within the normative system: avoidance of marriage on an individual basis. It is important to remember however, that this possibility is

---

[10] The reading "Akiva" appears in parallel sources and references — see gloss on the page in *Yevamot*. It is highly likely that the correct reading is in fact "Akiva", judging both from the parallel sources and the content of the statement: "so God created man in his own image" (*cf.* Mishnah, *Avot* 3, 14). This sharp condemnation of bachelorhood, attributed to Rabbi Akiva, is of course consistent with his philosophy, as described in the previous chapters.

not explicitly stated in the Talmud, which condemns bachelorhood in general and Ben Azai's behaviour in particular.

The atypicality of Ben Azai's bachelorhood, the criticism levelled at him by the Rabbis, and the rest of the talmudic discussion on this matter, reinforce the position that abstinence must be avoided even at high spiritual levels.[11] The talmudic account does not leave Ben Azai's case open, or Ben Azai himself a bachelor. The extreme opponent of bachelorhood in the end marries, enabling him to engage, per his definition: both in perpetuating the world and in studying Torah — the object of his soul's desire:

> "The daughter of Rabbi Akiva did so for Ben Azai (married him and enabled him to continue to devote himself to Torah study) — of which people say: ewe follows ewe (*rehela batar rehela* — alluding to Rabbi Akiva's wife Rachel), as the mother acts so does the daughter."
>
> BT, *Ketubot* 63a

The daughter of Rabbi Akiva (who began his career with her mother's love, and left her for more than two decades to study Torah) married Ben Azai and enabled him to continue his studies. She, who saw how her mother had supported her father's dedication to Torah study, followed her example in marrying Ben Azai. On the one hand, we see another example of the phenomenon of partial abstinence — also rejected by the Rabbis — and on the other hand, the message that bachelorhood is unacceptable even for a Torah sage as devoted to study as Ben Azai. Greatness in Torah does not justify failure to marry, as we see in Rabbi Huna's uncompromising position:

> "Rabbi Hisda was praising Rabbi Himnuna to Rabbi Huna, that he was a great man. He said to him: When he comes to see you, bring him to me. When he came, he saw that he did not spread a cloth [over his head in the manner of married men]. He said to him: Why do you not spread the cloth? He said to him: I am not married. He turned away from him, and said to him: See that you do not show yourself before me until you are married."
>
> BT, *Kidushin* 29b

Although Rabbi Huna desired Rabbi Himnuna's company and wished to converse with him as a great sage, he refuses to ignore Rabbi Himnuna's sin of bachelorhood, which he considers a fundamental flaw that precludes intellectual interaction with him as between two sages.

Halakhic authorities who discuss these talmudic sources are a bit surprising in their approach: they show understanding — under certain conditions and

---

[11] See *Yevamot* 63b-64a, which asserts, citing a tannaic source, that one who fails to engage in procreation impairs the Jewish People and causes the *Shekhinah* to depart from the People of Israel.

with certain provisions — for the type of extreme behaviour exhibited by Ben Azai, although they do not actually advocate it:

> "One whose soul continually desires Torah like Ben Azai, is ravished by it, cleaves to it all his days, and does not marry — has not sinned. That is on condition that he is not overcome by [sexual] desire. But if he is overcome by [sexual] desire, he must marry, even if he already has children."
>
> Maimonides, *Hilkhot Ishut* 16, 3[12]

Note Maimonides' use of words from the vocabulary of love: "soul desires" (the expression used by Ben Azai), "ravished", "cleaves"; through which he stresses the fact that human emotions particular to the love of a woman can in such exceptional cases be directed to love of the Torah.[13] The Halakhah shows understanding for this unusual phenomenon; since "he has not sinned" — such behaviour is not completely prohibited, but is by no means advisable. It is permitted because the emotional forces usually devoted to love of a woman, are focused on Torah study. If however, the desire for Torah study does not fill his entire being, overriding all other interests, and "he is overcome by sexual desire", he must marry — even if he has already fulfilled the commandment to procreate, since his situation proves that the completion of his soul can only be attained within the context of marriage. The Rabbis recognised this in establishing a general obligation to marry even if one has already fulfilled the commandment to "be fruitful and multiply": "Even if a man has a number of children, he may not remain without a wife" (BT, *Yevamot* 61b) — a position upheld by Maimonides and the other mediaeval halakhists.[14] Regarding Ben Azai and the like, Maimonides stresses the exceptional nature of the phenomenon, while recognising the fact that there are individuals who can indeed live a celibate life, focused wholly on Torah study, without being "overcome by sexual desire". In any event, such exceptional scholars are not considered to be on higher spiritual plane than their married colleagues.

In the Rabbis' discussions regarding the relationship between spiritual and intellectual development and marriage, the approach that abstinence is a precondition for spiritual enlightenment is unheard of. The debate over the relatively minor issue of the timing of marriage and Torah study, and the conclusions of the Gemara and the halakhists in this matter — barely leaving room for an unusual person such as Ben Azai — preclude any possibility of celibacy neither as a philosophy nor as an effective path to spirituality. The fact that there were nevertheless scholars who advocated celibacy as a way of life, and

---

[12]   See also *Tur Shulhan Arukh, Even Ha'ezer* 1, 4.
[13]   See Maimonides, *Hilkhot Teshuvah* 10, 3, in which he uses the same expressions to describe love of God.
[14]   Maimonides, *Hilhot Ishut*, 15, 16; *Hilkhot Isurei Bi'ah* 26. See also *Tur Shulhan Arukh, Even Ha'ezer* 1, 8.

that there were Jewish sects that lived such lives, should be viewed as contrary to the position of the Rabbis; and we should not rule out the possibility that the Rabbis specifically stressed their opposition to abstinence in light of such phenomena.

Chapter Five
MOSES' ABSTINENCE

> "And Miriam and Aaron spoke against Moses because of the Kushite woman whom he had married: for he had married a Kushite woman. And they said, hath the Lord indeed spoken only by Moses? Hath he not spoken also by us? . . . And the Lord came down in the pillar of the cloud, and stood in the door of the tabernacle, and called Aaron and Miriam: and they both came forth. And he said, hear now my words: if there be a prophet among you, I the Lord will make myself known unto him in a vision, and will speak unto him in a dream. My servant Moses is not so, who is faithful in all mine house. With him will I speak mouth to mouth, even apparently, and not in dark speeches; and the similitude of the Lord shall he behold: wherefore then were ye not afraid to speak against my servant Moses? . . . And the cloud departed from off the tabernacle; and, behold, Miriam became leprous, white as snow . . ."
>
> *Numbers 12:1-11*

According to midrashic interpretation, the prophet Miriam understood that her brother Moses had separated from his wife or even divorced her because of his desire to remain celibate. Miriam believes that there is no justification for such behaviour even when it is for the sake of heaven, for prophecy does not mandate celibacy. She speaks of the matter with Aaron, and stresses the fact that Moses' wife is a "Cushite", i.e. that she is beautiful — and according to the commentators beautiful without, and beautiful in deed and comportment — and Moses should have no reason to leave her.[15]

---

[15] Other commentators explain that Moses did not marry a daughter of Israel, but a Cushite princess — an act viewed by Miriam and Aaron as arrogant. God replies that Moses' marriage was not a matter of arrogance — because "the man Moses was very meek" — but of circumstance, since Moses married Zipporah when he fled from Pharaoh. See *Da'at Zekenim Miba'alei Hatosafot* on *Numbers 11:2*.

> "'And Miriam and Aaron spoke against Moses' — Whence did Miriam know that Moses had abstained from procreation? She saw that Zipporah no longer adorned herself with the adornments of women, and said to her: what is the reason that you do not adorn yourself with the adornments of women? She said to her: your brother does not care about it."
>
> *Sifre, Beha'alotkha* 12, 1

Miriam notices that Moses' wife Zipporah neglects her appearance and does not adorn herself. From this she understands that Moses has separated from her and they no longer have marital relations. She discusses the matter with Aaron, and is punished for the sin of evil speech (*lashon hara*). Note: she spoke the truth! According to Halakhah, the sin of speaking ill refers to giving a truthful account of someone's negative actions. According to the midrash, her intentions in speaking to Aaron were good: she meant to praise Moses for the dedication that led him to choose celibacy, but at the same time wished "to promote procreation", because she believed there to be no contradiction between this precept and devotion or prophecy. Her words to Aaron were not idle gossip, God forbid, and she did not mean to speak ill of Moses, but rather to promote a *mitzvah*: to get Moses to return to his wife and resume married life. Spiritual development at the level of prophecy is not conditional upon abstinence — what is more, abstinence from fulfilling a commandment, which should be unthinkable. Miriam therefore expresses her surprise:

> "'And they said, hath the Lord indeed spoken only by Moses?' — For God spoke with our forefathers as well, and they did not abstain from procreation; and he has spoken also by us and we have not abstained from procreation."
>
> *Ibid.*

This is the message in the words of Miriam and Aaron, who were prophets in their own right: even the lofty spiritual level of prophecy does not require celibacy. In this context it is worth citing Rabbi Saadia Gaon on sexual intercourse (in a chapter of that title):

> "And were it an obscene thing, God would have spared his prophets and messengers, peace be upon them, from it; for you see one of them say 'give me my wife' (*Genesis* 29:21) without shame, and one say "and I went unto the prophetess' (*Isaiah* 8:3) without disguise."
>
> *Book of Beliefs and Opinions* 10, 6

God's answer, as it appears from the plain meaning of the verses, as well as the midrashic commentary, is unequivocal: Moses' prophecy is unlike that of the other prophets, i.e. his level is unique, and will never be repeated in another. His is a level approaching that of an angel, enabling him to abstain from fulfilling the commandment of marital relations, and justifying the celibacy he has imposed upon himself.

The uniqueness of Moses' prophecy as justification for his celibacy appears in later sources as well, most notably in the *Zohar*:

" 'But as for thee, stand thou here by me' (*Deuteronomy* 5:27) — Henceforth, Moses separated completely from his wife, and entered [a state of devotion] and ascended to another place, of male not of female. Fortunate is the lot of Moses, a faithful prophet who attained lofty planes that no other human being has ever attained. Of this it is written (*Ecclesiastes* 7:26): 'one who is good before God shall escape from her'. What is good? That is Moses, as it is written (*Exodus* 2:2) 'that he was good'.[16] And since he was good, he ascended to another lofty plane."

Zohar III, 261b

According to the *Zohar* it is clear that Moses is unique in attaining such a lofty plane, only he is called "good before God", and therefore he alone ascends to another, highest level, on which there is no room for the feminine essence, thereby "escaping from her".[17] Maimonides also associates Moses' abstinence with his unique level of prophecy:

". . . None of the prophets prophesy at will. Not so Moses, who dons the holy spirit and is visited by prophecy whenever he wishes, without focusing his mind or preparing for it, for he stands prepared at all times, like the angels, and therefore prophecies at any time, as it is written (*Numbers* 9:8) 'Stand still, and I will hear what the Lord will command concerning you.' And this was promised to him by God, as it is written (*Deuteronomy* 5:27) 'Go say to them, get you into your tents again. But as for thee, stand thou here by me' — teaching us that when prophecy departs from all of the prophets, they return to their tents, that is to all of their physical needs, like all others, and they therefore do not separate themselves from their wives. And Moses did not return to his tent, and therefore separated himself from his wife forever, and from all similar things, and his mind became bound to the Rock of Ages, and glory never departed from him, and the skin of his face shone, and he became holy as the angels."

Maimonides, *Hilkhot Yesodei Hatorah* 7, 6

These words can be attributed to the influence of Ibn Rushd (also known as Averroes), regarding union with the Active Intellect. According to Ibn Rushd, the highest level of human perfection requires intellectual union, unhindered by physical needs. Scholars are divided as to the extent of this influence on

---

16   "And there went a man of the House of Levi, and took to wife a daughter of Levi. And the woman conceived, and bare a son: and when she saw him that he was good, she hid him three months" (*Exodus* 2:1-2).

17   The full verse in *Ecclesiastes* (7:26) reads: "And I find more bitter than death the woman, whose heart is snares and nets, and her hands as bands: one who is good before God shall escape from her; but the sinner shall be taken by her."

Maimonides, attributing his position to the neo-Platonic approaches that he adopted, particularly with regard to perfection of the intellect.[18] In any case, Maimonides appears to maintain that prophecy itself requires abstinence from physical needs at the time of prophetical inspiration — on the part of other prophets as well. While the others however, return to their tents when prophecy has departed from them, Moses does not return as they do, because prophecy never leaves him.

Elsewhere in the *Zohar*, further justification of Moses' abstinence — beyond his unique and lofty level of prophecy — is offered:

> "It is said of you [Moses] 'but as for thee, stand thou here by me, ' (*Deuteronomy* 5:27) — that all of Israel return to their tents (i.e. to their wives, after having refrained from sexual relations for three days prior to the giving of the Law at Mount Sinai), but you do not, until the final redemption. And who caused this? The mixed multitude (who caused Israel to worship the golden calf), on account of whom 'and he cast the tablets out of his hands' (*Exodus* 32:19)."
>
> *Zohar, Ra'aya Mehemna*, III 279a

The mixed multitude brought about the breaking of the first tablets, and Moses had to rectify the ensuing state of affairs, i.e. to maintain the same lofty spiritual/prophetic level that he had when he ascended to Mount Sinai in order to make the second tablets and ensure the final redemption. According to this midrash in the *Zohar*, sexual abstinence was not necessitated by Moses' unique level of prophecy, but was the result of the sin of the golden calf — caused by the behaviour of the mixed multitude. This is what prevents Moses from returning to his tent, to married life, like everyone else.

The fact that the Midrash devotes so much effort to justifying Moses' abstinence speaks of great discomfort and conveys a clear objection to abstinence in general, even for those on the highest spiritual plane.

We could leave it at that, and say that the phenomenon of Moses and his prophecy is the exception that reinforces the rule: with the unique exception of Moses, human perfection can only be attained through the union of male and female. The highest level of human development — prophecy — is also attained through union, not separation. This is undoubtedly the prevailing view in Rabbinical literature. It is worth noting however, that this is not unequivocal, and a number of *midrashim* leave room for the possible justification of abstinence among prophets, and in general[19] — for example:

---

[18] See Eliezer Schweid, *Iyunim Bishmonah Perakim Larambam* pp. 79-95; Moshe Idel, "*Hitbodedut Ke'rikuz' Bafilosofiah Hayehudit*"; and Dov Schwartz, *Philosophy of a fourteenth century Jewish Neoplatonic circle, 1996.*

[19] See E. Urbach, *Me'olamam shel Hakhamim*, "*Askesis Veyisurim Betorat Hazal*" pp. 437-458.

"'And God spake unto Noah, and to his sons with him. And I . . . establish my covenant . . . ' (*Genesis* 9:8) — Rabbi Judah and Rabbi Nehemiah; Rabbi Judah says: for he violated [the commandment to engage immediately in procreation], and was therefore humiliated. Rabbi Nehemiah said: he enhanced the commandment and acted in holiness."

Midrash, Bereshit Rabbah 35, 1

According to Rabbi Judah, it was Noah's failure to engage in procreation that resulted in his decline and humiliation, while Rabbi Nehemiah's interpretation implies that Noah's abstinence was a virtue. The two opinions are not entirely incompatible however, and the midrash on the whole, rejects sexual abstinence.

The sources pertaining to Moses however, would appear to preclude such hermeneutical compromise. According to these sources, Moses' exceptional level of prophecy fails to provide sufficient justification for his celibacy. The fact that Miriam's words are deemed "evil speech" (*lashon hara* — the halakhic definition of which is, as noted, the true account of a negative action) rather than "slander" (*dibah*), would seem to indicate something negative in Moses' behaviour, for if not, what was the subject of Miriam's evil speech?

The midrash cited above (*Sifre, Beha'alotkha*) indeed claims that God commanded Moses to abstain from sexual relations. There is another midrash however, that portrays Moses' abstinence not as a divine commandment, but as one of his own initiatives:

"Moses did three things of his own accord, and God agreed with him: He added another day (of abstinence prior to receiving the Torah), abstained from conjugal relations and broke the tablets."

BT, Shabbat 87a

According to this source, even Moses — on his unique and lofty level of prophecy — was not initially commanded by God to abstain from sexual relations. Only when Moses decides to separate himself from his wife on his own initiative, of his own accord, does God "agree with him". The mediaeval talmudic commentators stress that had he not abstained of his own accord, such abstinence would not have met with God's approval, since "man is led along the path he chooses".[20]

A later, more detailed version of the story appears in *Avot deRabbi Natan*:

"This is one of the things that Moses did of his own accord, by inference, and his opinion coincided with that of God. [He abstained from conjugal relations and his opinion coincided with that of God. He departed from the Tent of Meeting and his

---

[20] See *Tosafot, loc. cit.*, par. beg. "*Ve'atah poh amod imadi*": Rabeinu Tam.

opinion coincided with that of God. He broke the tablets, and his opinion coincided with that of God.] — He abstained from conjugal relations and his opinion coincided with that of God. How [did this come about?] He said: Regarding Israel, who were sanctified only temporarily and only in order to receive the Ten Commandments at Mount Sinai, God said to me: 'Go unto the people, and sanctify them today and tomorrow' (*Exodus* 19:10); and I, who stand ready every day and every hour, and I do not know when He will speak to me, day or night, all the more so that I should abstain from conjugal relations! — And his opinion coincided with that of God. Rabbi Judah ben Beteira says: Moses did not abstain from conjugal relations, but was told by God [to do so], as it is written (*Numbers* 12:8) 'with him will I speak mouth to mouth' — mouth to mouth I told him to abstain from conjugal relations and he did. Some say that Moses did not abstain from conjugal relations until he was told [to do so] by God, as it is written (*Deuteronomy* 5:27) 'Go say to them, Get you into your tents again', and it is written (*ibid.*) 'but as for thee, stand thou here by me'. He went back and interpreted [God's words], and his opinion coincided with that of God."

Avot deRabbi Natan 2, 3

The story in *Avot deRabbi Natan* differs from the legend in the tractate of *Shabbat* and is interested only in the lessons that can be learned from it. The authors of the later source try to reconcile the story with the halakhic norms of the day. First, the radical wording — "and God agreed with him" — is replaced with something softer and more in keeping with halakhic discourse: "and his opinion coincided with that of God". In other words, Moses examined the three issues closely, and drew practical conclusions from them — unsupported by explicit scripture, but based on logical inference. His reasoning is sound and his opinion manages to coincide with that of God.

Even this softened version of the story in *Shabbat* however, is not accepted by everyone. The text in *Avot deRabbi Natan* cites dissenting opinions as well, whereby Moses' abstinence was not, heaven forbid, his own initiative, but a direct commandment from God, supported by explicit scripture. These opinions do not seek to soften the talmudic legend, but rather reject it outright. Rabbi Judah ben Beteira's interpretation is close to the plain meaning of the text in *Numbers* 12. He interprets God's answer to Aaron and Miriam as referring to the commandment he had given Moses to separate from his wife. The other dissenting opinion presents further scriptural support for the same position. The concluding words "and his opinion coincided with that of God" are thus superfluous.

Another version of *Avot deRabbi Natan* preserves the legend within the framework of halakhic discourse:

"And how do we know that Moses created a fence around his words? For God said to him (*Exodus* 19:10) 'Go unto the people, and sanctify them today and tomorrow' — that is two days. Moses considered the matter in his mind and said: Perhaps a woman will discharge semen and come and stand before Mount

Sinai, and Israel will thus receive the Torah in a state of impurity. What did he do? He added another day, as it is written (*ibid. ibid.*) 'Be ready against the third day; come not near a woman'. And how do we know that God concurred with him? As it is written (*ibid. ibid.* 11) 'and be ready against the third day'.

> Moses reasoned and abstained from conjugal relations. He said: To Israel, who are not a special instrument and with whom he does not speak but for a time, God said to abstain from conjugal relations; I who am a special instrument and with whom He speaks at all times, and I do not know when He will speak to me — should I not rightly abstain from conjugal relations? How do we know that God concurred with him? As it is written (*Deuteronomy* 5:26) 'Go say to them: Return ye to your tents'. Was Moses also included in the leave [granted to Israel]? It is written (*ibid. ibid.* 28) 'But as for thee, stand thou here by Me' — say henceforth that Israel was given leave [to return to their wives] and Moses remained in his [state of] prohibition."
>
> *Avot deRabbi Natan* ver. 2 *ibid.* (Schechter, 1887)

This source presents yet another version of the story, without emphasising the independence of Moses' initiative. The subject here is the protective "fence" that Moses placed around the commandment that the Israelites set themselves apart for two days — to which Moses added a third day. The placing of fences is perfectly legitimate in Rabbinical tradition; the sages are in fact required to place a fence around the Torah; and there is scriptural support for the fact that God concurred with Moses in this matter. Regarding Moses' own abstinence, he concluded by reasoned inference that he must, by law, separate himself from his wife. This is however a personal law, pertaining to Moses alone, and stemming from the difference between Moses and all other Israelites: ". . . Israel, who are not a special instrument . . . I who am a special instrument . . . ". Moses reached the logical conclusion — due to the difference between himself and all the others — that he must separate from his wife. This conclusion is in keeping with halakhic norms, i.e. with the discourse to which the authors of *Avot deRabbi Natan* were committed and within which they operated.

In Rabbinic thought, very little value is placed on the connection between sexual abstinence and spirituality, and that mostly as a non-essential expression of the unique nature of the greatest of the prophets. Even at the highest, unparalleled level of prophecy attained by man — that of Moses — the ideal of conjugality, love and harmony between man and wife, remains absolute. Almost ignoring the spirit of the biblical text, the Rabbis do not spare Moses a certain amount of criticism, albeit very circumspect; or at the very least they do not present Moses' abstinence as a paradigmatic and unequivocal expression of spiritual perfection.

Chapter Six

ABSTINENCE: A PRECONDITION FOR LOVE IN THE PHILOSOPHY OF RABBI BAHYA IBN PAKUDA

In his popular book *Hovot Halevavot* (*Duties of the Heart*), Rabbi Bahya Ibn Pakuda (11th century) — influenced by sufism — makes a distinction between two types of Torah wisdom:

— The "duties of the limbs": manifest science, governing physical actions, i.e. the commandments by which man is bound.
— The "duties of the heart": veiled science, the internal knowledge that includes morality, devotion, knowledge of God, fear of God, and the most sublime — love of God.[21]

According to Ibn Pakuda, love of God is the supreme fulfilment of man's obligations, as evidenced by the first two verses of the "*Shema*" prayer: "Hear O Israel, the Lord our God, the Lord is one. And thou shalt love the Lord thy God . . . ". The first verse — Hear O Israel — calls for the unification of God, and the purpose of unification is love. Unification precedes love chronologically, as in the approach of Rabbi Saadia Gaon, who speaks of longing that follows knowledge of the idea of unity. Ibn Pakuda sees individual belief and its internalisation as a precursor of love. He concludes his book with the connection between the unification of God and love's component parts, as we shall see below.

Rabbi Bahya Ibn Pakuda is not alone among Jewish philosophers throughout the ages who have assigned the role of ultimate purpose and pinnacle of human achievement to love. He is nevertheless unique in his emphasis on certain conditions along the path to attaining the love, and the attitude a lover of God must have toward the precepts of the Torah. Love is the culmination of all religious duties and virtues, which serve as stepping-stones to its attainment. Prominent among the steps preceding love are abstinence and fear. The idea that fear immediately precedes love is common to many philosophers. Ibn Pakuda's approach to abstinence however, is unique. The essence of abstinence is the elimination of the attraction exercised by the world and all it contains, leaving the Creator the only source of attraction for man. Ibn Pakuda clearly distinguishes between physical and spiritual, matter and mind, base and lofty. Man, present in the physical world, must strive to raise himself to an existence

---

[21] Apart from being a common distinction in Sufi mysticism, the two types of "duties" — of the limbs, and of the heart — correspond to Rabbi Saadia Gaon's "revealed" (*shimiyot*) and "rational" (*sikhliyot*) precepts, although Ibn Pakuda does not use "intellect" (*sekhel*) in the same rational sense as Saadia Gaon.

between worlds. Eliminating the force of gravity — the downward pull toward matter — he may develop an upward pull toward the spiritual and the sublime, and so he should.

This upward pull is love:

> "Since we have prefaced . . . in the matter of abstinence from the world, and our intention was that the heart should be wholly dedicated to love of the Creator blessed be He, and yearn for His will . . . "
>
> *Duties of the Heart,* Gate of Love of God, Introduction

As noted above, the goal of abstinence is to facilitate love of God, by freeing the heart and dedicating it wholly to that end. The prefatory philosophical distinction between "duties of the limbs" and "duties of the heart" enables the author to develop his opinion that abstinence is justified and necessary. The precepts pertaining to the duties of the limbs ensure man's moral behaviour in the physical world, and his spiritual equilibrium in that world. They all pertain to the external, manifest, practical and material world. The duties of the heart pertain to the internal, veiled world, which requires — if one wishes to enter and fulfil the obligations it entails — a change in attitude to the external world, expressed through abstinence.

On the antecedence of abstinence to love in the hierarchy of human behaviour, he adds:

> "And we have therefore anticipated the Gate of Abstinence to this Gate, for love of the Creator cannot settle in our hearts alongside love of the world. And when the heart of the believer is void of love of the world and free of its desires, in conscience and understanding, love of the Creator will settle in his heart and be fixed in his soul."
>
> *Ibid.*

Love of the world and love of God, according to Ibn Pakuda cannot coexist. Abstinence frees the soul from love of the world and enables love of God. Abstinence however, does not mean celibacy, i.e. that one who loves God must completely forswear the physical aspects of this world. The change brought about by abstinence is manifested in the fact that one's earthly activities are limited to that which is necessary for existence:

> "He gives the world its necessary due, and to the Torah — his entire being."
>
> *Ibid.*

This does not imply total withdrawal from the world — the necessary connection remains. What is this necessary connection? It is not the satisfaction of basic needs, without which life cannot be sustained. That goes without saying. Emphasis here is placed rather, on another connection to the physical world, one that stems not from that which is essential to existence, but from its "essential duties", i.e. the precepts of the Torah, man's duty toward which cannot be compromised by abstinence. Among these precepts is that of *onah*, which requires a man and wife to have sex on a regular basis.

In the Gate of Abstinence, Ibn Pakuda stresses his opposition to celibacy, and the fact that the abstinence he advocates is not celibacy: "completely abandoning population of the earth is not consistent with Torah law" (Gate of Abstinence, chapter 3), i.e. celibacy is a violation of Torah law. Nevertheless, man must follow the path of "general abstinence, employed for the improvement of our bodies and order of our affairs".

Abstinence is of vital importance, and a necessary condition for attaining man's ultimate purpose: love. In the distinction he makes between abstinence and complete celibacy, Ibn Pakuda deviates from the Sufi beliefs that influenced him. The Muslim mystics believed that when one reaches the level of lover of God, he is no longer bound by the duties of the limbs, making celibacy an acceptable possibility, albeit an exceptional one, even within Sufism. Ibn Pakuda does not go that far, asserting rather that one's ladder must be "set up on the earth" — i.e. it is morally imperative that one preserve a minimal connection to earthly life — even when "the top of it reaches to heaven".

The influence of Rabbi Saadia Gaon is evident in the limits Ibn Pakuda places on abstinence. Saadia Gaon was critical of abstinence that leads to celibacy, claiming that it runs counter to basic human existence and the population of the earth. He concludes that the prohibitions imposed by the Torah are sufficient:

> "That which is beneficial to man is that he use abstinence in its place, and that is if he should encounter a forbidden food or a forbidden sexual encounter or forbidden property, he will apply it, that it might keep him from it."
>
> *Book of Beliefs and Opinions* 10, 4 (Kapah edition)

Rabbi Yosef Kapah, in his notes on the text, remarks:

> "That is to say that one need not take upon himself further prohibitions and restrictions, for in observing that which the Torah has forbidden he is already practising abstinence, and it is sufficient that he adhere to that, and that is what Maimonides says in chapter four of his commentary on the tractate of *Avot*, see my edition, p. 383 *et seq*. And similarly in *Hilkhot De'ot* 3, 3: 'So said the Sages: Is what the Torah prohibited not enough for you, that you take upon yourself further prohibitions?' And no further comment is necessary."
>
> *Ibid.* n.80

Ibn Pakuda cannot be said to oppose these assertions. The emphases in his approach are different however, both because his philosophy is not critical like that of Saadia Gaon, Maimonides or Judah Halevi, and because his opposition to extreme abstinence is expressed within the context of a thorough investigation of human ability. He observes three different types of love of God: two are motivated by gratitude and self-interest; while the highest form is that of love of God per se, not for what one receives from God, but an ardent desire to cleave to God and bask in his sublime light.

Ibn Pakuda asks whether pure, perfect and unselfish love of God is humanly possible. The test of man's love of God lies in his willingness to make sacrifices for it. If he is willing to sacrifice his property or some of his physical needs, then he will have passed the test of a lover of God—a test that is within the realm of human ability. Some outstanding individuals have even been prepared to make the ultimate sacrifice: to offer their lives on the altar of love of God—although beyond human ability and against nature. Pure love of God thus does not depend solely on man's efforts and is not within everyone's grasp, because it depends upon the divine grace that man enjoys as a result of his previous efforts.

Chapter Seven
RABBI JUDAH HALEVI'S REJECTION OF ABSTINENCE

Rabbi Bahya Ibn Pakuda's approach does not contradict the approaches of Rabbi Saadia Gaon and Maimonides—based upon self-control and the power of the human spirit in general—which leave a certain amount of space, albeit limited, for abstinence. Ibn Pakuda's philosophy cannot however, be reconciled with that of the great critic of abstinence of all kinds: Rabbi Judah Halevi (c. 1075-1141).[22] In his poetry and in the *Kuzari*, Halevi strives to vindicate imagination and the emotional—as opposed to intellectual—experience. Man approaches and loves God through creativity: poetry, music, and above all, the precepts of the Torah. Abstinence is not love of God, and Rabbi Judah Halevi sharply criticises all forms of asceticism:

"The divine law imposes no asceticism on us. It rather desires that we should keep the equipoise, and grant every mental and physical faculty its due, as much as it can bear, without overburdening one faculty at the expense of another . . . Our law, as a whole, is divided between fear, love, and joy, by each of which one can approach God. Thy contrition on a fast day does nothing the nearer to God than the joy on the Sabbath and holy days . . . that thou shouldst be pleased with the law itself from love of the Lawgiver . . . and if the joy lead thee so far as to sing and dance, it becomes worship and a bond of union between thee and the Divine Influence."

Kuzari 2, 50 (tr. H. Hirschfeld, Routledge, 1905)

---

[22]   My understanding of the *Kuzari* as an anti-ascetic work, and Rabbi Judah Halevi as an opponent of abstinence of any kind contrasts with diverse and even opposing readings. See Dov Schwartz, "*Perishut Kitzonit Vesagfanut Bemishnato shel Hug Parshanei Hakuzari Beprovence Bereshit Hame'ah Ha-15*".

Abstinence violates the harmonious balance between extremes, and is not the Torah's way to divine service. The Torah prescribes "the equal path" — creating harmony between body and soul, neither preferring nor neglecting either element. One must thus strike a balance between two key concepts: fear and joy. Neither is superior to the other: fast days such as *Yom Kippur* express fear, but the fearful in their fasting are no better than those who celebrate with joy, food and drink, music and dancing.

Although Halevi speaks of striking a balance between fear and joy, the above passage is not balanced, but rather favours joy and its component parts, as "worship and a bond of union between thee and the Divine Influence". The above was undoubtedly written in apologetic style, against abstinence and the human tendency to see the ascetic as a greater servant of God than one who takes joy in worldly pleasures. Joy and its physical causes are no less divine worship than "spiritual" or other behaviour, to which people tend to ascribe greater value. The theme of joy plays a central role in Halevi's philosophy and, together with love of the world, constitutes the principal source of perfect divine worship. Pleasure is a positive thing, if it is not automatic or instinctive, but given the attention that makes it human rather than animal. The blessings recited over food and other sources of physical pleasure — rooted in the gratitude that endows life with optimism and a greater sense of enjoyment — are therefore fundamental. The obligation to bless God for all that is beautiful in the world, brings one to contemplate what he is about to enjoy and the grace of God who has granted man such pleasures.

Halevi's unequivocal rejection of abstinence and asceticism stems from his belief — contrary to that of Rabbi Saadia Gaon and Maimonides — that love is not the result of knowledge, because knowledge does not require emotion, but a response to sensory experience:

> "We see that the human soul ... is ... attracted by a beautiful form which strikes the eye, but not so much by one that is only spoken of. Do not believe him who considers himself wise in thinking that he is so far advanced that he is able to grasp all metaphysical problems with the abstract intellect alone, without the support of anything that can be conceived or seen ... Were it not for the sensible perception which encompasses the organization of the intellect ... that organization could not be maintained. In this way, prophets' images picture God's greatness, power, loving kindness, omniscience ... "

Ibid. 4, 5

The fact that the highest level of human achievement depends upon the senses and the emotions, leaves no room whatsoever for a philosophy that advocates even mild abstinence. The question of abstinence for those who have attained a high level of spirituality — or in the case of a select few, a particularly elevated spiritual plane — does not even arise, since abstinence, and certainly asceticism, obstructs spiritual growth. The senses and the emotions do not lose their importance and their decisive role at a higher spiritual level. On the contrary, knowledge of God, the Tetragrammaton, is expressed in emotion and taste.[23] The Muslim philosopher Al-Ghazali uses the concept of "taste" in a mystical sense: a kind of reception or deep recognition, not through the mind, but through one's internal nervous senses. [24] Rabbi Judah Halevi cites the verse "O taste and see that the Lord is good" (*Psalms* 34:9), in Al-Ghazali's mystical sense, defining it as the internal eye, the internal sense of man, connected to the power of imagination or perhaps even the power of imagination itself. Halevi does not believe that intellectual knowledge is the highest form of knowledge, but that there is something above and beyond it: love of God — "the Divine Influence" — the knowledge called "taste". Contrary to the Aristotelian philosophers and to Maimonides, he ascribes a fundamental cognitional role to the power of imagination.

Rejection of asceticism also entails rejection of the melancholic, pessimistic element of the approaches that advocate asceticism and abstinence. Rabbi Judah Halevi thus makes an original and innovative contribution to the wisdom of love. The weight that Halevi gives to emotional experience and to the possibility of the creative expression of love, recognising that creativity does not stem solely from intellectual knowledge, but from all of the powers of the soul and the imagination — constitutes an important, unique innovation, that affords love ample room for expression in Jewish thought. The strong emphasis Halevi places upon joy offers a test of love's sincerity, and for those who identify with his approach, a guide to a life of creativity, love and optimism.

Chapter Eight
SUMMARY: MAINTAINING BALANCE

Jewish sages throughout history have addressed the tension between the idea that one must live a life of intellect and spirit, based on abstinence and asceticism; and the idea that a complete sage must live in harmony with his wife. Sometimes, the discussion has led to the development of a philosophy of abstinence and to the creation of groups that have put such philosophies into practice. This phenomenon should be ascribed to the natural tendency to see the spiritual man, the sage, the worshiper of God, as one set apart from ordinary people, and therefore from the ordinary pursuits associated with

---

[23] *Kuzari*, 4, 16-17.
[24] See Yisrael Efrat, *Hafilosofiah Hayehudit Biymei Habeinayim — Tekstim, Munahim Umusagim*, p. 190 *et seq.*

physical needs and desires. To this we must add the great influence of Islamic philosophy upon Jewish thought.

Rabbi Bahya Ibn Pakuda, Rabbi Abraham son of Maimonides and others, were influenced by the Sufi stream in Islam, and adopted its principles of abstinence as a precondition for spiritual growth. Sufism also exerted considerable influence upon the kabbalists — especially evident in the writings of Rabbi Abraham Abulafia and others influenced, in turn, by him. The influence of Ibn Rushd and the idea of union with Active Intellect — justifying detachment from the physical existence that obstructs the attainment of perfect knowledge — can be found among intellectualists as well. Jewish philosophical ideas on abstinence were also influenced by the neo-Platonism prevalent in mediaeval Christianity and Islam — whereby the soul, deriving from a lofty source, is imprisoned within the physical world. Naturally, the rabbis and philosophers were not indifferent to the spreading phenomenon, but attacked it and fought against it as best they could. We must keep in mind however, that such philosophies were never a part of mainstream Judaism, as asserted by Dov Schwartz, in his article "Extreme Abstinence and Asceticism among *Kuzari* Commentators in early 15th Century Provence":

> "... We must recall that the ascetic tendency never managed to fully pervade the writings of Jewish philosophers. Even those who advocate extreme practices, at the same time continue to support the moral golden mean as a general rule, as well as the obligation to participate in social and family life ... The ascetic tendency is thus reflected in sporadic remarks ... "

Schwartz 1993 pp. 79-80

The absurdity in adopting extreme abstinence without renouncing the golden mean — including marital relations — shows the difficulty in developing ascetic tendencies that will be compatible with the normative position of the canonical sources.

Abstinence is a common method to repress desire, to liberate oneself from the physical while yet living in the physical world, and aspire to lofty spirituality. It is based on a dualism that distinguishes between the "base" — matter, and the "lofty" — spirit. It is important to note that even among those who reject abstinence, some accept the dualistic approach, but reject abstinence for practical reasons, claiming that man — comprising both matter and spirit — is inherently incapable of such restraint. Instead, they propose a balanced existence, according to the Aristotelian golden mean.

Total rejection of abstinence however, comes from the advocates of harmony, who reject the dualism of the physical and the spiritual, make no distinction between "lofty" and "base", and see man's moral challenge in the harmonious integration of matter and spirit. Advocates of this approach stress the fact that the Creator did not invest man with negative proclivities, and see lust for example, as a positive emotional characteristic. Man enjoys free will, and may choose to follow a positive or a negative path, employing his natural tendencies, like lust or jealousy, for a positive end — for example, deepening his relationship with his wife; or for a negative end — having an illicit affair and inflicting suffering upon his wife. The following midrash captures the essence of this approach:

> " 'And God saw every thing he had made, and, behold, it was very good' (*Genesis* 1:31).
> And it was good — that is the good inclination.
> And it was very good — that is the evil inclination.
> How can the evil inclination be very good? Were it not for the evil inclination man would not build a home, take a wife or have children."
>
> *Bereshit Rabbah* 9, 7

This midrash reflects the approach that all of the qualities and proclivities with which man was endowed were meant to serve good and fitting behaviour. Even characteristics and tendencies that appear to be negative, are for the better, and without them, the purpose of all creation, entrusted to man — i.e. populating the world — could never be realised. The wording of the midrash is slightly problematic, since it preserves the expression "evil inclination", even as it highlights its positive aspect. The tone of the midrash however, is obviously defensive, in response to the dualistic approach that views some human characteristics as wholly bad and others as wholly good.

The Rabbis saw harmonious married life — including a physical relationship, crucial to the creation of such harmony — as a precondition for spiritual fulfilment. A similar message arises from the early *midrashim* that speak of the tremendous inadequacy inherent to bachelorhood, and of the fact that one who is not married is incomplete and his life not worth living; and from the harsh talmudic condemnations of sexual abstinence. Such abstinence, even partial and for the important purpose of Torah study, can sometimes be fatal. Beyond serious consideration of women's feelings, there is a clear message here: no aspect of life — as spiritual and lofty as it may be — can replace marriage or come at its expense. Nothing can compensate for the deficiencies of bachelorhood or sexual abstinence. Moreover, a Talmudic source ascribes to the sages of Eretz the position that marriage is a sine qua non for spiritual growth.

In the Rabbis' discussions regarding the relationship between spiritual and intellectual development and marriage, the approach that abstinence is a precondition for spiritual enlightenment is unheard of. The debate over the relatively minor issue of the timing of marriage and Torah study, and the conclusions of the Gemara and the halakhists in this matter — barely leaving room for an unusual person such as Ben Azai — preclude any possibility of celibacy as a philosophy, as an effective path to spirituality. The fact that there were nevertheless scholars who advocated celibacy as a way of life, and that there were Jewish sects that lived such lives, should be viewed as contrary to the position of the Rabbis; and we should not rule out the possibility that the Rabbis specifically stressed their opposition to abstinence in light of such phenomena.

In Rabbinic thought, very little value is placed on the connection between sexual abstinence and spirituality, and that mostly as a non-essential expression of the unique nature of the greatest of the prophets. Even at the highest, unparalleled level of prophecy attained by man — that of Moses — the ideal of conjugality, love and harmony between man and wife, remains absolute. Almost ignoring the spirit of the biblical text, the Rabbis do not spare Moses a certain amount of criticism, albeit very circumspect; or at the very least they do not present Moses' abstinence as a paradigmatic and unequivocal expression of spiritual perfection. The principle that human perfection can only be attained through marriage, and that a man is incomplete without a woman, was undoubtedly a revolution in prevailing thought and culture.

Beyond its significance as a comprehensive system, the power of the wisdom of love in Jewish sources lies in the connection between legend, myth and philosophy on the one hand, and halakhic praxis on the other. This combination of thought, imagination and practice resulted in a winning formula, almost impossible to dismiss or ignore. Legends, myths and philosophy are contradicted and rejected by different and opposing views, and are even forgotten over the course of time. The daily practice of moral principles and the application of philosophical beliefs to one's actions within a love relationship however, make abstract thought a part of reality, ideas a firm and lasting fact of life.

Thus, although certain elements within Jewish society over the generations may have adopted approaches far from the rabbinical ideal of love, there has always been the possibility that they might return to the wisdom of love as expressed in the canonical sources. The prevailing view throughout these sources is that love, marriage, spiritual and physical harmony are in fact, the height of human perfection.

BIBLIOGRAPHY

Aristotle. *Nicomachean Ethics* (Sefer ha-midot le-Aristo, translation by H. Roth), Jerusalem, 1983.

Biale, David. *Eros Vehayehudim* (Heb), Tel Aviv, 1995. English edition: *Eros and the Jews: from Biblical Israel to contemporary America*, New York Basic Books, 1992.

Boyarin, Daniel. *Reading sex in Talmudic Culture*, Berkeley, 1993.

Boyarin, Daniel. "Internal opposition in talmudic literature: the case of the married monk," in: *Representations* 36 (1991), pp. 87-113.

Brown, Peter R. L. *The body and society: men, women, and sexual renunciation in early Christianity*, New York, Columbia University Press, 1988.

Bultmann, R. *Urchristentum in Rahman der Antiken Religionen*. Trans. as *Primitive Christianity in Its Contemporary Setting*. New York, 1956.

Chadwick, Henry. *Augustine*. Published: Oxford; New York: Oxford University Press, 1986.

Cohen, Jerome. "*Mitzvat Periah Ureviah Umekomah Bapulmus Hadati*," in: I. Bartal and I. Gafni (eds.), *Eros, Erusin Ve'erusim*, 5758 (1998), pp. 83-96.

Crescas, Hasdai. *Or ha-shem* (Heb), Eliezer Schweid ed. Original from the Ferrara edition, Jerusalem, 1970.

Dan, Joseph. *On Sanctity: religion, ethics and mysticism in Judaism and other religions* (Heb), Jerusalem: Magnes Press, Hebrew University, 1998.

Efrat, Israel. *Hafilosofiah Hayehudit Biymei Habeinayim — Tekstim, Munahim Umusagim*, Dvir publication, Tel Aviv 1969.

Eisenshtein, J. *Otsar Midrashim* (Heb), Jerusalem, 1969.

Elior, Rachel. *Temple and chariot, priests and angels, sanctuary and heavenly sanctuaries in early Jewish mysticism*, Jerusalem, Magnes, 2002.

Feintuch, Joseph. *Mesorot Unus'ha'ot Batalmud*, Jerusalem, 5745 (1985).

Flusser, David. Judaism *and the Origins of Christianity*, Magnes Press, Jerusalem, 1988.

Frenkel, Yonah. *Darkhe ha-agadah veha-midrash*, Givaataim, Yad la-talmud, 1991.

Fridman, Mordechay. *Jewish polygyny in the Middle Ages* (Heb), Byalik Publication, Jerusalem, 1986.

Fromm, Erich. *The art of loving*, New York: Bantnam Books, 1967.

Gafni, Isaiah. "The Institution of Marriage in Rabbinic Times," in: *The Jewish Family*, (ed. David Kraemer), New York, 1988, pp. 13-30.

Gasset, Ortega, Y. J. *Estudios Sobre el Amor*, Madrid, 1991.

Goody, J. *The European family: an historico-anthropological essay*, Oxford: Blackwell, 2000.

Greenwald, Itamar. "Nokhehuto Habilti Nimna'at shel Hamitos — Masat Petiha," in: H. Pedayah (ed.), *The myth in the Jewish thought* (Heb), Ben Gurion University Press, 1996, pp. 15-28.

Gutrie, W. K. *The Greeks and Their Gods*, London, 1950.

Harvey, Warren. "Mitos Batar Mikra'i Uvatar Filosofi," in: H. Pedayah, (Ed.) *The myth in the Jewish thought* (Heb), Ben Gurion University Press ,1996, pp. 112-117.

Homer. *The Odyssey*; translated by Edward McCrorie; with an introduction and notes by Richard P. Martin, Baltimore: Johns Hopkins University Press, 2004.

Hunt, Morton M. *The Natural History of Love*. New York, 1993.

Idel, Moshe. "Seclusion as a concentration in the Jewish Philosophy", (Heb), Shlomo Pines Jubilee Volume, *Meḥkere Yerushalayim be-maḥashevet Yiśrael;* 7, 9 1988, pp. 44-57.

Josephus Flavius. Jewish antiquities, Cambridge, Mass, Harvard University Press, 1998.

Karelitz, Avraham Yeshayahu. Hazon Ish — Orach chayim, Bnei Brak, 1957.

Karelitz, Avraham Yeshayahu (Hazin Ish) *Teshuvot u-ktavim* (M. Greineman ed.) Bnei Brak, 1991.

Kook, Rabbi Abraham Isaac. *Be'oro — Iyunim Bemishnato shel Harav Avraham Ytzhak Hakohen Kook ZT"L Uvedarkei* (H. Hamiel ed.) World Zionist Organization Publication, Jerusalem, 1986.

Leibowitz, Yeshayahu. *Sihot Al Pirkei Avot Ve'al Harambam*, Jerusalem and Tel Aviv, 1979.

Leon, Hebreo. *Śiḥot al ha-ahavah*, translated from Italian by Menaḥem Dorman. Mosad Byaliḳ, Jerusalem 1983. English edition: *The philosophy of love* : (Dialoghi d'amore, translated into English by F. Friedeberg-Seeley and Jean H. Barnes) with an introduction by Cecil Roth, London: Soncino Press, 1937.

Liebes, Yehuda. "Mitos Ve'ortodoksia — Teshuvah LeShalom Rosenberg," in: *Mada'ei Hayahadut* 38, 5758 (1998), pp. 181-187.

Lieberman, Saul. *Yevanim Veyavnut Be'eretz Yisrael,* Jerusalem, 5723 (1963). English edition: Greek in Jewish Palestine: studies in the life and manners of Jewish Palestine in the II-IV centuries C. E. New York: P. Feldheim, 1965.

Linder, Amnon. *The Jews in Roman imperial legislation,* Detroit, Mich. Wayne State University Press; Jerusalem: Israel Academy of Sciences and Humanities, 1987.

Neusner, J. *Aphrahat and Judaism : the Christian-Jewish argument in fourth-century,* Atlanta, Scholars Press, 1971.

Midracsh Tehilim (Shohar Tov, S. Buber Ed.) Vilnius, 1891.

Nathan Ben Yehiel ha'romi, Aruch Ha'shalem, New York, 1955.

Nooman, John T. *Contraception: Ahistory of Its Treatment by the Catholic Theologians and Canonists.* Cambridge, Mass, 1965.

Pedaya, Haviva (Ed.) *The myth in the Jewish thought* (Heb), Ben Gurion University Press 1996.

Plato, *The collected dialogues of Plato,* including the letters, Edited by Edith Hamilton and Huntington Cairns. With introd. and prefatory notes. [Translators: Lane Cooper and others.] New York: Pantheon Books, 1961.

Safrai, Shmuel. *Rabi Akiva ben Yosef, hayav u-mishnato: pirke halakhah ve-agadah,* Byalik Publication, Jerusalem, 1971.

Schechter, Solomon. *Agadat Shir ha-shirim,* Cambridge, 1896.

Seadya ben Yosef, Gaon. The book of beliefs and opinions, translated from the Arabic and the Hebrew by Samuel Rosenblatt. New Haven: Yale University Press, 1976.

Sefer nitshon yashan, (English & Hebrew), *The Jewish-Christian debate in the high Middle Ages,* with an introduction, translation, and commentary by David Berger. Edition: 1st ed. Published: Philadelphia: Jewish Publication Society of America, 1979.

Rosenberg, Shalom. "Mitos Hamitosim," in: *Mada'ei Hayahadut* 38, 5758 (1998), pp. 145-281.

Rothenberg, Naftali. *Be'ikvot Ha'ahavah* (Heb), Karmel Publication, Jerusalem, 2000.

Rothenberg, Naftali. "Ve-achal ve-chai le-olam: al ahava, yrah, yediah ve-avoda be-kitvei ha-rambam," in: *Sinai* 99 (1986), pp. 57-74.

Ricoeur, Paul. *The Symbolism of Evil,* Boston, 1969.

Schremer, Adiel. "Ben Shemonah Esreh Lehupah? Gil Hanisu'in shel Yehudei Eretz Yusrael Bitkufat Habayit Hasheni, Hamishnah Vehatalmud," in: I. Bartal and I. Gafni (eds.), *Eros, Erusin Ve'erusim,* 5758 (1998), pp. 43-71.

Schremer, Adiel. *Male and female He created them* (Heb), Merkaz Zalman Shazar Publication, Jerusalem, 2003.

Schwartz, Dov. *Philosophy of a fourteenth century Jewish Neoplatonic circle* (Heb), Mosad Byalik, Jerusalem, 1996.

Schwartz, Dov. "Perishut Kitzonit Vesagfanut Bemishnato shel Hug Parshanei Hakuzari Beprovence Bereshit Hame'ah Ha-15," in: *Meḥkere Yerushalayim be-maḥashevet Yiśrael* 11, 1993, pp. 79-99.

Schweid, Eliezer. *Iyunim bi-Shemonah perakim la-Rambam*, Jerusalem, Aḳademon, 1965.

Smith, W. A. *Dictionary of Greek and Roman Antiquities*, London, 1875.

Thought, Bailey, Derrick Sherwin. *Sexual Relation in Christian Thought*. New York, 1959.

Tishby, Isaiah. *The wisdom of the Zohar:* an anthology of texts systematically arranged and rendered into Hebrew by Fischel Lachower and Isaiah Tishby; with extensive introductions and explanations by Isaiah Tishby; English translation by David Goldstein. Published: Oxford [Oxfordshire]; New York: Published for the Littman Library by Oxford University Press, 1989.

Urbach, Ephraim E. *Ḥazal, pirke emunot ve-deot*. Jerusalem: Magnes Press, Hebrew University, 1969. English edition: *The sages, their concepts and beliefs*; (translated from the Hebrew by Israel Abrahams. Published): Cambridge, Mass.: Harvard University Press, 1987.

Urbach, Ephraim E. *World of the sages : collected studies*, Magnes Press, Hebrew University, 1988.

Wright, W. *The Homilies of Afraates, the Persian Sage*. London, 1869.

Yehuda ben Shemuel, ha-Lewi. The Kuzari: in defense of the despised faith, (translated and annotated by N. Daniel Korobkin) Northvale, N.J.; Jerusalem: J. Aronson, 1998.

Zohar, (translated to Hebrew by J. Rosenberg), Bilgoray, 1924-1930.

INDEX

Printed in the United States
219863BV00004B/3/P